Love Me True

CAITLIN PRESS INC.
8100 Alderwood Road,
Halfmoon Bay, BC VON 1Y1
www.caitlin-press.com

Text design by Shed Simas / Onça Design
Cover design by Vici Johnstone
Printed in Canada

Caitlin Press Inc. acknowledges financial support from the Government of Canada and the Canada Council for the Arts, and the Province of British Columbia through the British Columbia Arts Council and the Book Publisher's Tax Credit.

LIBRARY AND ARCHIVES CANADA CATALOGUING IN PUBLICATION

Love me true : writers reflect on the ins, outs, ups and downs of marriage / Jane Silcott & Fiona Tinwei Lam, editors.

ISBN 978-1-987915-66-2 (softcover)

1. Marriage—Literary collections. 2. Love—Literary collections. 3. Creative nonfiction, Canadian (English). 4. Canadian poetry (English)—21st century. I. Silcott, Jane, editor II. Lam, Fiona Tinwei, editor

PS8237.M37L68 2018          C810.8'03543          C2017-906533-5

# Love Me True

## WRITERS REFLECT ON THE INS, OUTS, UPS AND DOWNS OF MARRIAGE

Edited by

Jane Silcott

& Fiona Tinwei Lam

CAITLIN PRESS

# Contents

# Struggles

# Partings

# Death

# Celebration

# Preface

*"Chains do not hold a marriage together. It is threads, hundreds of tiny threads, which sew people together through the years."*
—Simone Signoret

Marriage: A beautiful weave of disparate threads as lives intertwine over time—or a gnarled mess, something to avoid or cut yourself free of as quickly and gracefully as you can?

There's no single answer. All that's clear is that it's never been clear. In a world that's still arguing about gay marriage, that still has arranged marriages, that still looks the other way when young girls are married off to old men under the guise of religious belief, marriage is a complex topic, with legal and cultural dimensions, as well as deeply personal and intimate ones.

Although there are academic studies of the social, economic and anthropological significance of marriage through time, we wanted to create a book that used personal narratives and poetry to examine the real challenges and issues that arise in contemporary marriages. So we have brought together a broad range of pieces by diverse authors about the intricacies of committed partnership. We've chosen to organize the collection through eight admittedly overlapping lenses: the evolution of marriage in our time, the decision to get married (or not), along with explorations of commitment, passion, struggles, parting, death and celebration.

In Western culture, marriage has evolved from the *Mad Men* fifties of the wife at home in her apron and the husband at the office with his cigarettes and tie. Roles have changed. And so have laws: gay marriage is legal, and life partners who cohabitate are recognized in law. Marriage is no longer structured around a sole breadwinner and an orbiting spouse who is a cross between an executive assistant and a virtual domestic servant. People no longer need to deny their individuality, their aspirations or their sexuality.

Still, it's not a step to take lightly. Joining your life to another's is risky. Joseph Campbell called it "the ordeal," and he meant that in a good way. We don't know what's going to happen, where it's going to take us or if we'll be able to keep going in that same direction. What if one person changes dramatically along the way? Marriage may mean adopting a new role, becoming a parent to someone else's child or learning to love and let go. As Bill Moyers

1

said, "In marriage, every day you love, and every day you forgive. It is an ongoing sacrament, love and forgiveness."

So, why do it? Is passion behind it all—that inexplicable and often irresistible draw to another person? Sure, we're fuelled by hormones, pheromones and need, but can passion survive the mundane—the chores, the bills, the kids and the passage of time? How do we find the will or the way, and what happens when the eye and the heart wander?

According to several sources, including fridge magnets and Pinterest, "Marriage lets you annoy someone special for the rest of your life." Certainly, relationships have challenges—minor to monumental: irritations that balloon, truths that morph into lies, arguments that flare, silences that descend, impenetrable as concrete. But as poet and philosopher George Santayana put it, "familiarity breeds contempt only when it breeds inattention." If both parties listen, are willing to reflect and change, with or without the assistance of counselling, those rifts can sometimes be bridged. Other times, philosophical divides or emotional damage might be too profound.

We know from divorce statistics that some marriages don't survive. In our "Partings" section, writers explore what has gone awry, describing how marriages disintegrate from discord or abuse. Some authors grieve the unravelling of a long-standing partnership, while others express relief as they regain a sense of self and purpose.

Those who remain will eventually come face to face with the vows "in sickness and in health" and "until death do us part." How do couples cope? Some of the authors write about the comfort that spouses find in each other's companionship and care; others about the toll of caregiving and the impact of the devastating loss of a child or spouse.

Finally, we look at the rites of celebration, whether it is by marking each year that passes in a committed relationship, or in participating in a ceremony witnessed by family and friends. Whether conducted in the living room or backyard, a church or temple, city hall, a community garden or a maximum-security prison, the commitment that comes from words and deeds has import and significance much wider than ourselves.

We've chosen poems and personal narratives and essays that don't shy away from difficult truths. Some narratives follow the trajectory we might expect; others carve an unexpected, perhaps refreshing, alternative path.

The anthology has, of course, only begun to scratch the surface of a broad and ever-changing subject. Stories necessarily vary with circumstances, cultures and personalities. We offer this collection as a tapestry of voices reflecting the doubts, joys, sorrows and struggles that are an integral part of love and commitment, a weaving of many threads, dark and light and all the shades between.

Jane Silcott & Fiona Tinwei Lam
February 2018
Vancouver, BC

# Evolution

# Let's Get Married

**RONNA BLOOM**

It would be a quiet affair, a small dinner at home.
It would be a lavish affair with hooped skirts and high-necked collars.
It would be a farmers' feast with fresh beets and rutabagas.
Sheep smiling.

It would be June, of course.
There would be travel and tongues
of Romance languages,
pillow books, courtesans, and tarts.

There would be scandals and finger-wagging.
Friends would be shocked, secrets revealed,
undergarments kept under and thrown over balconies.
There would have to be balconies,
with both confessing love.

We would be like birds
simply looking at each other from rooftops.
Then flying over.
This one there, that one here.
There would be flight and plumage.
Singing and clapping.

And with it, an era tiptoeing,
gently making its way to the bedroom—no, no not the bedroom—
quietly making its way to where love goes when it's most tender
and surprising in its magenta feathers,

where it is kind,
and its silence is so wide it engulfs us all
in a music we can't hear or identify but know,

and we walk away humming.

# The Evolution of Marriage

## LUANNE ARMSTRONG

At the summer wedding of one of my son's friends, I sat outside with the other older women under an umbrella to keep off the hot sun. We drank wine and gossiped while the August sun glazed the dusty grass with heat. People were either in the kitchen cooking or outside decorating tents.

One of the other women leaned over to me and asked, "Have you noticed who is doing the child care?"

I looked around the yard. A tent had been set up and filled with toys. The men there were looking after their own and each other's children, besieged by small people wanting drinks, walks, arbitration in disputes over toys, or to be picked up and carried. One young man walked my four-year-old granddaughter down the driveway several times so she could check out a black stump that might just, at any moment, turn into a bear.

I got up and wandered into the kitchen where both men and women were cooking, chatting back and forth about recipes and restaurants. Outside, the women were mostly decorating the tents and an arbour, but some men were also helping with that. It was all very peaceful. People did what they were good at. Then the women disappeared to help the bride get dressed. And the grandmas smugly sat on in their comfy chairs and drank wine to the sunset.

When I was a child, my mother's best friend was in an unhappy marriage. She would come for tea and I would be sent outside. But I was my mother's confidante and usually the only person around that she could talk to so she would tell me the details after her friend left. I would sit on the stool squirming.

"Oh, poor M. She won't let her husband touch her anymore. She's so afraid she might get pregnant again. She hated having babies. She said that trying to nurse a baby made her throw up."

It turned out that M also hated doing laundry, dishes and vacuuming. She spent much of her time dressing up (she dressed amazingly well) and having tea with the ladies in town. My father had told my mother that her husband "had a skirt in every town."

But they couldn't divorce, these two, even though their fighting was renowned among the neighbours. It wasn't done, said my mother. No one would talk to them again. The husband would lose his business and never again would M go to have tea with the ladies. And what would happen to their kids? It wasn't to be thought of.

Nor could my parents divorce.

My mother and father fought bitterly, most of the time over money. They fought over Christmas, over going to movies, over buying school supplies, anything that might cost extra money. Every possibility of a family celebration was fraught. My father hated to do anything that wasn't work on the farm. Driving to town for a movie meant spending money on treats. He hated buying food from a grocery store that the farm hadn't produced.

When I was seven, my mother asked me if she should leave my father. She had asked my father for money to buy new linoleum for the kitchen. He refused. She began tearing at the linoleum herself, ripping it up, blue linoleum with ragged flowers.

"Help me," she said, her face purple. "Come and help."

It was a transgression, going against my father, tearing up the floor. I was caught, as I was so often, between my father, who made the rules, and my mother, for whom I felt sorry. The linoleum tore easily.

As we were kneeling side by side, my mother asked, "Should I leave your father?" It was a real question. She went on, "I could get a job as a hairdresser. But where would we live?"

I thought about my mother and father, the differences and the bitter angry words that flew between them. I thought about how my father made the farm work, about how his unrelenting persistence, hard work and ferocity made everything go the way it was supposed to—how he bullied the cows into milking and forced the balky tractors to run, how he swore at things until they gave way.

My mother was always in the house, also working but tied to the house by invisible strings. I was always trying to get her to go out so I could show her the fascinating farm stuff: the new kittens, the first dandelion, how shiny and clean my horse looked from brushing and polishing. But even when she came out, her eyes narrowed. She would look around the yard as if she had never quite seen it before and then say, "I've got to go in. I left a pot on the stove." She would hurry away to the house as if it might catch fire from a moment of her inattention.

So I said, "No, I don't think you should go."

I knew it was the wrong answer and also the right answer. I knew she had asked me because she was afraid of what would happen, afraid to leave in spite of her rage at my father. For years after, she would say, "You told me to stay," whenever she was in a screaming rage at my father, and I dared to say anything in his defence.

As a child, I saw this side of marriage. I saw the trapped women as flightless birds trembling in their kitchens. There might have been other places where women were far more free, but I was in a small rural community where the lines were drawn, the roles were set: women were bitches and men were tyrants. On the whole, I preferred the men. I did the same things they did; I was outside where the world was made into work and straight lines. And outside was a place of escape, a place, it seemed, to which my mother couldn't go.

Then, later, there was a long time when I was a single parent. There seemed to be a lot of us. My friend Sam and I used to wonder where all the good dads had gone. We knew a few among our friends. But we knew so many kids, like our kids, who had no dads at all, dads that existed but didn't send child support or birthday cards, dads that didn't visit, dads that had no presence in their kids' lives. This was in the seventies and early eighties. There was a lot of talk in the media about the nuclear family disappearing altogether. There was a way-out-on-the-fringes group who called themselves the REAL Women of Canada (REAL was an acronym for realistic, equal, active, for life). REAL women went around declaiming that such things as abortion rights and feminism and gay rights would destroy the family altogether. I found them exasperating, not because they were so extreme but because of their appropriation of the word "family." In their view of the world, there was only one kind of family: mom in the kitchen, dad out working, and 2.5 clean and obedient children with clipped hair reciting Bible verses.

One afternoon in 1986 I stood on the steps of the Hotel Vancouver. I was making a presentation to the secretary of state on behalf of the feminist organization I was working for. The law banning abortion was still being discussed by the Supreme Court. All kinds of women's groups were there making presentations about themselves, including REAL women.

I was outside for a break. One of the REAL women stood on the steps beside me, watching the traffic, perhaps waiting for someone.

I moved over to her and said as nicely as I could manage, "I have a family too. A pretty good family with four great kids." I had prepared a whole nice speech in my head, just for her.

She ignored me. I might as well have been speaking to the cars driving by.

But it was true. Families were indeed disintegrating. It seemed as if everyone wanted to claim their own definition of that word. Marriage seemed to be headed for the hills. No one got married anymore. They just had "relationships" of varying lengths and configurations. In the Slocan Valley, a friend of mine said it was as if everyone in the valley had slept with everyone else in the valley at some point. It made party planning complicated.

Families were also rebuilding. Gay people were focusing on the right to adopt. Extended families were becoming more the norm. It is impossible to survive in North American society as a single parent without an extended family. In my case, I had my mother and a wide network of friends who kept me fed and sane. In many rural communities in BC, people experimented with all kinds of family configurations; this meant that family dinners got more and more interesting with partners and ex-partners and stepchildren and half-brothers and half-sisters all mingling together over the lentil and tofu turkey. The seventies and eighties were a cultural coleslaw when it seemed everything was shredded and mixed into rainbow colours.

And somewhere, somehow in there, dads discovered dadding. Perhaps it was the New Age movement. Perhaps it was the emphasis on the new way of giving birth. Perhaps they all got lonesome.

Dads discovered they could be in the delivery room. They could bond with their new babies. They could do their share of child care and housework. They could even cook. Men had always cooked but usually because they were getting paid by someone. But now, urged on by feminist magazines and wives, they began to live in their own house instead of coming into them, as my father always had, as a place to eat and sleep and then leave again early in the morning.

I lived through all this in various ways. I tried marriage three times and failed marriage three times. I never actually wanted to be married or have children. I did both out of some confused sense that it was what I was supposed to do. And even when marriage made me feel safe, which I had never before felt, and when the words "my husband" rolled in my mouth plummy and rich; even when I loved the person, it didn't keep me from being frantic with claustrophobia. It wasn't until I became a feminist and a writer that I understood myself and the world well enough to realize I never actually wanted a relationship or a marriage. I wanted books. To read them, to write them. To do that, I mostly needed to be alone.

Finally, I became single, stayed single, and I had all these children—who are now grown.

I worried that I had put them off marriage forever. They didn't have models. They didn't have fathers. Their friends didn't have fathers. They had a community full of various kinds of families. They had my parents, who had hung together but who still had some monumental and quite terrifying wars.

But I mustn't have done too bad a job. Now, much later, three of my children are in good relationships. My youngest son and his friends are all married, with children. They were serious about getting married and are serious about staying married. They are good at marriage, good at children, good at finances and mortgages and owning houses. The men never even question the idea of doing child care, housework and cooking. They just do it. In fact, they love doing it. These families are solid and serious. And often worried. About the future and their children's future. But in the meantime, they are all working so hard to pay for everything, they don't have much time or energy left over for worrying.

Marriage has moved on. All through the seventies and eighties the culture wars raged with the right gloomily depicting the death of the nuclear family—of marriage, of society. Instead, what happened is that marriage reformed itself—marriage turned out to be amazingly resilient. The idea of standing up in front of your family, friends, community, children and associated pets and declaring your allegiance to one of the structural essentials of community proved irresistible. True, marriage went through a period of being "fashionable," something you could spend far too much money on. But even that has faded as fashion has moved on and people have less money to flash around on turquoise bridesmaids' dresses.

Family is probably the most durable connection humans make. Biologist E.O. Wilson believes that humans and ants have a lot in common. Our most basic instincts are to create a "nest" and then to defend it. We do both of those things extremely well. And the human community is based on the need to care for and nurture children. Despite whatever future technical global apocalyptic weirdness North American culture evolves into, that fact will remain timeless. And marriage, in all its present multiple iterations, has evolved by turning in circles and more circles and thus remains much the same. The difference between marriage now and the marriage of my parents' generation is simple: choices, lots and lots of choices. Maybe too many but at least no one is staying married anymore because they will be culturally shunned for not being married.

My children's generation mostly seems to be getting married because they want to—it's important to them. Often both the man and the woman have jobs—they may have small children and a dog. Or not. They share things. They talk to one another. In every way, this is an improvement over those whispered prisons of my parents' generation.

Today, marriage is more of an affirmation of what is already in place and working. It's a way of saying, yes, here we are, part of you, part of us, part of humanity.

It works this way for same-sex marriage as well. I was initially surprised by the demand for same-sex marriage. I supported it. I understood the need for shared health and pension benefits, I understood the need for gay and lesbian partners to be allowed into the hospital rooms of partners, which was a huge deal during the AIDS crisis.

What I didn't understand, until I saw it working, was how much same-sex marriage would normalize LBGT people. I didn't understand until I saw my previously homophobic, prissy, closed-minded small town happily accept not one but two married gay couples, one of women and one of men. After the town took a look and realized these people had careers, mortgages, kids, lives, lawns, yards, clipped hedges and nice cars, and were also quite willing to volunteer and be part of the community, they were absorbed into the life of the town.

Marriage is a cultural narrative. It tells us a lot about what we value and how we organize ourselves. It changes with almost every era and every generation. It changes with status and money and location.

But I haven't heard anyone complaining lately that it's disappearing. I haven't heard any rants about the nuclear family dying off. Instead, my small, once racist, once homophobic town is full of nuclear families, married men and married women of various backgrounds with small children, and the schools, once universally white, are full of non-white children.

The world may be going to hell with climate warming and insane US politics but marriage, it appears, whatever shape it takes, is here to stay. It probably will continue to face some new challenges, to morph and take new shapes. In the end, it will still be about people committed to making family, making community and making it work; and willing to stand up and say so in front of everyone. There will always be mothers and fathers and grandparents weeping and shuffling around while the happy couple of whatever mixed genders heads out the door.

As I sit in my overstuffed chair under an umbrella in the sun, I raise a glass to all of them. And wait for the next iteration of marriage to come floating by.

# On the Piano

## JANE EATON HAMILTON

---

When the neighbours spit my way over the fence, I just kept carrying the sandwiches out to Joy, raised my voice and said, "Darling, how did it go at the *lesbian* library this morning? Did you put *lesbian* gas in the car? Come and sit down on your *lesbian* chair. Put down your *lesbian* spade and eat some *lesbian* food. Honey, here's your *lesbian* tomato and cheese sandwich. May I have a sip of your *lesbian* Coke?"

I could have been worse, really. I'd let the 'phobes off lightly. I could have said sex things.

Joy and I had talked about how it might go being two of the thirty-six litigant public faces in a court case against the federal government for same-sex marriage in Canada. Our pro bono lawyers, barb findlay and Kathleen Lahey, estimated it would take us about seven years, start to finish, for the cases, which they felt we had a good chance of winning thanks to Canada's living tree constitution, the Charter of Rights and Freedoms. There were three cases, one each in Quebec, Ontario and BC. Did we have that kind of tenacity? Did our kids? Would our kids, now cuspal adults, get pulled in, and would they feel safe, at all times safe? Joy and I talked about the kinds of things that had happened to queer activists around the world—the loss of homes and jobs and custody, the beatings, the murders.

We could be killed. Anyone could be killed, any one of the women or men stepping forward to insist that it was our time.

But I had advancing heart disease and Joy had had breast cancer, so death figured differently for us. Personally, I'd seen death's face so many times that every time the scythe swung my way I just stepped aside. *Grim Reaper calling? Go suck lemons, Hoodie-Hat.*

Being in the case meant being a professional queer, and being a professional queer meant being out in a whole new way. This was not just being out at school with your kid's teacher or at work with your supportive colleagues or out with your family members—this was everybody, not just queers and allies, but prudes and know-it-alls and right-wing zealots and thugs who thought they oughta knock or rape a little straight into lezzies knowing who we were. At a restaurant? Walking on the street? Using a public washroom? At the supermarket? In the dentist's chair? At the car wash? At a client's house? Taking out your garbage?

We could be targets.

In 2000, it wasn't a friendly world for queers. It was only three years since Ellen had come out on *The Oprah Winfrey Show*, two years since Matthew Shepard had been tied to a Wyoming fence and tortured. Here in Vancouver, a gay man named Aaron Webster was still to be beaten to his death in Stanley Park. In Iran, in those days, queers had the choice of death by stoning or jumping off a cliff.

All over the world, we heard repetitive messages: *You are bad. You deserve to die. You are pedophiles. You are abominations. You are going to hell.*

Queers assimilated other, subtler messages too from the things said around us:

*We don't invite you to family events (because you embarrass us).*

*When we talk about our husbands, don't chime in with stories about your partner; it's just not the same.*

*No, you can't be at her bedside. You're not family.*

Our photo was not on the piano at my not-in-law's house.

To think there is not a caustic backlash to being treated as invisible, as embarrassments, as second-class is as absurd as thinking that spaghetti is not food. This treatment erodes couples. This treatment is acid poured on a queer family, slowly and steadily consuming its health and stability.

It is hard to stand up tall when your own people continually cut you down. It is hard to assert the loveliness and glow of your relationship when people everywhere are telling you your partnership is filthy and hazardous to your children.

It's hard, but queers did it. We developed a fuck-you, bite-me, we-don't-give-a-frig-about-straights swagger. And we really didn't. Sod straights anyway. We had our own community where our heads, when we weren't actually giving head, were held up high and proud, where we could love our own ways, where we could be the outlaws we'd always been told we were.

Still, there was bullying. Family rejection. Trouble at school. Foster homes. Homelessness. Dropouts. Low self-esteem. Stereotyping. Discrimination. Sketchy relationships. Instability. Poor housing. Poor mental health. More stress. Poor physical health. Time spent in mental institutions, in reclamation camps, in sad hetero marriages. Often someone lost their job, or their apartment, when someone found out they were gay. Sometimes someone got beaten on the street. Sometimes someone killed themselves. Sometimes someone was murdered.

Sometimes a "gay panic" defence was used. *I killed him, but only because he came on to me.* And mostly, in those years, a gay panic defence worked to set murderers free.

In those days, most straights didn't even realize they knew any queers. They didn't know a lesbian personned the mammography machine. They didn't know three of their letter carriers were queer. They didn't know two out of eight tellers went home to same-sex partners every night, and two more partied till dawn in gay clubs three nights out of seven.

We had Pride in 2000, but we didn't have visibility.

Visibility was my mantra. Visibility was the key to unlocking the cages straights had shoved us into. Visibility would throw open the doors.

It had once been illegal to be gay in Canada, and punishable by death (though this had not been enforced). This law was repealed in the late 1800s, replaced with an act forbidding "gross indecency between men," which stuck until PM Pierre Trudeau turfed it in 1969. In 1984, after Trudeau pushed through the new Charter, thanks to activists and their lawyers, equality rights blossomed. It was contentious—some queers wanted to keep our outlaw community intact; some thought gaining rights meant selling out, aping hets. Some just thought it meant safety. Some rights stole money from queer pockets, as when lovers, newly considered a couple, got only one benefit cheque instead of two. But ultimately, every Canadian citizen, and every Canadian couple, needed to be governed by the same laws.

I didn't believe benefits that accrued to married couples should exclude single people (why on earth could a single person not pass along their pension to their kid, or their friend, the way married people could their spouse?) but I thought that whatever was enshrined had to be enshrined across the board. I didn't think marriage was without its problems—among them its origins as an institution where women were property—but, thanks mostly to feminists, Canadians had altered marriage to suit modern times. The mothballs were gone, the webs dusted off. Despite its problems, marriage remained a potent institution. It was, among other things, a family-maker, and a scaffolding under which to raise children. Some of the power disparities common in het marriages wouldn't be issues in queer marriages, since no one went in with a predetermined role.

In September 2000, Joy and I and bill bissett went to Vital Stats in Vancouver and applied for a marriage licence, which was denied. Other couples across the country were doing the same. The cases launched. BC's was heard first, in Justice Ian Pitfield's courtroom. It lasted two weeks. Joy and I heard every nasty bit of business the right wing had to say about queers: *We would ruin marriage. Marriage had been one man and one woman since time immemorial. If we were able to marry, we would so sully the institution that no straights would ever be able to wed in Canada again. Next, we'd be asking to marry animals. Next, we'd be demanding to marry corporations.*

It was the sort of thing we needed support to tolerate. We needed to be able to feel the groundswell of our community shoring us up as the right wing ripped off our skin. But the eight couples from BC didn't have our queer communities behind us; our queer communities hung us in the harsh winds of homo-hate.

We'd rubbed some people wrong, and editorials were published against us in vitriolic diatribes week after drubbing week. Jane Rule, lesbian author, came out against equality.

It became cool to be against marriage. For us, it felt like a big schoolyard pileup. Vancouver queers leaped on top to squash us like bugs.

Our spirits flagged. Was a quickie really as meaningful as a long relationship? Were we actually ruining queer culture forever?

Were we really *those* fags and dykes, assimilationist and boring and living in suburban homes with 2.5 kids? Our vibrant out queer histories were scrubbed with a magic eraser.

We sat around my living room together, the Vancouver couples, and we pulled questions we were likely to be asked from a jar, and we practised over and over and over again, cobbling together reasoned responses. Not just to the hets who would be asking, but, alas, to the queers.

And then we set ourselves loose into the questioning hands of reporters, into the fray of the rainbow community, into the jagged het community.

*I saw you in the newspaper*, people said. Or they said nothing, but just stared, recognizing us from a newspaper or magazine or TV spot, their cheeks turning rage-blue. Guys in vans shouted hate as they pushed down their gas pedals.

And then we not only lost our case, we lost badly.

Meantime, Joy's mom died suddenly, fracturing the family, and we celebrated Thanksgivings and Christmases alone.

The pain was like crunching razor blades.

Ontario's lower case won in 2002, and the government was given two years to change the law. Our appeal was heard in the spring of 2003, in front of three justices, a shorter hearing, and this time when the verdict was rendered, we'd also won. The federal law holding that marriage was between one man and a woman fell.

But wait.

We won, sort of, but we didn't, exactly. What the court called "the remedy," marriage, was put on hold for fifteen months.

Joy and I considered flying to Belgium, which had just enacted same-sex marriage, the first country in the world, but my mom had just died and I was too wrecked.

In the middle of May, we celebrated our tenth anniversary.

A scant three weeks later, on June 8, 2003, Ontario's appellate court issued its ruling. The federal law was changed effective immediately. Marriage performed by religious banns became retroactively legal, and marriages began in a gay frenzy.

We reapplied for licences in BC, twice, figuring if there was only a federal impediment to marriage, and it had fallen, same-sex marriage ought to be legal everywhere.

But BC, absent the feds forcing them, would not issue licences.

We got together with our friends Tanya Chambers and Melinda Roy, another litigant couple, and decided, all four of us, to travel to Ontario.

So we hopped a red-eye to city hall and were given a bona fide marriage licence; after our prior rejections, Joy and I, Melinda and Tanya all wore shit-eating grins. A Tokyo TV reporter bought us flowers from the corner store, stiff dyed mums; our friend Maggie divvied them up as only a lesbian could do, still plastic-wrapped, and thrust them into our shaking hands. Five in a row with our daughter Meghann at our side, in front of a gay judge, we spoke our legal vows.

I know of no legal impediment why I, Jane, may not be married to you, Joy—

I know of no legal impediment.

## Epilogue

It's been fourteen years since Canada changed the law prohibiting same-sex marriage, and twelve years since we codified it. Queers didn't all run out and marry our dogs, as the wrong-wingers told judges we would, and we didn't marry corporations either. Even though a rabbi said no Jewish people would ever be able to marry again because of how we had sullied the institution, Jewish people—surprise!—went on getting married.

Queers said marriage would wreck our culture, and that, perhaps, has come true—although who's to say leaping toward security and certainty is a bad thing, really? A lot of us have craved it. We age, we change, we settle down, our goals alter. And within marriage, everyone is still called on to be vital; hopefully everyone is on the streets with placards and resistance.

But are the only acceptable queers the lesbians down the road with the 2.5 kids and the SUV in the drive?

People wonder what my thoughts on marriage are now, since eight years into mine, and eighteen years into our relationship, my wife wanted out, a development that crushed me body and soul, and from which I am still recovering.

Yet, I still believe in the general good of enfranchisement, and therefore in queer marriage. The power of vows is real, the power of community-witness is life changing. I do believe, will always believe, there is great value in standing together, sometimes with children, to enjoy the wonder and ride out the storms. It is certainly true that time, commitment and struggle bring unions to a deeper intimacy.

I'm not sure what to think about queer divorce, which I have seen get every bit as acrimonious, expensive and time-consuming as the heterosexual equivalent. In some ways, I yearn for the old days when we broke the way of the Ferron lyrics: "You give me the furniture, we'll divide the photographs / Go out to dinner one more time / Have ourselves a bottle of wine / And a couple of laughs." We figured it out however we figured it out, and then we went our separate ways with no continuing financial involvement.

Overall, it's good that we consider each other's futures, isn't it? In the splits of old days, vulnerabilities like disability and children were overlooked. People aren't on equal footing at the start of relationships, and there's no reason to assume they will be at the end either; thus we've joined a heterosexual regime which already realized this.

We're here, we're queer and we love each other. We never marry corporations or dogs, and our cats, well, they remain aloof, never even seeming ready to pop the question.

# Cover to Cover

## FIONA TINWEI LAM

---

*cover: cover ground; cover up; blow cover; duck and cover; cover the field; under cover; break cover; take cover; cover to cover ...*

The Free Dictionary

### Cover ground

During the first four years that Ted and I cohabited, I swung back and forth about getting married. From the start I'd felt completely safe and at ease with him, more than I had felt with anyone else. Here was a man who could be vulnerable and open, who would never harm me with words or deeds or malice of any kind, a man who could make me laugh so hard with his sly irreverence that I'd use up half a box of tissue. A cabinetmaker whose clothes smelled of freshly cut wood when he came home from his work, whose strong, lithe hands I loved to hold, whose weathered face I loved to touch. It had been eighteen years since the end of my first marriage, but it still took a long time for me to articulate the dread and unease that came over me whenever the subject came up.

"I'd like us to get married, but I don't want to be called a wife," I said.

Ted seemed nonplussed.

"Just think about what people's perceptions would be if I called you my wife?" I said. "It's not a neutral word. It implies subordination. "

Ted chuckled and shrugged. Why couldn't we both wear the pants—or skirts for that matter? He wasn't one to analyze categories—that was my department.

### Cover up

Although I didn't declare myself a feminist until I went to law school, I was already aware of women's subordinate legal status historically. From the Middle Ages until the late nineteenth century, a married woman had the legal status of *feme covert* or literally "covered woman" under English common law, which melded Anglo-Saxon traditions, Catholic canon law and the legal traditions of the Romans and Normans. In the eighteenth century,

William Blackstone articulated the principle in his *Commentaries on the Laws of England*:

> By marriage, the husband and wife are one person in law: that is, the very being or legal existence of the woman is suspended during the marriage, or at least is incorporated and consolidated into that of the husband under whose wing, protection, and cover, she performs everything. … And her condition during her marriage is called her coverture. … And therefore all deeds executed, and acts done, by her, during her coverture, are void.

English common law (which was also the law of Canada and other British colonies) only allowed widows and unmarried adult women to own and manage property and have standing in court. Once married, women had none of those rights. The law changed slowly in Canada until the passage of Married Women's Property Acts in various provinces in the late nineteenth century, giving women the right to control their own property. And until 1983, marital rape was not considered a criminal offence: a husband could be charged with assault, but not sexual assault.

Since that time, the concept of marriage has changed with the rise of women's rights and individual freedom, especially in liberal Western societies. But a certain residue of social convention, expectation and tradition around marriage persists, such as when a woman takes on her husband's last name, something I've always considered regressive (except in cases where the woman is escaping a family history of violence or abuse). To a limited extent, I could accept the ancient philosophical notion of a couple forming two halves of an idealized whole, as was set out in the myth of Aristophanes in Plato's *Symposium*: "Love is born into every human being; it calls back the halves of our original nature together; it tries to make one out of two and heal the wound of human nature." But if two people indeed become one, why does modern society still expect the two to become *him*? And why would a modern woman allow a man's identity to veil—or swallow up—her own?

Confucian philosophy was no better. When married, a woman would be expected to leave her family of origin and become part of her husband's family, managing his household, serving his parents, bearing his sons to continue his line and tending to his ancestors' graves. I could vividly recall my mother's rants about the injustice of not being allowed to work as a doctor, of being expected to be my father's housekeeper, receptionist and secretary. After his death, she had never once considered getting remarried. "I don't have the time or energy to take care of a man and his children," she had told us. "Never depend on a man to support you." She remembered the dependent status of her own mother, who had been a young, uneducated teahouse singer brought into a large household as the fourth concurrent wife of the owner of an herbal medicine company in Vietnam and Hong Kong. In the family hierarchy, my grandmother ranked at the bottom.

I was born in the year of the dragon. According to a Chinese astrology book, "a dragon daughter is not desired because a female dragon won't submit willingly to the Confucian 'three virtues for women' that demand obedience to father, husband, and in old age, eldest son." When I was in my twenties, I consulted a Chinese astrologer on a whim during a summer break. He advised me not to become a lawyer, even though I hadn't mentioned I was in law school.

"You must soften yourself with men," the astrologer urged. "Not be so strong."

I tried not to roll my eyes. I had just started dating a Caucasian classmate who I thought would be untainted by the sexism in Chinese culture. We were incompatible in a few significant ways, but I thought this would dissipate with time. At the end of third year, getting engaged seemed to be the best way to cement our bond while I returned home to Vancouver to work as an articling student and he went on to pursue another degree in Windsor. But over time I started having doubts. The initial strong attraction between us had flatlined and I was having flashbacks of my parents' rocky relationship.

Two weeks before the wedding, I shared my growing misgivings with a friend.

"It's just nerves," she reassured me. "You'll be fine."

It wasn't, and I wasn't. But the proverbial runaway train couldn't be stopped. I put a lid on my gut instincts and kept careening toward the cliff. On the morning of the wedding, the seamstress was still adjusting and sewing the hems of the bridesmaids' dresses. At the ceremony, my grandmother frowned at my non-traditional wedding dress and lack of a veil. I forgot to kiss my groom at the altar. After the ceremony, several older Chinese guests were confused by the absence of a sit-down meal at the afternoon cocktail reception and left. At the Chinese banquet that evening, the waiters abandoned us so they could serve two larger wedding feasts in the same restaurant. My mother, in the early stages of dementia, remained in a confused haze. During the honeymoon in Ireland, I was in a confused haze myself due to the extra-strength old-style antihistamines I had to pop regularly because of a record high pollen count. A few months after the ceremony, my wedding ring flew off my wet finger in a restaurant bathroom and landed with a distant clang. I'd never see it again.

### Blow cover

About four years later, we left Vancouver for Ottawa where my spouse was to receive French-language training prior to being posted overseas with the Foreign Service. Soon after our arrival, I picked up a newsletter published by the Foreign Services Spouses Association. The newsletter featured articles on property division after marriage breakdown and handling culture shock. At one of the association's gatherings, women commiserated about having to uproot every three to five years just when they were starting to make friends and establish a sense of community. Some felt they were akin to executive assistants and housekeepers, chauffeuring their kids to schools and hosting social events for their husbands' colleagues when required. Many were lonely, exhausted and isolated. There were tears and hugs. Only one woman had managed to find short-term non-profit work as a consultant. One male spouse had also found work in his field. A staff liaison urged me to consider joining the Foreign Service myself, despite my lack of interest. The closer the time came for choosing my spouse's posting, the more unbearable my feelings of suffocation and panic. Finally, the tight cover over my misgivings, doubts and resentments blew up and off. I fled.

### Duck and cover

In the middle of the divorce, I attended my first cousin's wedding. There were five hundred guests at the formal ceremony presided over by both archbishop and bishop in a historic Toronto Anglican church. A professional soprano sang "Ave Maria." At the wedding reception at the Royal York, a string quartet played while waiters circulated with endless trays of crispy suckling pig skin and dainty dim sum.

I felt as if a big scarlet "D" had been stitched to my chest. The last family wedding that many of the guests had attended had been my own. Few people talked to me—maybe because I was constantly ducking behind my siblings. I took cover at the buffet tables, stuffing my mouth with food so I didn't have to speak to anyone.

### Cover the field

Six years after my divorce, to the further horror and consternation of some of my older, tradition-bound relatives, I became an unmarried mother, raising a child without a spouse. Meanwhile, a succession of friends and family members went through legal separations. The divorce rate in Canada had increased to 41 percent of marriages ending by the thirtieth wedding anniversary, with the average marriage lasting 13.7 years. I stopped feeling like a pariah.

Then, fourteen years after my divorce and seven years after having my son, I met Ted. He became an integral part of my life and my son's over the next four years—making gingerbread castles, building a bookshelf to hold my son's huge collection of books, moving into our home, taking us on road trips near and far. I wanted my other family members to accept him fully as an indispensable part of our household and an honoured member of our family. He and I had both passed the midpoint of our lives—a point on the curve on the graph of life where losses and regrets would soon start to accumulate. Why not take the opportunity to celebrate life and love despite it all?

The legal differences between cohabitation and marriage had dissolved by this time too. British Columbia's provincial government adopted legislation that made it clear that common-law relationships of two years' duration or more were equivalent to marriage when dividing property during divorce and separation. The goal of the legislation was to protect dependent parties when long-term relationships dissolved. Instead of requiring lawyers to cite evidence of committed spousal relationships and shape arguments about constructive trusts in drawn-out expensive courtroom battles, the legislation would simply deem a cohabiting long-term couple to be spouses, responsible for each other's care. With the economic consequences resolved, what remained was the social and cultural significance of marriage.

In addition, the legal recognition of gay and lesbian marriages underlined how marriage rites were still valued as a public way for partners to demonstrate their long-term devotion to each other and to demonstrate their intent to fully share their lives. It seemed to show a growing understanding and acceptance that the fundamental structure of a marriage relationship no longer had to be based on a division of labour defined by gender. A marriage of two men or two women might possibly involve one partner taking on the stereotypical role of wife, the other the role of husband—but perhaps partners could now negotiate a relationship of equally shared and integrated roles custom-tailored to their abilities, interests, schedules and needs.

### Under cover

A month before my wedding to Ted, I combed through the various forms of vows sent to me by my friend Julie, a United Church minister who would be officiating.

"I'd prefer it if you didn't use the terms 'husband' and 'wife,'" I told her.

I had used the term "partner" to refer to Ted since he had moved in with me four years earlier. Being over fifty years of age, he had outgrown the label "boyfriend." Although the word "spouse" had a bland, bureaucratic ring, I occasionally used it. The term "life partner" sounded needlessly formal and strange. My lesbian friends always used "partner" to refer to their committed long-term live-in lovers, so I figured I could too. Anyone who felt unsure about whether the term was meant in a business or romantic sense could eventually figure it out.

She agreed to this, and promised to keep the event secret from our friends until after the ceremony since I wanted to completely avoid the usual pre-wedding hype and buildup. As the date got closer, it was hard not to blurt out the truth to my close friends. When the day arrived, I took the bus downtown to get my hair cut (not even informing my hairdresser about the wedding), bought a few bunches of dahlias from a corner grocery store to decorate the house and then returned home to make a lopsided *croquembouche* for dessert before throwing on a favourite ten-year-old summer dress. Ted wore one of his two suits. My teenaged son decided to stay barefoot for the day.

After the vows had been exchanged in our backyard, Julie dutifully addressed the nine close family members whom we'd asked to attend. "As we are living in the age of gender neutrality, Fiona and Ted have requested that they not be called 'husband and wife.' So please refer to them as spouses, partners or newlyweds."

*The diehard pagan feminist strikes again*, I imagined my family thinking as I gazed at their stoic expressions. I hoped that they'd spread the word to other relatives: no wifeliness for me.

### Break cover

The day after the ceremony, I finally informed friends and relatives about the nuptials. Congratulatory greeting cards from both sides of our family soon arrived—addressed to Mr. and Mrs. Ted Belch. A wedding cheque was even written out this way. Four months later the Christmas cards came. When I fumed, Ted just laughed.

When one unsuspecting friend initially asked me whether I was changing my name, I wrote three long indignant paragraphs in response about the patriarchal custom of subsuming a woman's identity. Then I pressed Delete, and thanked her for her good wishes instead. I added that Ted wouldn't be taking my last name and I wouldn't be taking his, and blending our last names—"Blam" or "Lelch"—just didn't sound very good.

Had these folks somehow missed the evolution of women's legal status over the past two centuries? Did they know nothing about me and nothing about our relationship? Why had they assumed that I would be willing to throw a cover over all that I had worked for and regress into anachronistic traditional and stereotypical roles?

"Does it feel different being married?" both married and single friends asked.

Strangely, it did. Somehow the public statement about our long-term commitment and caring for each other made us feel closer. Ted seemed subtly more confident and relaxed: my occasional blips of impatience and frustration no longer alarmed him.

During those first few months after the wedding, we'd sometimes poke each other in the arm at bedtime. "Howdy, pardner," we'd say in mock cowboy accents.

### Take cover

For four years, I had mulled over the pros and cons of remaining common-law versus getting officially married, while navigating the inevitable ups, downs and plateaus of our relationship. But the major turning point in our discussions occurred about a year before the wedding, when Ted received a diagnosis of stage 2 colorectal cancer. His sister had died of the same kind of cancer eight years before. A friend of mine was in its terminal stage and was undergoing experimental treatments. We wondered how long his body had been under siege from within, and how it would cope with a possible barrage of toxic drugs and radiation that would hurt his healthy cells as well as the malignant ones. It was unclear from the tests and scans if the cancer had spread to Ted's lymph nodes.

Prior to his scheduled surgery, we took a trip to Haida Gwaii, touring some of the ancient villages by Zodiac. At night, we held each other close and talked quietly about what might lie ahead. Worry kept shadowing his face—future bills, monthly rent for his carpentry workshop, possible chemotherapy and radiation and its harsh side effects, the risk of long-term unemployment, the arduous years that his sister went through trying treatment after failed treatment. I reassured him that I could assist with any health or work expenses that arose.

"Guess you must regret being saddled with me," Ted said half-jokingly, but then grew serious. He paused, his eyes searching my face. "I don't want to ever be a burden."

I looked back at him, stroking his kind, humble face—familiar angles of chin and cheekbones, noble nose, easy smile, gentle blue eyes that gazed at me with a radiant tenderness. This time around, at this stage in my life, with this relationship, I was going to follow my instincts and intuition, which said, *To have and to hold, in sickness and in health.*

I smiled, put my arms around him and whispered in his ear, "I want to be with you, no matter what. No need to worry—I've got you covered."

# Dear Son

## BETSY WARLAND

Dear Son,

Now that you are nineteen, I am writing you quite a different letter than the weekly ones I wrote you after Mom S and I split up.

Given your increasing interest in experiencing an intimate relationship, it's time to give you glimpses of mine. Why? You have likely absorbed—through a kind of osmosis—the notions of love that I gained from my past relationships, and so you should have a sense of these stories. Also, you have always had such a large capacity to love. Just as we talk openly about sex, I want to be open with you about love.

This letter won't prevent you from making similar mistakes but it may help you to identify the causes of suffering that we inevitably encounter with a partner or lover. Recognition is important. Then we have a chance to consider alternative ways to express our hurt, as well as our love.

In my sketches of my five relationships below, I'm signalling an insight at the beginning and end of each sketch alongside a real-time glimpse of each relationship via a poem written during each one.

**1. There was, and still is, this romantic illusion that all you need is each other.** Years ago I began to get a glimpse of this falsehood, but it still took two more decades for me to see it clearly.

As you know, I grew up on a farm. Our social circle was pretty small and most of it was with my mom's and dad's extended families. "Going to town" was going to a town of 363 people. No one divorced. I didn't even know of this concept until much later. There were only two single women ("spinsters"). One was a schoolteacher; one the postmistress. One lived with her widower father; one with her widowed mother.

A woman living on her own was inconceivable. My parents' and my own assumption was that I'd be married by the time I graduated from college (I was), and that I would remain married my entire life. It didn't turn out that way.

My marriage was pleasant and agreeable but underneath it was quietly troubled. Our life passions were too disparate, including our emotional and sexual ones. As I became a writer in Toronto, I also became actively involved in the women's community of straight and lesbian feminists, particularly in the feminist literary community. After eight years, my marriage finally hit the wall. I moved out. Within a few months I fell in love for the first time. I thought I had been in love before, but I had only been in love with an assumption—that if I was married I must be in love. When I fell in love with J, I understood why my body had never fully responded to sex during my marriage. This lack of deep intimacy had been disheartening to both my husband and me.

Small Stranger

as i lay in bed last night
      i discovered my hand
clenched in a tight fist
                  my own hand
a hard cold rock
          next to me
it felt as though
it took a long time
         to open up
i hardly dared breathe
fearing i might wake you
              and you'd find
                      this small stranger
in our bed
this hand
a mirror
        i didn't want to look in

I've not read this poem for decades. Just now, as I was keying it into this letter, I began to cry. This took me by surprise. That particular sadness was so poignant, so impossible to express, talk about, share with others. We did try. But the absence of a mutual vision for our future—or a sensual closeness—persisted. We had been drawn to one another by our idiosyncrasies, our not-quite-fitting-the-norm college selves, but over the years his aspirations grew more normative and mine more aberrant.

**2. If you recognize a deep and persistent sadness, take heed.** Accepting that message was perhaps the most important thing I learned from my marriage.

**3. Be careful not to idealize lover/partner relationships.** Early on with J, we didn't yet recognize how some of a lesbian couple's challenges don't differ much from heterosexual ones.

As J and I figured out our sensual and erotic life, it was exciting but also challenging. Can you imagine never having seen a sexual or erotic image that reflected your eroticism; never having read about one except in a fleeting, metaphorical way; never having talked with anyone about sexual intimacy? At that time, there were some underground publications for male homosexuals but not for lesbians.

We had to figure it out as we went. Invent.

**4. Don't expect to be friends after a breakup.** It's rare for ex-couples. But you, dear son, intimately know the outcome when ex-lovers can: J is family to us some thirty years later.

My split-up with J was very different from my divorce. At that early stage in the lesbian feminist community, we were just beginning to understand how lesbian intimate relationships were both similar and dissimilar to heterosexual ones within the relationship, as well as in the larger, public world.

One problem was that we merged too much because we could identify with one another far more effortlessly. Eventually, there was a popular joke about how quickly we moved in together after a romance began.

Q. "What does a lesbian bring on her first date?"
A. "A U-Haul."

Also, if you become too cozy (having similar haircuts, adapting too much to one another's way of dressing, being together most of the time), the electricity of attraction and surprise often loses its charge. One night J and I had an identical dream. In each dream we were stripped naked in public. Our merging combined with the pressure around our intimacy made us both feel too exposed.

J became involved with another woman. I was heartbroken but J gently insisted she wanted our friendship, for we enjoyed so many things together: music, film, literature, nature. After licking my wounds for numerous months, I agreed.

apart    i become aware
we had been a sky with no earth
            a sun with no sunset

On the heels of our breakup I decided to do something I'd never done before: I became intentionally non-monogamous. I needed to protect myself for a while. Also, I needed to better understand my erotic self. Over the next year and a half I was involved with several women (lesbian and straight). At one point, I was involved with two Toronto women and three Vancouver women. Everyone knew. It was acceptable then as we were part of a young community figuring it all out. I learned a lot and was surprised that it is possible to care about and be intimate with more than one person at a time.

Yet it proved not to endure.

**5. Couples can't flourish in their own little worlds for any length of time.** They are affected by the political and cultural time they dwell in, both positively and negatively.

I met Daphne, a Vancouver author, at the first feminist writers conference in Toronto in the fall of 1981, where we both read. We agreed to have a coffee together after I arrived in Vancouver.

The attraction between us was palpable. Daphne was still in a relationship of many years but it was in slow decline. Hardly anyone (including me) was aware of this. When Daphne first leaned over from the driver's seat and kissed me, I instantly knew I was no longer non-monogamous.

as you read love poems to me

i saw the audience shudder
saw my old lover shoot down the aisle      her pain
your last lines
"this place full of contradiction—you know, you knew
it was the one place i meant"
                                    stunned we clapped
in horrible awe
as you struck/each poem
and blazed
            yourself aflame

During our twelve years together, Daphne and I created a precious sense of a blended family. In tandem, we worked flat out. The eighties were an intoxicating time for feminist thinkers and creators of culture in the Western world. We were creating art never created before. It felt like anything was possible. In 1984, our books of erotic love poems were published and we gave readings from them across Canada. That had never happened before, and to my knowledge, no Canadian lesbian couple has written companion erotic love collections since.

When cultural support and acceptance became conservative again, our options as feminist lesbian artists took a big hit. It often put us at odds with one another.

**6. Differences are inevitable.** They enrich a relationship. When others, however, continue to show high regard for one and little regard for the other, this can erode a relationship over the years. If you encounter this dynamic, consider it carefully as it is not likely to change.

Susan and I met in September 1992, not long after I arrived in Saskatoon to be the writer-in-residence. When we met, Susan's relationship of many years was very uncertain and her partner was away for a number of months. That summer I had acknowledged to Daphne that I was no longer committed to being monogamous.

Within a few months, Susan and I realized we were drawn to one another. We shared some significant influences in our lives: we both grew up in the church, were deeply involved with our extended families and had trained as visual artists. Landscape was another bond. Susan revelled in the Saskatchewan prairie and big sky and it reminded me of the Iowa landscape I grew up in. We immersed ourselves in it as much as possible.

> there is this spaciousness about you, in you, with you which
> words litter like satellite and shuttle debris each letter forever
> floating aimlessly

Once we were lovers, we also discovered a deep interest in having a child, and that interest became you! We were legally married in Vermont when you were two and a half. Joy radiated from you and we were happy being your moms. There were, however, a series of tough turns over those first seven years: you almost dying in the first weeks of your life, medical mistakes and their life-long repercussions for you, an extended litigation, moving from one sublet to another as we figured out health issues, including my being diagnosed with cancer, financial stresses and the crushing realization that I needed to remain in Vancouver and Susan in Saskatoon in order to continue our professional lives.

**7. When a couple goes through a long period of multiple challenges, it's common for both people to revert to how they navigated hardship as kids.** These approaches can be incompatible and inflexible because there's just too much going on.

Regardless of it all, both your moms loved—and love—you fiercely. As hard and sad as the endings of my other intimate relationships were, the pain of our family breaking up was the most devastating.

**8. It's not a good idea to start a new relationship before you've ended an existing relationship.** This caused additional pain and complications for everyone that lingered on, often for years. I vowed never to do that again to myself, or others.

For nine years I remained single, uncertain that I would ever have another intimate, committed relationship. During those years my focus was on nourishing our mom-son relationship from two provinces away, and I travelled to visit you in Saskatoon about every six weeks.

Gradually I began to enjoy my daily life as a solitary person, reorienting myself and rethinking my assumptions and expectations about a committed intimacy. I referred to myself as a recovering romantic. This helped me identify what I needed to do differently if I were to be in a committed, intimate relationship ever again.

Clack/clack

Why is grasshopper flying?
Because she fell in love?

How romance turns the world upside-down!

Again. Again. Grasshopper flings herself into sky
(thinks herself swallow)

       does she not hear clack/clack of her wings?

Ahh, no!

Grasshopper believes it's beloved's applause for her

       jerky

              boisterous

flight.

A crucial understanding was that a new partner had to respect your centrality in my life. Also, I wanted her to have her own relationship with you.

So, when I fell in love with Ingrid it was a very, very slow process. As you know, we had been good friends for a long time and she was very close to you. I had always been mystified by how good friends could become lovers. It proved, however, to be a real plus to already have established a tender knowing of, and respect for, one another that spanned over twelve years of numerous changes in each of our lives. I think now that at the heart of every healthy relationship is a good friendship, whether between kid and parent, teacher and student, sister and brother, or employer and employee.

As older lovers in our sixties, we knew we needed to bring a great deal of respect to the well-formed lives we both have apart from our love. For me, my being freed up from the expectations of the romantic script has made every aspect of my intimacy with Ingrid an exploration. During these years I also found a new self-acceptance as "a person of between" and took Oscar as my second given name.

From part 37, sections 14 and 15 of *Oscar of Between*:

For the first few weeks, Oscar and Ingrid take frequent long walks on the park's trails then wander more and more off trails. ...

Categories of groomed trails, park map in hand and safety-maintained trees on either side give way to nature's fervent instinct to survive, thrive, endlessly reinvent, redefine itself.

This is the nature of committed relationships: our intimacy can run deep but our interpretations and "instinct to survive, thrive" will be diverse. That said, the person from whom I have learned the most about love and respect is you, my dear son.

Your Mom B

# Decisions

# By the time you listen to this, I'll be gone

## CHELENE KNIGHT

———

## Side A. 1999

I never wanted to get married. Two friends gave it a shot. I admired them. I missed them. I watched them do things like tuck their shirts in, iron jeans, put the kettle on, set the table, burn bridges, build new ones. I watched them leave their lives behind. Sit down in prayer, hands clasped together, *Lord grant me the strength*. We are only young once. But when you've barely left high school and your old seat at the back of the class is still warm and even your mother had her doubts, do not worry about your fear of the sexless existence between two people whose loose lips spew pleasantries over a mashed-potato dinner, keep secrets in their tailored pockets, permanent-marker foreheads with the usual: *how was your day, the kids are asleep, what time are you coming home,* shopping lists, soccer games—falling into a dark pit of societal expectations, noose around the neck, ball-and-chain games, you'd never play—

## Side B. 2017

by the rules. Pull the sheets up around my chin. Another wedding. *I didn't want to be like them.* Open bar. I'll sit at the back tweeting about how amazing her dress is. Long lace sleeveless sheer back, empire waist—she's slamming champagne and smiling. I post a photo for proof. Thirty-four likes and sixteen retweets later, the first dance slaps me in the face when I realize they were playing *my* song—I *did* want to be like them, absorbing speeches, future blessings. I want them to be happy but this isn't how I pictured myself at thirty-five. The bus ride home forces a handwritten story to slowly tattoo itself somewhere on my body that I cannot see. Eyes shut. Three shots of whisky before sleep comes. Morning coffee blacks my tongue. Jeans too tight—a reminder that my old tricks no longer work. Dim the lights. My eyes brighten. Watch me part my hair in the other direction while three grey hairs shake their heads. *Tick tock.* Maybe I just wanted someone to ask me. *Tick tock.* And mean it. Maybe I just wanted someone to *not* leave. Stay. I'm okay now. I'm okay with my choices. I'll sit under the sun bare-legged and smiling. So go ahead and pour me two shots of gin to erase my thighs, stomach—a folded and used road map for the places I've been. I'm free here and content with never staying long enough to learn their names.

# Beach of Love and Death

**YASUKO THANH**

"I need to do this," I told my friends before leaving. I was twenty-five and felt I had accomplished something just by getting on the plane alone with a one-way ticket. I still wanted to make it to Peru, ride on a *cayuca* through the Amazon, penniless and happy, relying on the generosity of river people to survive, surrounded by pet monkeys and brown slippery children. But I was waylaid in Zipolite by Jesse—his smile, his sea-green eyes, his hands as solid as the wooden table he placed them on.

An American anthropology major, he spoke fluent Spanish and German. Bipolar and paranoid, he'd escaped across the Mexico–us border on a motorcycle after leaving his San Fernando halfway house two years ago. His charges stemmed from an armed carjacking that Jesse described as a "misunderstanding."

One day, early on in the relationship, we sat on the beach and watched couples smoke joints as the sun was setting. Kids laughed in the turned-over cavities of fishing dories. Catholic school girls pulled at the white shirts of boys with hungry hands. The scene mocked me as I waited for something missing. There was an edge here in Zipolite. Junkies passed out on the street while cars tried not to run them over. Drunks scared tourists for cash. People with the crazed kind of eyes seen on born-again Christians, both full and empty.

Jesse invited me back to his cabana to smoke a joint. His beach house had a lime-treed courtyard, furnished with gnarled, bleaching driftwood. River stones separating his exotic plants from the others glowed like cairns marking a path on the moon. Ghost crabs skittered across his garden like alien invaders. He was only renting this home. He planned to build another on an arid slope of land by the *tortillería*. I was yet to discover that he had slept with every beautiful woman from here to Mexico City and could memorize languages as easily as phone numbers. He had bought the land by saving his construction wages, and put it in a friend's name because foreigners couldn't own ocean property.

He talked about the expansive coral reef, the exquisite delicacy of purple sea fans, his love of the sea. Then we walked along the beach, our bare feet slapping the wet sand like paddles. It was easier to walk on this hard-pack than the shin-deep flour, but I was intensely aware of the sucking sound of each step—*shloop, shloop*—as incoming sheets of seawater tried to glue us in place. The moon looked silly, the *shloop* was silly. His arm around my shoulder swept a wide circle keeping others back. I felt giddy in his embrace, swaddled and safe from harm.

To get to the land, *el terreno*, I had to take a *camioneta* to the post office. I'd walk up a steep path to my left following the smell of cook fires and recorded sounds of Los Tigres del Norte. There, Jesse would be digging holes in the earth with a small shovel.

We'd been together a month, maybe two. I brought him support beams he propped with an assortment of rocks. The frame measured six hundred square feet. Balanced unsteadily on the roof he barked contradictory orders. A Texan, to whom we sold drugs, laughed when he thought Jesse wasn't looking. Later we drank mescal as fish cooked slowly over the coals.

Jesse—to love him or not. His full lips were always smiling, even when his eyes were worried or sad. His stomach was so lean that I could run my hands up and down his torso and fit my fingers in the washboard spaces when he held his breath. It had frightened me at first, when we met, how hard he felt, like something not human, too perfect to be real.

He had an immense capacity for forgiveness; I could call him the vilest names and he carried on without a blink as if he hadn't heard a syllable.

But I'd also seen Jesse rigid on the bed, catatonic, unable to speak for fourteen hours, muscles flexed to maximum capacity, eyes wide open like a doll's. He would put his hand to his neck, to find patterns in the beats of his pulse, an emotional tension within him making the exercise vital. People wanted him dead for secrets only he knew: they had planted spies in bookstores, cafés and taxis. He recorded his findings in a spiral-bound notebook, writing in a code so that no one else could read it. His pseudo-research gave him a connection to something larger than himself and a lifeline to place: in this way I envied him.

But his search for patterns and meaning where none exist shattered his idea of the known world, so that his lust for unity became a destructive force, a fatal disturbance—a riddle without end for us both. Still, I admired his insatiable hunger for anything extraordinary, his ability to produce psychological fictions. He was dying to be impressed.

His identity encompassed the two extremes of my desire: I wanted intimacy, but without the price tag of disclosure to my friends and family back home. His compulsive need for closeness, his fear of committing, his manic depression made avoiding disclosure easy. I loved how, without believing in what I wished for, we could talk about going to Mexico City and then back to my home. "I think I can get used to being a Canadian," he said.

Sometimes I wondered how long I'd find his vulnerability endearing. I'd gotten into the habit of ignoring his delusions about the Illuminati and about his teeth growing too big for his mouth. Six months into our relationship, I'd begun to flirt with other men, fantasizing that someone besides Jesse could be that magnet, first pulling, then repelling me.

Sometimes I dreamed, not about Jesse, but someone who looked exactly like him, holding a suntanned toddler with sun-bleached curls in his arms. Seen like this, Jesse resembled the capable altruistic men like the doctors I had met on the beach, young and handsome, on vacation with their European families.

Or I'd dream that he was calling my name. It would be morning with few people on the road and the concrete bricks of the eastern wall yellow with sunlight, the air still cool, not yet water-thick. He would be standing there dusty and alone at the gate, wearing his navy-blue T-shirt with the white V-neck, holding his luggage, a sun-bleached lock of hair hanging over one sunburned cheek. He'd have lost his red coral necklace somewhere. I'd hear his voice echoing as if from another dimension. Yet I'd feel no urgency to respond and pretend it was a lullaby, letting the sound soothe me.

Even when he wasn't sick, paranoid or hearing voices, I found myself thinking, why me? We lived as opposites. He was wide awake when I went to sleep and still wide awake when I got up. He claimed he was guarding me. He held my head and put me to sleep with bedtime stories about poisonings. When he was manic, I wouldn't wake up, preferring to curl up in his rigid embrace and float away from coherent thought.

The severity of his bipolar disorder enabled him to live on two planes at once, and sometimes I thought my low self-esteem could be almost as dangerous.

After the Texan left for his hotel, we listened to silence, crickets, crashing waves. He screamed at the top of his lungs at intermittent intervals. He wouldn't let me leave *el terreno* because he wanted to protect me from demons. When I tried to go, he said, "I can't let you leave. Don't you understand?" He looked at me as if I were a child. "It's for your safety."

We'd lasted this long—six months—because Jesse wanted a traditional marriage and children, and also because I knew that with him I'd never get either. His protective hands, his eyes wrapping me in their warm clutch in the same way a spider cocoons a ladybug, his confident voice insisting on all the things he could teach me. When we tumbled into bed, breathless as wrestlers, it was compelling and passionate partly because I never knew where I stood, and partly because I never knew if he was going to be around, or if I would be, the next day. He drew something out of me—that degree of self-sacrifice essential to any worthwhile relationship, his needs drowning out the annoying buzz of my own. But there was an element of desperation in our attachment, like the *shloop* of wet sand sucking at our feet.

Still, I could play at being the good wife while simultaneously breaking away from the role. Together we were the kind of couple that made people stare, good-looking, confident. His studied nonchalance, his exquisite symmetry fulfilled my need for adventure. Our sex, up to seven times a day, didn't involve true abandonment of oneself in another, as much as it involved constantly skirting the line between love and hate, making it so primal, so animal. Had we been animals we'd have already eaten each other like animals feasting on their own. This consuming appetite, this desire for each other, translated into something that felt, at least in the moment, more pure, more true than anything I'd had with anyone else, and kept me coming back for the easy way our bodies moved together like swimmer and river, our hair twining, hands clutching. I'd ignore his put-downs and affairs in exchange for what was immediate and simple and perfect, precisely because it could never be as complex as love. I felt absolute sacrifice and longing when he was inside me, longing even then, which seemed to become only more profound over time.

Jesse and I made a living selling drugs in Zipolite, and in the months since we'd partnered, we'd taken numerous trips together in claptrap buses to obscure parts of Mexico in search of new product, the better deal. At least every few weeks we bused the half day to Oaxaca, over the mountain road to Tehuacán, through Puebla to Teotitlán de Flores Magón, Tuxtepec to Huautla de Jiménez, where Jesse held my head in his hands en route, muscles straining as I slept. He never let me drop as the bus bounced over potholes. In his embrace I began to swallow down sadness, like the little girl I used to be who played Barbies alone in the stairwell of an apartment project, scribbling their faces the colour of blood and only sometimes bandaging their wounds. The bus skirted black sands that sounded like sea spray against the bus panels. I tried not to think of my parents but sometimes, looking out the window, I did. We ate bananas and bruised tomatoes from roadside sellers who boarded at each stop. In this way we passed time without ever speaking a word.

In the cabin where we stayed, I asked the owner what his pet turtle ate and if I could take it for a walk. When the owner refused, Jesse bought me a pair of silver turtle earrings as small and delicate as he made me feel.

Oaxaca City's nervous, polluted streets provided a mindless distraction from a coast filled with demons, from mountains thick with ghosts. The capital boasted more museums per capita than anywhere else in the state and instead of the repetitive folk art, the galleries featured photographic exhibitions of boys who dreamed of being television wrestlers. Sometimes we came here for relief, like a vacation. One day, on our last trip to Oaxaca, he refused to get out of his chair, insisting that the floor was covered in an invisible poison. Whenever I left the hotel room to buy food, I had to ask his permission, spell out my itinerary, my travel route and expected time of return. Often I would buy enough tuna and *charras* to last for days because I would never be sure if he'd allow me to leave before we ran out of supplies.

Below us lived street musicians, and next door, a young man who shared his room with his mother who made and sold jewellery. There was a heroin dealer down the hall and vendors from out of town.

Frijol, the stray dog we had lured home with a taco, sniffed for crumbs on our concrete floor. I sat on the tattered, knobbly bedspread, with half a beer in front of me, while a radio blared from down the hall where our neighbours were high. I set up things in a circle around me that reminded me of myself— my sheet music, my notebooks, my guitar. I looked at postcards from old friends and wrote a list of all the things I used to like to do, trying to convince myself that the person I used to be still existed.

Outside the window slats, night was falling on the courtyard, and I could see the colonial buildings of the town square with the mountains in the background looking like a crumpled piece of paper tossed from heaven. In 1763, a Franciscan priest declared that God had put all the remaining mountains in Oaxaca after creating the world.

"I'll be in the bathroom," I said.

He held his breath as I crossed the room and closed the door.

Across the hall from our room was the out-of-service toilet. The management had told us not to use it, but I had used it in the past anyway, not wanting to run the gauntlet of other rooms to the in-service bathroom. But now I passed the bathroom and hurried toward the end of the hall. Through the small window at the end of the hall, I could see the glowing lights of the liquor store.

Out on the street, I looked longingly at the bottles. If only I could have a drink, this might all seem funny: Jesse's voices, his visions, the stories he told, like the one about his mother, his childhood, where they were crossing the United States by car.

He was six, maybe seven. For the most part, the journey excited him: amusement parks and corn dogs, the carnival-like blending of towns, one into the other. They slept on the side of the highway. Once he woke up in the middle of night. The doors were locked and he was alone.

"Why were you on the road?" I had asked at the time, as if the answer itself was important.

He thought for a moment. "I think we were looking for something."

"Maybe she went to buy milk," I said, "or smokes."

"She was a prostitute," he said.

How do you know, I wanted to ask, but I knew this line of reasoning would spiral into a deep pool of misunderstanding from which we would never emerge, as it always would. The two of us were a habit, a symptom, not an emotion, as we moved toward a now or never.

Out on the street, out front of the liquor store, I flagged a cab. Asked the driver for a pen and paper. Wrote Jesse a note and told the driver to give it to the desk clerk. Then I got in and told him to go.

I couldn't stop crying. I told the driver that I'd left my lover. "I have to disappear. Take me somewhere I can blend and vanish into a crowd."

He nodded his head knowingly. "I see," he said, not seeing at all. "You need to talk to your *paisanos*." He drove to the tourist district, where I vowed I'd simply get drunk and talk to no one.

Before I got out of the cab, I asked him, "Will it always be this way?"

"We make our lives happy or sad," the cab driver said. "But yes, it will always be this way. *Así es la vida*, such is life."

Squinting in the yellow/white light particular to this city, I watched families go into the Iglesia de la Compañía de Jesús. They strolled holding hands, bought candles and saint cards from the vendors outside and shared a devotion I did not have but craved: it wasn't that I didn't want to believe, it was that I'd forgotten how. I'd heard that inside the chapel a statue of the Virgen de Guadalupe was adorned by prayers written in Spanish, English, Nahuatl and four dialects of Zapotec. Instead of praying, I smoked.

The night became cold, and sitting in the centre of the square, I tried to forget what it felt like to have a pair of arms around me to ward off the chill.

I listened to a marimba band. Children selling *chicle* and toy birds saw my face and stayed away; so did the women with *elote*, the men with crutches; even the blind accordion player seemed to feel my confusion and did not hold out his hand.

Jesse found me in the *zócalo*. He had been looking all over town, wearing his board shorts and a heavy parka.

He said: "I love you more than I've ever loved anything."

He said: "You needed something to love that much and I'm it."

He said: "I want to be together in fifty years."

He said: "We'll get married in June."

I lowered my head, raised my eyebrows. "Who says?"

"What if you got pregnant? Think about that." He grabbed my wrist and clutched it till it hurt.

Months later back in Canada alone, I would recall the heat of our last day on the land. I was helping Jesse build the roof. He had curtained one side of the *ramada* with a layer of palms and wanted me to hang my hammock inside. I refused. It was an unstable structure and I knew better than to trust myself to something so unbalanced.

"Don't cry ma'am," said the Texan, who had once told me that his civic government had selected him for a learning-to-speak-English-better program sponsored by their Ministry of Agriculture, which made me laugh. "Please don't cry. It'll be okay, ma'am." He put his hand on my shoulder. "Don't cry."

I passed Jesse palm fronds knowing they would never keep the rain off this floor. I knew one strong wind would send the fronds crashing on our heads. Knew this house would never be completed, would never be real.

# Finding a Way Out

## JAGTAR KAUR ATWAL

I join the assembly line, taking up my task of helping my sisters, Raveena and Gurjeet, with filling the samosas. Mum is rolling out small pieces of beige dough to the size of a saucer before slicing them in half. She keeps looking over to make sure we're not slacking; the other family will be here soon and I know she wants the samosas to be perfect and it'll be her first sign the day will go her way. The window is pushed open and the fresh scent of the early morning rain catches a ride on the breeze gliding into the kitchen. The leaves hanging over the window sway with the wind; I wish I could glide out. Mum is talking to me, but I'm not hearing her. I'm too busy trying to get my part of the job done quickly so I can go and hide in my bedroom before they arrive. I press the edges of the semicircle into a hollow triangle and spoon the diced potatoes, peas and spices into the empty space. I place the last dull-looking samosa on the silver tray for frying later, and shove the heavy platter into the fridge—lopsided.

My lilac *salwar kameez* is already pressed and neatly folded on my bed. Mum must have been in my bedroom. I grab the silky material that reminds me of what I have to deal with today, and throw it hard at the chair. It pisses me off when people come into my room. It's the only place where I don't have to pretend to be someone I'm not.

I look out of the window at the Derbyshire hills overlooking the bungalow rooftops, where blackbirds rest before they stretch their wings and soar through the clouds. If I squint really, really hard I can see the dark grey towers of the old power station in the distance. When I zigzag down a few streets from my house, I'll find the Derby County Football Club. During the football season the cheers and boos sweep through the normally quiet side streets. I could do with the sounds of roaring fans today to lift my spirits.

I sit cross-legged by my bookcase, which I placed in front of the Victorian fireplace a few years ago. I decided to block the fireplace because during the winter nights the cold wind would find its way down the chimney, howling angrily. It sounded like a family of ghosts rushing down to give me nightmares. Those were the nights when I would bury myself under the quilt and try to dig myself deeper into the mattress until the howling was just a whisper.

I let my finger lightly brush the creased spines of Agatha Christie paperback books—my prized possessions—stopping when I reach my palm-sized notebook. I know Mum will be pissed if she catches me not getting dressed, but I just want to forget. As I turn the pages to the last entry I made, I hear someone rattling the lock. I don't say anything, hoping whoever it is will just go away.

"What're you doing?" My younger sister Raveena tries the door again.

The Indian suit catches my eye. "I'm getting dressed."

"Well hurry up, Mum wants to talk to you."

"I won't be long."

I bring *Why Didn't They Ask Evans?* to my nose, gently fan the yellow stale pages and inhale the old mustiness trapped between the lines. I begin to write the forty-seventh title I own in the notebook. I bought the second-hand Agatha Christie book yesterday at the flea market; it cost me less than one pound, which isn't bad considering all the pages are fully intact.

I'm twenty-two years old and I've never been to a friend's party, never sat in a movie theatre and never been to a restaurant. "What are people going to say if they see you walking the streets alone?" my parents say. Instead, my sisters and I are expected to learn things I don't give a shit about—how to cook a tasty dhal, prepare fluffy rice and bake the perfectly round roti; how to iron a man's shirt and pants; or how to best scrub away stains in a kitchen sink so I can become the perfect Sikh wife. In Agatha Christie's world of murder I'm so much more. I'm a fearless detective travelling the world solving mysteries, partying with people of high society and flirting with life. When I close the book I come back to a life ruled by my parents.

"Mum wants you downstairs NOW," Gurjeet shouts from the bottom of the stairs.

"I'm coming down, I'm just combing my hair." I quickly place the book next to *The Murder at the Vicarage*, and dress before Mum decides to start knocking on the door.

I catch my reflection in the long mirror: my body trapped by the lilac *salwar kameez* with its age-long traditions and expectations woven into the fabric, binding me to my future as a married woman. I wish my parents would cut some of the fine threads so I can breathe a little easier. But that won't happen today, because today I have to meet a boy for marriage.

Gurjeet had an arranged marriage nearly two years ago. It was the first for my parents. She seems happy with Rambir. I was hoping she would say no, because each no would have meant more time for me. Raveena's the lucky one, because she's the youngest and lives in London at the university campus working toward a nursing degree. She doesn't have to deal with any of this until she's finished studying.

Mum looks up at me from the bottom of the stairs, thirteen steps separating us. "Don't forget what I said," she says.

"I haven't." I have no idea what she is talking about and I really hope she doesn't decide to repeat it.

"The family will be here in a few minutes. Make a decent cup of tea, not too strong or too milky." Mum turns her head toward the glass-stained front door as we hear a car pull up.

It's Dad. He comes in and says nothing to me. He never does, Mum is his messenger. I take the thirteen steps down as Mum and Dad disappear into the living room, and I hide in the kitchen.

A sudden continuous ringing from the doorbell kicks my heartbeat to double its speed. I look out through the crack of the door. Mum brings her palms together as if she is praying and welcomes the guests. All I can see are flashes of colourful outfits passing by as she says a series of "*Sat sri akaal ji.*"

I close the door and try to steady the rhythm of my heart by breathing in deeply until my lungs are ready to burst before I let out the air. My fingers tremble as I turn the dial on the gas stove and a rush of orangey flames spreads across the bottom of the wok. It isn't long before the intense heat rises up from the golden liquid, coating my face. I watch the oil swallow the samosas.

I was twelve when I decided I needed to talk to Mum about how I was feeling. I don't remember what I wanted to say but I was clogged with sadness. It was a Saturday afternoon. Mum walked into the living room with a wet dishcloth to wipe down the coffee table.

"Mum, can we talk? I feel sad," I said.

I thought she would take time out and we'd sit on the sofa, with her arms wrapped around me. Instead, her face creased up with frustration.

"What do you have to be sad about?" she said, slamming the door behind, not bothering to wait for an answer.

I've done nothing since then but swallow, swallow, swallow.

I hear the rusty door hinges creak as Raveena peeks around. "Mum wants you to bring in the samosas and tea."

"I don't care what anyone wants," I snap.

"Don't annoy Mum and Dad," she says as she sucks on her lower lip, her eyes begging me to hold it together.

"Easy for you to say. All this"—I wave my hand over the fine china—"is a waste of my time."

"Keep your voice down." She closes the door behind her.

"When we go in the room will you stay?"

"I can't, Mum said."

"Why?

"So they don't get confused. They might think it's me who they've come to see."

"God help me."

"Please don't do anything silly."

I take a deep breath.

I watch her place the steaming samosas on the white serving plate with light pink roses circling the edge that matches perfectly with the teapot, teacups and saucers.

Alone again in the kitchen, I hold onto the sink edge, wondering if I could crawl out of the window without hurting myself or breaking the china.

I hold onto the heavy tray, my knuckles turning white from the grip as I stare at the closed wooden door before I kick it open. Silence falls in the reception room as if someone had pressed the mute button. I place the tray on the coffee table. I scan the faces quickly before I head straight to the farthest armchair. The silence continues. Six sets of eyes are on me. I feel like my clothes are being torn off me until I'm stripped and left bare. My cheeks heat up with the attention as they inspect the goods. I've read my mum's weekly *Des Pardes* Punjabi magazine on the odd occasion and under the matrimonial section the parents look for girls who are light-skinned (I'm no Casper); tall (I am five feet four inches); slim (I'm all curves); homebodies or professionals (I'm neither).

My future husband looks like Magnum PI from the 1980s TV show. He is tall and his well-kept moustache enhances his good looks. I wonder what's wrong with him that he needs help in finding a wife.

Mum offers him tea, the steaming liquid splashing into the tiny cup, and a large hand with a set of long masculine fingers accepts the saucer. Magnum's pinky flares out as he takes a sip. I choke back a laugh.

The room fills up with unfamiliar voices. I pick at the gold sequins lining the bottom of the *kameez*. I don't know what I will do if I end up having to marry him. I shudder at the thought of the wedding night. I squeeze my thighs together.

Mum told me they were coming last night, while my dad was eating. They left it to the last minute so I wouldn't have time to make up excuses. My stomach turned and twisted. The words "I'm gay" won't pass my lips.

I do want to get married and have children one day, but nowhere in our tradition is there a path carved for a person like me. If I continue to pretend to be like my sisters I will end up getting married to a man and spend the rest of my life feeling more miserable than I already am. Shame has become my second skin, and when I think about living life openly as a gay woman, that skin tightens until I can't breathe.

My lips feel the heat of the tea, steam washing my face. Magnum's mother's stern face looks directly at me, her eyes drilling me as the hot tea stills in my mouth. I wouldn't just be marrying him, but the family as well. I would be the family's cook and maid—and his whore.

There are more quiet spells in the conversation. They want to get down to business—that's why they are here.

"We have to go soon—" Magnum's mother breaks the silence.

"*Han jii, bacha* can go in the other room and talk," my mum suggests.

"We have to go in ten minutes."

Magnum stands and walks toward the door. The bushy caterpillar on his top lip wiggles as he says, "Okay, I won't be long."

It is the first time I have heard his voice. It's croaky, as if he has a permanent sore throat.

Before anyone adds anything more, I'm up and crossing the threshold into the corridor, relieved the prying eyes are left behind. Now I only have one set to contend with.

I don't care if Magnum follows or not. I sit nearest to the patio doors so I can feel the heat hugging me, even though the sun is hiding behind some clouds. I watch his reflection on the black TV. The lanky figure walks in and takes a seat on the old brown armchair nearest to the fireplace. His head moves left to right, scanning the photos hanging from the picture railing circling the room.

The faint aroma of him tickles the fine hairs in my nose. He smells spicy. My nostrils puff and blow him out. I force him to speak first by keeping silent.

"Do you want to get married?" he asks, looking straight at me with his big brown eyes.

I tuck my hands under my thighs and look down at my knees. "Yes. Do you?"

"Yes, I'm ready to settle down."

I curl my hidden hands into two tight fists.

"Will you find it difficult to leave England?"

I frown. "Why would I leave England?"

"We're from New Zealand."

"Oh, okay." Why can't he find a wife in his own country? Don't they have women?

An uncomfortable silence stretches longer than it should as I realize that I may have just found my way out of this marriage; I will just tell my parents I don't want to leave England. Surely they can understand that.

Sunrays break through the patio glass into the room, exposing the dust motes dancing in mid-air.

"Do you want children?" His left foot stops tapping the air and instead swings gently to the left and then right like windshield wipers.

I nod my head as I look away.

"Is there anything you want to ask me?"

I stare at the photo above his head of my parents' wedding day: Mum sitting cross-legged on the floor, dressed in her pink *salwar kameez*, her mini beehive hairdo covered by a *chine*; Dad beside her in a dark two-piece suit and a badly wrapped turban. They look frightened.

I want to ask Magnum what he's thinking and whether he's going to agree to the union. I want to tell him to say no. Instead I shake my head, too afraid he'd tell his mother, who would then tell mine.

"I better get going." He leans forward and pushes himself to his two feet.

"Okay, well, have a good trip back," I say in a way too cheery voice.

I don't get up from the sofa. I don't care if he thinks I'm rude. I let him find his own way back. I get up and sneak a look into the corridor before darting up the stairs. I lean against the locked door and let out the breath I'd been holding since the morning—it's over.

"Well what did you think?" Mum asks as she pushes past me in the kitchen the following morning.

"About what?" I turn to switch on the kettle. I knew it was coming. I had overheard the phone conversation Mum had with the other family—they had called last night.

She reaches for the small cup on the drying rack. "The boy. He said yes to you."

I turn and step into the small pantry and pretend to look for a snack. "Oh, he's nice."

She looks at me with hope in her eyes. "So you like him."

I concentrate as I stack up the cups on the first shelf on the top cabinet. All I want to do is smash each cup against the kitchen sink. "I just said he's nice."

"Is it a yes?"

I look up at her as I clutch the last cup. "Mum, you do know that he lives in New Zealand?"

"So?"

I slam the cabinet door. "Well, I don't want to leave England."

"Why not?"

"I just don't want to." I walk away leaving the kettle boiling.

---

In the evening our Indian neighbour comes over. After getting a rundown from Mum of the visit yesterday, she sits opposite to me in the reception room trying to change my mind.

"I don't want to get married," I say to the heavy-set woman. She reminds me of an armoured tank, crashing through my life without stopping to think of the damage she will leave behind.

She leans forward and fires a shot. "Why?"

"He lives in New Zealand!" I'm wondering if anyone has looked at the world map lately.

Another shot. "Don't you want your parents to be happy?"

"Of course I do."

"You told your mum he's nice."

It seems as though she is inching closer and closer to me with every passing minute. When she came in to talk, rather than sitting on the other armchair, she dragged a small stool and placed it in front of me and now our knees are kissing.

"He is, but I don't want to marry him."

She fires another shot and this one nearly hits me. "You're stopping Raveena from getting married."

"No, I'm not."

Her hand is now on my knee. It's big and I can feel the hardness of her palm through my jeans. "People will think there's something wrong with you and the family."

I'm so tired of people not listening to me. She keeps saying the same thing over and over again. I want to get out of the room and I know there is only one way to get out of here.

"Yes. Okay. I'll marry him," I say as my head drops down.

She slaps her hands on my knees and gives them a squeeze and leaves to share her success with my mum. I try not to cry.

Upstairs in my room, I fall to my knees in front of the bookshelf and begin to haphazardly grab books; my fingers have a mind of their own as they tear through the softbacks. I flip through the pages and fling it to the side. Flip, fling, flip, fling.

There it is. The blue small bank book, stuffed between the pages of *The Man in the Brown Suit*. I turn the pages quickly until I get to the last entry. I can feel a teardrop balancing on the bottom of my eyelid, blurring my vision. I'm left with only one choice. If Mum and Dad won't hear my words, then running away is the only way I can scream at them. A fresh tear escapes from the corner of my eye, running along the eyelid until it finally pushes the old tear over the edge. I watch the tear fall until it splashes onto the number in the book.

£934.00.

A blackbird lands on a chimney across the street. I saved the money from when I worked for my uncle at the dealership, dreaming one day I would spend a year travelling the world, never thought I'd use my life savings to run away.

The blackbird hops onto the ridge, balancing on the terracotta tiles on its two twig legs. I pull the neckline of my top and rub my wet eyes and clean my snotty nose. Tomorrow when Mum and Dad go to work, I'll sneak to the travel agency downtown and find the cheapest ticket to a country that's farthest away from here. I'm trying not to think about what I'll do once I land, in case I talk myself out of it and into a marriage.

As the blackbird tips its head up at the sky, the stretched wings slap the air—and then it's gone.

# The Marrying Kind

## AYELET TSABARI

It's your wedding day, and you're barefoot in a deep blue sari, hunched over a cigarette outside a North Vancouver home. It's a cold, wet December day, and the snowy path had to be shovelled before guests arrived. You take a few urgent puffs, like a high school student in a bathroom stall, and flick the cigarette onto the pavement. You rub your henna-painted hands together and breathe into them to keep warm.

Your new brother-in-law pokes his head out the door. "You okay?"

"Yes," you say, forcing a smile. "Just getting some fresh air. I'll be right in."

You're not going back in. Not quite yet.

Inside the house, thirty-odd guests you just met are pretending to be your family. Looking at them through the steamy windows, you're almost fooled. They could be your family—a bunch of olive- and brown-skinned people with dark hair and dark eyes. From where you're standing, it's hard to tell that the women wear saris and that everybody looks more Indian than Israeli.

You look Indian too. You look Indian to Indians in Vancouver who ask you for directions in Hindi or Punjabi on the street. You even looked Indian in India, where the locals thought you were a slut for dressing like a Westerner and walking around with white boys.

You've never looked more Indian than you do today. Your wrists are heavy with elaborate bangles, and you're neatly tucked in six metres of shimmering silk embroidered with gold and red stones. Your boyfriend's cousins helped with the sari, wrapping it around you as if you were a gift with many layers, draping one end over the shoulder and stuffing the other into your skirt. You're only wearing a thin line of eyeliner, and your fingernails are chewed down and unpainted. You're barefoot, because you don't wear heels. You catch your reflection in the window and eye it with satisfaction, tossing your hair back like a Bollywood starlet on the red carpet. The door swings open, letting out warmth, broken conversations and the smell of curry. Your boyfriend (now officially husband) steps out and looks around suspiciously, as if expecting to see someone else.

"What are you doing?" he asks.

"Nothing, I'm coming in."

You take one more look at the empty suburban street. It is frozen still: the snow-topped houses, the parked cars, the cotton-ball bushes. Your feet start to feel numb. If you had shoes on, you might have walked away, down the trail, up the slushy road. Your bangles would jingle as you strode off, and the free end of the sari would flutter behind you, a splash of blue against all this grey and white.

"Are you coming?" He's holding the door open for you.

When you met a year and a half ago, you weren't thinking marriage. You were sitting outside your bungalow in southern India when he walked by. He looked a bit like Jesus, skinny and brown, long-haired and unshaven. He carried a guitar case and a small backpack slung over his shoulder. When you started talking, you discovered he was an Indo-Canadian from Vancouver who didn't speak a word of Hindi.

One night you shared a bottle of cheap whisky around a beach bonfire, and talked until everybody left and the fire died out. After one week, you were throwing around *I love you*'s in both Hebrew and English. After two weeks, you called your families to announce your state of bliss. You wandered through India delirious and glossy-eyed; made love in guest houses infested with rats and monkeys and cockroaches as long as your index finger; cooked food outside straw huts; shared sleepers on overnight trains; and licked acid stamps at parties on sandy beaches.

You separated at a crowded train station in Pune, a classic scene from a Bollywood film: a woman holds on to her lover's hand, extended from between the metal bars of the train's window. They utter declarations of love and cry. They vow to meet again. The train conductor blows his whistle, and the train starts chugging away slowly. The woman runs alongside the train until she can't continue. The train fades away into a cloud of smoke.

You spent the next seven months waitressing in Tel Aviv while he planted trees in northern British Columbia. You wrote each other long sappy love letters, and sometimes, when he was out of the bush, you spoke on the phone. When you made enough money for a ticket, you flew to Canada to be with him, lugging a suitcase filled with Hebrew books and tie-dyed tank tops you'd bought in India. You were hoping to travel in BC for a while and then find a job. Maybe you'd stay for a year or two if you liked it. Who knows? You'd been living like a nomad for the past four years so you wouldn't mind the change.

Vancouver was beautiful that summer, warm and golden, and the days long and lazy. You'd never seen the sun setting that late before. You found a one-bedroom apartment in the West End, facing English Bay and a daily display of sunsets, bought IKEA furniture and a foam mattress. An old American car. A set of Teflon pots.

One night after dinner, you started talking about the future. "Maybe I could go to college here," you said.

Your boyfriend glanced at you carefully. "Here's the thing—" he said. He had done some research these past few days. Apparently, the only way you could stay in Canada, get a work permit, study, was to get married.

You tensed up.

You were twenty-five. You never planned on getting married; never understood why people bothered. You blamed your father who died when you were nine for your textbook fear of abandonment and string of bad relationships. But your tourist visa was running out and so was your money, so you knew you had to make a decision. Fast.

"I don't want to get married," you whined over the phone to your sister in Israel. "Why do I have to? It's not fair. Why does it even matter? It's just a stupid piece of paper anyway."

"If it's just a stupid piece of paper," your sister said, "what difference does it make?"

"Okay," you told your boyfriend as you lay in bed that night. He looked up from his book.

"Okay," you repeated. "If we absolutely have to get married, then I want it to be really small, just us, no big deal. Nobody has to know. We're doing it for the papers. That's all. And …" you paused for emphasis, "there's going to be no husband-wife talk. You're my boyfriend. Not my husband. Is that clear?"

Your boyfriend grinned.

A few days before the ceremony, your boyfriend called his father to tell him about the wedding and inform him that he was not invited. In fact, nobody was. It was just a little thing you had to do to sort out the papers. You heard his father yelling on the other end (you could make out the words "customs," "tradition" and "community") and watched sweat gathering over your boyfriend's brow as he struggled to throw in a word. Finally, he slouched onto the couch and nodded into the phone, defeated.

"My dad is throwing a party," he said after he hung up, rubbing his temples. "Just close family members, nothing big."

Within days, his father arranged a catering service, a cake and an outfit for you to wear. Fifty guests were invited, and your boyfriend's aunt volunteered her large North Vancouver home. He wanted you to have real wedding bands, replace the 150-rupee rings you'd bought each other in India, but you refused; you liked yours, his was shaped like an Om and yours like a flower with a moonstone in it. You called your mother in Israel and assured her that there was no need for her to borrow money to fly to Vancouver. That it was just a formality. Your mother sighed but didn't push. You figured she was so relieved to see you married off that she chose to pretend it was the real deal, or at least hope it would turn into one.

On the morning of the wedding, you woke up at 3:00 a.m. flushed with sweat, remembering a visit you made to a fortune teller in the mountains of Israel the year before. You and your best friend had driven her beaten vw bug two hours north of Tel Aviv and up precarious mountain roads to see her. It was a hot day and the car wasn't air-conditioned. The fortune teller greeted you in jeans and a T-shirt—not quite the mystical character you had expected—and led you to her living room, which had no crystal balls or velvet curtains. Children's toys were scattered on the carpet. She opened your cards on a table marked with crescent-shaped stains left by coffee mugs, and then leaned over to examine your palm. Her face lit up.

"Good news!" she announced. "You're going to be married by twenty-five!"

You leaned back, laughed a long, healthy laugh and explained to her that that was impossible, that you did not intend to ever marry.

"She really doesn't," your friend affirmed. "She's not the marrying kind."

The fortune teller smiled knowingly and said you must invite her to the wedding.

"What a waste of time," you muttered, rolling your eyes, as you stepped out of her house and into your friend's car.

You woke up again at 9:00 a.m. with a jolt, heart racing as if you'd been running all night. It was raining outside. It took forever to put on your sari, and it ended up looking stupid: the front pleats were uneven, and the part that draped over your shoulder kept loosening up. You pinned the fabric to your blouse with safety pins. It would have to do until your boyfriend's cousins fix it later this afternoon.

Your boyfriend came out of the bathroom wearing his brother's suit. "It's too big," he groaned. A red dot adorned his cheek where he'd cut himself shaving. You swore he looked fine and helped him tie his hair in a neat ponytail. Your maid of honour, a male friend of your boyfriend's, showed up with a bottle of champagne, and you downed a glass with your morning coffee.

The wedding ceremony was held in your living room. The only guests were your maid of honour and your boyfriend's brother. A poster of a contemplative

Bob Marley was your backdrop as the justice of the peace, a grey-haired lady you'd picked from the phone book, performed the ceremony. You'd picked her because you liked the sound of her name, and because she was a woman. Jewish wedding ceremonies are traditionally performed by men, so having a choice is just one advantage to marrying out of faith. Not that either of you care much about religion. Your spiritual affinity is the kind one picks up on one's travels, along with mass-produced Buddha statues and incense sticks. It's summed up by statements such as *Everything happens for a reason* and *The universe takes care.*

The early morning glass of champagne made you tipsy and you giggled like a teenager at a school dance and avoided your boyfriend's eyes. You felt silly repeating these English lines you'd heard a million times in movies. Eventually you fixed your gaze on the justice of the peace. She had icy blue eyes, like frozen puddles. You exchanged the same rings you'd been wearing for the past year and a half. Then the woman said, "I now pronounce you husband and wife," and your stomach turned. Your boyfriend smiled at you. You kissed quickly and hugged.

Now your boyfriend is holding the door open, looking at you narrowly. "Are you coming or what?" he says.

You walk in. He follows.

Inside, the house is warm and smells of turmeric and steamed rice, coriander and perfume. The guests wander around, taking dozens of variations of the same photo, lining up by the buffet table to heap vegetable samosas and lamb curry on their plastic plates. Your boyfriend's buddies form a row of white boys as they sit against the wall on their best behaviour, clad in suits, empty plates in their laps. There is no alcohol served, which you find peculiar and cruel. Your boyfriend's young cousins chase you around the room, admire your henna and grab the free end of your sari. Finally, you escape to the washroom. You lean on the sink and stare at your reflection.

"You're married," you say. "How does it feel?" Your reflection shrugs. The truth is you feel nothing, except for a dull pain over your right eyebrow, a remnant of a champagne-induced headache.

"You're married!" you persist. "You're someone's wife!" Your reflection flinches. For a few seconds it's hard to breathe, as though a foot presses on your chest, but then it passes.

After the buffet, everyone gathers around for the ceremonial portion of the day. You enjoy the traditional rituals for the same reason you like wearing a sari: you see them as an anthropological experience, like some weddings you attended in your travels; only now, you're the one on display. You let your new family feed you Indian sweets and shower you with rice. You and your boyfriend break little clay cups with your feet while the guests cheer. The custom is that whoever breaks the first cup will be the boss of the house. For the next four years, you will both remember breaking the cup first.

In the late afternoon a cake is brought out, a massive creamy thing, with your names written on it in pink. At this point you're exhausted, your cheeks ache from smiling and your eyeliner is wearing off, along with the effects of the Advil. The party reminds you of a distant cousin's bar mitzvah you were dragged to by your parents. You feel like pulling on your mother's sleeve and nagging, "Is it over yet? Can we go now?"

The guests gather around, prepare their cameras and wait for you to cut the cake, holding the knife together as you bend over the cake and feed it to each other as newlyweds do. This is the one ritual in the party that you recognize from your own family weddings, from movies and television. As you stand next to your boyfriend, your sari tightens, clinging to your skin, making it difficult to breathe. You feel nauseated just looking at the icing. You breathe in deeply and slide two fingers between your petticoat and your skin to allow for air circulation; startled by the cold touch of sweat. You lean toward your boyfriend and whisper, "I'm not cutting the cake."

He turns to you. "What? Why not?"

"Because I think it's stupid. That's why. I'm not doing it."

"It's not a big deal. We're almost done."

"I'm not doing it. And I'm not feeding it to you or being fed either. Anybody who knows me even a little bit would know I hate this shit."

He doesn't tell you you're being ridiculous. He sighs. His aunts are whispering into each other's ears. A murmur spreads around the guests, growing louder as moments pass. Nobody is sure what's going on. But you won't budge. You have given up enough. You never wanted to get married in the first place; you never wanted a party and now you want a drink and you can't have it, and you will not cut the fucking cake!

Your boyfriend (as you'll call him for the next four years, never your husband) ends up cutting the cake with his brother, not quite the photo op the guests hoped for. You stand beside them and smile like a bride should, feeling as if you won one battle amid many defeats.

A couple of days later you pick up the wedding photos and browse through them quickly, pausing only to admire your outfit or to discard the ones of yourself you don't like. You're posing beside strangers you cannot name, smiling the same smile in all of them. Except for one. In the picture, your boyfriend leans over the cake with a knife, smiling goofily, as his brother pretends to fall over it. You're standing in the shadow looking smug; the smile you thought you mastered so skilfully appears frozen and forced. You feel that pressure in your chest again, but this time it stays. It's like someone has your heart in his fist.

You call your brother in Tel Aviv that night and recount what forever will be known as "the cake story." You do it in a light, amused tone, as if it were some funny tale for dinner parties. You think you're being clever and charming. You expect him to appreciate the hilarity, to share your distaste, knowing well enough that you're better than those cake-cutting brides.

But your brother isn't laughing. "I don't get it, it was just a cake," he says. "What was the big deal?"

You're quiet for a moment, while your mind races in search for an answer, then say, "Whatever," and change the subject.

You hang up the phone and look over at your boyfriend. He's stretched out on the couch, switching channels on TV. He catches your gaze and smiles. Your husband. From this angle he looks like a different man, a handsome stranger, the kind of man you'd meet on a tropical island for a holiday fling.

*Your husband.*

You feel that weight in your chest again, and this time you know: it's doubt. This won't last, it tells you. It's not the cake, it's you. You're going to screw it up. Can't you see? He likes the cake; he likes the husband-wife talk; he *is* the marrying kind.

"What?" Your boyfriend's smile turns to a frown.

The moment is gone. You bully doubt into a dark corner and shut the door. "Nothing," you say.

You wear a big smile and join him on the couch.

# Commitment

# Arrivals, Departures

## RUSSELL THORNTON

First a guarded corridor, then fifty feet
of floor and different glass walls between us—
me arrived, waiting for you, you detained,
passport and visa from the wrong country
confiscated, luggage and plane ticket
confiscated, flight back home changed.
There you were in your multi-coloured
homemade coat, a slender Slavic Venus,
Tartar cheekbones, brilliant yet soft blue eyes,
troubling the *frontiera polizia*.
After a while, we were having a shared dream—
a week of me on one side of a world, you
on the other side, where all you could do
was walk around and around in circles,
then try to sleep curled up off in a corner,
as you tried to avoid the guards and their taunts.
In your country, you grace a theatre—
here it is assumed you are a visiting *prostitute*,
and I your pimp. We become two humans
trapped in separate clear containers,
still trying to join by instinct, slipping
and falling, again and again. Two children
trying to climb opposite sides of a hill
of sand that only sweeps us lower. Two numbers
trying to occur together and solve an equation.
No point in mouthing words back and forth—
it is too far away for either of us to see.
But you reach out and frame my face. I realize
I am blowing kisses to someone. You forced
to live in a part of an airport for five days—
the first three days without food. Me forced
to make appeals to officials who ignore me.
Finally, I put a bribe into the right hand—

I am let through to cross from *bella Italia*
into a departure lounge. We can say nothing,
but twine ourselves around each other
across airport seats for an hour, allowed
entry into a silence we now know in ourselves,
making a place of no arrival or departure.

# Every Stepfather Has His Day

**KEVIN CHONG**

---

Family Day: the store-brand cola of holidays. How easy it would have been to ignore it. You don't even work Mondays. But here's everyone—the woman you'll marry, her son and you—on this day of legislated fun, snowshoeing on Cypress Mountain.

Throughout that afternoon, snowball fights end with Joe calling a truce—then breaking it. You're cool with it. You're always cool.

You've signed another armistice agreement at the end of the trail. You're checking your email on your phone when another snowball from Joe wings your head. It gets under your glasses. You see only slush. You're fed up. You bring a bowling ball of crusty snow up to shoulder height.

"New truce?" you ask.

Of course he nods. Joe is nine, heading out of the age when kids delight adults with their big eyes and mispronunciations ("cap-a-city" for "capacity") and into the one when they become electronics-obsessed golems.

You drop the snowball on him. You don't throw it too hard. You don't think you do. But then the boy's expression shifts. His eyes crinkle. Is he laughing? Tears run out. The snowball has winded him. His mother, who rushes toward him, tells him to breathe. Slowly he begins to gasp between his sobs. Step-patricide fills his eyes. You've turned him into a preteen Hamlet.

You want to scoff at those tears. He had it coming. That's what your own father would say. The way the boy's feelings run hot—like his mother's—makes you feel like a Vulcan. Or an Asian.

You end up letting him take a freebie shot to your face.

You know from the start that Holly has a child. At what point do you consider being a step-parent?

In the early days courting Holly, it's only the two of you. On what you will retrospectively deem to have been your first date, you go to the racetrack. For the last race, Holly places a two-dollar bet on every horse in the field to guarantee a winning ticket; a long shot wins, so she finishes ahead.

Holly wants you to see her as a love object, not someone's mother. The two of you go for cocktails. Later on, you enjoy unhurried breakfasts and extended coffee breaks. You take overnight trips. This is the life you already

64

know, the one where, if you sleep in, or leave the house late enough in the evening, everyone you run into is another childless adult.

It feels dishonest now. Holly was never a carefree single gal. Nor were you ever the kind of bachelor who swung nimbly from dazzling social engagements to new romantic interests. You ate at your desk at home. You brought laundry back to your mom.

The first time you meet Joe is on the beach. You take your parents' old Labrador retriever along with you. You show Joe, then seven, the catapult you use to play fetch. If you launch a ball into the water, the dog will charge after it. Except that the dog is old and the water's cold. Both of you watch the ball float into the ocean until it's a Day-Glo orange speck.

In the coming months, you become a tertiary character in the life of a boy still aching for his parents to reunite. You bring over a new iPad loaded with video games, and Greek custard pudding for dessert. Then, one day when Holly has a late meeting scheduled, you pick him up from school and conjure chicken piccata for the second time in your life.

Holly compares that moment to a challenge on a reality-TV show. Instead of a rose or a box of steaks, you receive a tangle of new obligations: meals to be cooked, school pickups and drop-offs at karate.

You will marry after four years of dating Holly, but you become a stepdad sometime earlier. As a literary construct, the stepfather is narrative shorthand for villain: Humbert Humbert in *Lolita*; Robert Mitchum's character in *Night of the Hunter*; Dwight from *This Boy's Life*. Murderers, pederasts, bullies. Oedipus is his own stepfather.

And who are the good stepdads? Liam Neeson's character in *Love Actually*. Good stepdad, shitty movie. And a cream puff alongside his counterpart in *Taken*—a biological dad, of course.

To avoid bickering, you find the perfect friction point of step-parent housework: more than you think you ought to do, but not enough that you feel like a martyr.

You chafe in your role as an authority figure. Your default mode as a substitute parent has been benign non-intervention. Try not to let him see you being a jerk. Do no harm. *Let Holly handle it.*

You don't want to discipline Joe. And he doesn't want you in that role. But then there come times like when Joe, upset about a frustrating math quiz that he and his mom are practising at home, throws a pencil at his mother.

When you call him out, he snaps back (using one of his preternaturally adult sentence constructions): "You have no place in this."

You insist that you do.

To love a woman with a child, you have to assimilate into an already established family unit. You adhere to the habits of their pre-existing household. You play board games. You come to understand that hot-tempered outbursts blow away quickly. You get teary yourself now. You need to ask before you take the last pork chop if anyone else wants it. In your own family, you just took it.

One summer day, the three of you arrange to meet a friend of Joe's at the park. Joe's friend is joined by his mother, his three younger brothers—triplets—and their stepfather. You watch the stepdad slather sunscreen across the cheeks of one of the fair-skinned triplets. A nose nuzzle would be no less physically intimate. By contrast, you need an air traffic controller to guide the half-hugs you give Joe. It's like this other stepdad has leapt across a chasm, while you stand on the other side, clinging to the cliff face.

In what will be the last year of his life, on a boys' getaway to New Orleans, your father convinces you and your brother to make a stopover in Houston.

It's only when you've left Vancouver that he tells you why you're going to Houston. "We're visiting the woman I almost married before I met your mom," he says.

You arrive in Houston, unhappy to be there. The friend calls your father at the hotel, and he heads down first to meet her. You take your time. When you emerge from the elevator, you see your father and his former fiancée standing ten feet apart. It's only when this woman sees you that a flicker of recognition lights across her face. You look more like your young dad than your dad does now.

You all board her husband's minivan for lunch. This woman is dreamier, more bookish than your mother, who prefers Cantonese soap operas to literary fiction. She tells you she married an American, in part, to leave Hong Kong. It was too crowded for her.

Her Guangdong-born husband is mild-mannered but voluble as a host. As he guides the car down the interstate highway, he tells you about growing up in Texas in the 1960s. Asians could visit the doctor through the front door; blacks came through the back.

"Why are you visiting Houston?" she asks your dad.

"The plane stops here from New Orleans," your father explains. "There are no direct routes."

Both of them are being disingenuous. Your father wanted one last glance at his former flame. She knows. Their reunion is innocent, stilted. Your father might have wanted to reminisce but there's no chance for them to be alone.

"We should probably set you two free," your father tells his friend at the end of a day spent visiting the Johnson Space Center and eating barbecue.

Later on, you think that hitting the eject button on his visit was an attempt to get a reaction from this woman, to wring some feeling from her. He succeeds. She's stunned. "Oh," she says. "We were expecting to go for dinner."

On the elevator ride up, your dad claims to be relieved to be done with his ex. "I can't believe how much she's aged," he says. "Your mother looks much younger."

Your dad is ridiculous in his last year. He's a deeply flawed husband. But he's your dad. He did your taxes for your entire life. He loved you enough to remortgage his house so you could get (eye roll) your MFA. For you he will always be the cocksure voice you hear in your own head. The one that competes against the bitingly critical voice of your mother, that fuels your self-loathing—and which keeps your feelings permanently at half-volume.

When that self-hatred grows too strong, you remember riding in a car with him once in Chinatown. Some white guy was in the other lane, screaming at him for some traffic misdeed. You remember your dad with his eyes on the road. You remember the way he stretched out his arm in front of your face and extended his middle finger.

The goldsmith texts to say that he's completed the engagement ring. You determine that you need to get the proposal right, to make a moment for the two of you—and for Joe.

The first time you propose to Holly is in your bedroom, when you're both in your pyjamas and exhausted after hosting a party. You slip the ring on her finger.

Then you ask for it back. The ring's returned to the box. The next day, you tell Joe of your plan to propose. While Holly goes out for a manicure, the two of you get flowers for your surprise.

Joe beams on the walk back from the florist's. "I'm so excited," he admits. He quickly adds, "I feel like a traitor." You don't ask him whether he feels as though he's betraying his father or the family that preceded this one, nor do you openly acknowledge his own psychological acuteness.

Holly returns home to the flowers and openly speculates about why you've bought them. Joe executes the plan and suggests a board game. Inside the Dominion game box are envelopes addressed to Holly and Joe. "Look behind you," you've written in letters to each. Behind Holly, on the living-room bookshelf, you've hidden the box with her ring in it. Behind Joe, on another shelf, you've placed a gift for him, a watch that you purchased that afternoon.

As you did the night before, you propose. But Joe isn't happy. He wants you to propose again, now for the third time, so he can take a photo. He wants you down on one knee. So you oblige. There are two of you in the photo, but, from the way you both look at the picture-taker, he may as well be in it.

You don't know beforehand how much you will feel, a year and a half later, on the day your daughter is born. People say your life will change, but it already did a few years earlier. Eventually, you will take as much pleasure when people compliment her long eyelashes as you do when they laugh at the way she resembles you when she scowls. Sometime soon, this baby will be the root of everything.

But on the day she's born, you're tired from getting up so early for the C-section. You're embarrassed to wear a hairnet in the operating room. You're rubbing your tongue against the tooth you cracked on a stale granola bar.

Joe arrives at the hospital with your mother. He's upset that it's taken you so long to call them. He's upset at the doula who says something he feels is patronizing. He holds the sleeping baby in his arms and he's got this pained look. He seems angry that everyone's looking at him. He's upset to be so emotional in front of so many strangers.

You know what a big day it is. But he's the one who feels it. He already feels the way you should.

# The New Sacred

## MONICA MENEGHETTI

I find S in one of his usual dungeon master's occupations: colouring a hand-drawn map. He shows me the umpteenth otherworldly kingdom of his creation, pointing out the valley in which his gamers will take some serious hit points, if not die.

"I've been invited to submit to *Love Me True*. It's an anthology." I pause for effect. "About marriage."

This gets both of our soft bellies jiggling.

The humour lies in the irony. S and I "live in sin." Not only have we been doing so for decades now, we gave up monogamy eighteen years ago. And rather than non-monogamy being a detriment to our relationship, as many assumed it would be, it is one of the reasons for our longevity.

So maybe it *is* funny for someone like me to be included in this anthology. The invitation implies I have something to contribute to a conversation about real love, commitment and family-building. Why is that funny? Monogamy isn't necessary for any of those things.

When I share this analysis with S, he smirks—for a different reason this time.

"Well, you *are* sort of married, to three people, in a way …"

I laugh. Yet something is buzzing, an annoying whine at the furthest range of my hearing.

By 3:00 a.m., his comment, like that lone mosquito that gets into your tent before you can zip it back up, has wormed into my sleep and stung me awake: Holy shit. Am I *married*? To *three* people?

I finally manage to fall asleep as sunrise nudges between the slats of the blind. In the morning, I tell him about my hour-of-the-wolf anxiety.

"I guess your comment really got under my skin."

"Yes!" he says, doing the universal gesture for hockey-player-just-scored.

And I realize it's one of his jokes, the teasing, sorta-true-but-not-all-true kind—one of his patented techniques for jovially provoking enlightenment.

So now? Well, now the essay I was going to write for this anthology is derailed because I can't shake his joke. *Why does the idea of being married bother me so much?*

I was twenty-one when my thirty-four-year-old boyfriend proposed to me, about three months into our relationship.

"I won't be marrying you, or anyone. I have issues with the institution of marriage." I went on, citing the usual suspects: patriarchy-misogyny-economic control-et cetera.

We settled on cohabitation. Before long, he started suggesting we could remake marriage in our own image. Forget the rings. Write our own vows. Make it something different from our parents' marriages. Subvert the institution from the inside. So, after a few years, I agreed to get married. I was an idealist. Anything was possible, right? Plus, the idea of thumbing my nose at the mainstream was irresistible. So was the chance to piss off my dad, who disapproved of the relationship. I didn't see any of this at the time, of course. No, no. I made *my own* choices, thank you very much.

On our way to tell my family, nausea gripped me. Motion sickness, I told myself, but light-rail transit had never made me sick before. In the months after the announcement, the crisis line attendant dismissed my panic attacks on the toilet as cold feet. Never mind my attraction to a new friend, the first lesbian I'd ever known. Never mind my dad's negative opinion of my fiancé—I would do what *I* wanted, Dad couldn't control *me*! Never mind the fourteen-year age difference and numerous incompatibilities. Never mind any of it. Because announcing an engagement is like pressing "play" on a continuous playlist of societal expectations fuelled by romantic myths. No one ever says, "Hey, you're allowed to change your mind you know." Instead it's "When's the wedding?" which tends to merge into "Where's your honeymoon?" into "When are you going to buy a house?" into "When are you going to start a family?" into "Who's your marriage counsellor?"

Since year zero of AMT (Adult Monica Time, roughly 1989), I have used the most minimal object to carry my essentials. If I needed anything else along, I would use a backpack instead.

I still remember the first time S said, "Don't forget your purse."

"I do *not* carry a *purse*! It's a wallet. A wallet on a string."

"Does it have more than just money in it?"

We looked at the keys, inhaler and lip balm bulging against leather.

"See? Definitely a purse."

This exchange became a comedy sketch we'd perform as a duo, varying our ripostes each time. After a while, we didn't even need to say the whole script, just the punchline. Grey eyes twinkling, corners of his mouth twitching, he'd bait a hook with that word "purse," cast it into the space between us and wait with the corners of his mouth twitching like the tip of a fishing rod getting a nibble. I'd delight him by taking the bait—all the while wondering, *Why does the idea of carrying a purse bother me so much?*

My mom and dad got married on the longest night of the year—"How romantic!" thought the Romeo-and-Juliet-obsessed Monica of Yore. To this day, one of my favourite pictures of Mom is a monochrome wedding photo. She is mounting the marble steps of what must be an Italian cathedral. Snowflakes are floating down around her white suit and white fur hat and landing on her white pumps. She is escorted by an unknown man in a dark suit and black overcoat. My aunt is the only one still alive who may be able to identify him, so I better ask her soon.

Me, I got married in 1992 at twenty-five, for the first and only time, in a southern Alberta hamlet. I wore a white suit, white pumps and nothing in my hair. Bright petunias lined the flower beds along the pathway to the venue. At least, I think they were petunias. It was hard to tell with all the fresh snow. Snowfall on the morning of my late-August wedding felt like an homage, or maybe even a visitation, Mom's way of telling me, "I'm with you today." Within a year, I would see it instead as pathetic allegory, a sign I was doing something unnatural. But from the perspective of AMT? Snow on flowers is perfectly natural in August at that altitude. Shit happens. Sometimes snow is just snow.

We gathered our guests at a small restaurant bearing the same name as a cult in southern California: Heaven's Gate. Our ceremony was a secular one with spiritual sprinkles. My betrothed was a practising Tibetan Buddhist, so a singing bowl was played briefly to complete the ceremony, and a friend offered us white Khatas from their mutual teacher, a former monk who sadly was too ill to attend. My dad called me afterward, asking about the significance of these ritualistic elements. He was suspicious, as though I'd joined some sort of cult.

My recollection of how I felt that day? Numb. And yet, I believed it was the right thing to do. We loved each other, and love is all you need, right?

The marriage lasted ten months. I waited years to finalize the divorce. By then, all but one member of Heaven's Gate had committed mass suicide. My dad, ever the irreverent jokester, found the coincidence hilarious and couldn't resist a quip when I announced the paperwork was concluded. His dark humour wasn't very funny to me at the time. I won't go into why because this essay isn't a purse.

The marriage commissioner had married us with the bare minimum statements required by law. Our customized vows did not promise till-death-do-you-part, nor sexual exclusivity. We didn't exchange rings or start a joint bank account or plan to own property or have children. None of that short-circuited the script. Keeping my maiden name resulted in people calling my husband Mr. Meneghetti. Those who didn't assumed I was Mrs. HisLastName. The government still expected me to finance his education rather than granting him a student loan. People still reacted strangely when they found out we took some of our vacation time separately. If I showed up to an event alone, people would ask where he was, or act strangely because they assumed we were fighting. I was no longer invited to do anything independently of him, though we had always done many things separately. I was now expected to prioritize time with his family. On and on. And when I left, everyone—including my husband—acted as though I were violating vows I had never made.

I hadn't realized how much sheer work it would take to subvert a centuries-old, enshrined institution from the inside. Our families, our books and films, our communities all instilled lessons in how to be married before we had a chance to decide for ourselves. It took constant vigilance to be aware of this conditioning, lest I find myself carrying out the marital script. At times, I dedicated more energy to fighting against this societal programming than to the actual relationship, which hardly helped us thrive. For me, getting married was like signing up for one of those "free" holidays where all the angles are invisible until you're at the resort grimacing through Chase and Sanborn coffee and a relentless time-share sales pitch.

Like many misfits' lives, mine hasn't exactly been a point A to point B kind of journey. It's been full of stops and starts, confusion and utter clarity, distraction and pinpoint focus. My life energy is like an alternating current. My body gains and loses the same pounds. I turn over new leaves only to turn them back again. I sabotage then nurture myself, court epiphanies but resist them. I've courageously roared my truths quite a lot; does that make up for the one and only time I cowered on the bathroom floor, incapacitated? Times of great struggle or quasi-numbness give way to contented peace or triumph or pleasure. Nine-to-five has taken its pound of flesh even as it's healed me. I've also lived with minimal routine, feeling intensely alive. Fierce love, deep wounds and complete conviction as well as floundering, pondering, questioning and losing myself in perfectionism and self-pity—that's me, AC/DC.

Anxiety has been with me through it all. So has Writing. Actually, those two are my life partners. When I pick up a pen, my heart rate drops. I exude words like sweat, shed them constantly, like skin cells. Writing takes my hand and guides me to my truth, my passion and direction, whereas Anxiety is my staunch defender, the partner who keeps me safe. Whenever I overextend or someone breaches my boundaries, Anxiety rests fingers on my neck and gives counsel—sometimes in a whisper, sometimes in a shout. I should write an ode to Anxiety and Writing. But I don't want this essay's string to snap.

S and I will celebrate twenty-two years together soon. When I share that, sometimes folks imply it's not much of an accomplishment because we haven't been exclusive. It's true, ours is a different kind of accomplishment. One not many understand enough to appreciate.

We were both twenty-eight when we met in Banff. Following a science-fiction-infused flirtation, we fell in love and U-Hauled it three months later, like a pair of lesbians. In our early days together, I would know it was morning by the needle dropping onto our favourite Black Sabbath album, and his trip outside for the first hand-rolled smoke of the day. Our first place together was on Muskrat Street—as locals, we said we lived "on Rat." Our rundown basement suite was in a building we dubbed the Half-Wit House. Our basement suite's main attraction was the wood stove. It came complete with a supply of used wooden chopsticks left behind by the previous tenant, who had collected them from the sushi restaurants in town for an art project. While the chopsticks burned, we spent hours on the futon, holding each other, watching science fiction and having sex. Our kitchen window was level with the front lawn. Sometimes an elk would be grazing just the other side of the glass, his antlers nearly rapping on the pane. In that kitchen, we made countless grilled cheese sandwiches from orange processed cheese on cracked wheat 'n' honey bread from the local market. As so many new lovers do, we fell into unconscious monogamy and imploded into our own world, our uniquely woven cocoon of love. Our time together flowed as naturally and essentially as an exhalation. So that one day, I was surprised to notice some of his chest hairs had turned white and realized how much time had passed.

I've been in and out of love with others many times, and here he and I still are—together. We've never had a single major fight or breach of trust. We joke about everything, we cry, we fuck, we get anxious, we laugh at ourselves and never tire of each other's company. He actively supports me in my life and my loves, even when it isn't convenient, or easy or fun. If that's what "husband" means, then I have one.

To be polyamorous is to drink an emotional power shake daily, blended and stirred by love of various stages of depth, challenge and development. The vulnerability, the gratitude, the humility and awe of such nourishment have brought me to my knees more than once.

People say it takes a village to raise a child. Well, I believe it takes a community to raise a relationship. I didn't realize this until I stepped outside the institution of monogamy. Suddenly, there are no water-cooler chats or casual advice given out in the coffee lineup, and very few films and books that reflect and validate your reality, that tell you, "You're okay and good for society." Polyamorous folk need to actively seek out others who understand our joys and challenges, who love us and support what we are trying to build. Because there are times in any relationship when you need outside support. That's where friends come in, where community steps up. We need others to believe in us. We need them to help us stay positive, to remind us how much we have already overcome and how much we have going for us. We need to feel them rooting for us. Sometimes a person needs to talk about a problem without having to explain the entire context first. Other times, it is as simple as being able to share your stories without facing judgment, censure, confusion or hostility.

Those who do not live the way I do often focus on what they imagine I get from multiple partners. Their first thought seems to always be the sex. They rarely think of what I give, of all the emotional output it takes to nurture multiple intimacies. I often contend with—and transcend—fear in its many guises, in myself, my partners and broader society. It's challenging, certainly, more akin to being in a family than in a couple relationship. Often, it feels like being in a relationship with love itself. My life is rich, abundant, stimulating and rife with support, interaction, pleasure and growth—as well as the usual challenges of a relationship—times three. When Anxiety and I are dancing well, this life is deeply fulfilling, it connects me ever more deeply with Spirit, the divine, whatever you want to call that numinous and primordial something that flows constantly and everywhere. When Anxiety is dominating our jagged tango, I flounder. Yet I don't have a choice. I am of the nature to love multiply. All I can do is persist, keep building a life in which that quality is welcomed.

Years later, I finally saw my dedication to purse-free living for what it was: a rejection of gender stereotypes. Okay, so I happened to be a double-x carbon unit (well, triple-x really, but that's another, naughtier essay). Did that mean I had to do silly things like hobble around in foot-destroying high heels and further encumber my movement with a designer handbag worth more than its contents? (Yes, I did eventually address my internalized misogyny, too. And wound up embracing stereotypically feminine clothing and shoes as fetish items. But let's not try to stuff too much in here.) Further down the path of my seemingly endless coming-out process, I understood how a purse can make me even more invisible as a queer bisexual than I already am.

When reading glasses joined my list of essentials, I started using ever more purse-like objects. And as long as they don't encumber me, and are amenable to being shoved into a pannier or backpack, I'm actually okay with purses now.

I met T at a drag king show in Calgary. During intermission, a disembodied voice told me, "Ask her to dance." A voice from above or within? I only know it wasn't my own voice. The dance floor was minuscule and vacant, the music decidedly undanceable. I ignored the command. She'd been flirting, sure, but I wasn't even aware of being interested. Five minutes later, I heard the voice again so I listened. As soon as I was holding her in my arms, the attraction became obvious. As the show resumed, I hit the bartender up for a blank strip of credit card chit and slipped her my contact info. It was terrible timing. I had just started graduate school.

"Are you seeing anyone?" she asked after the show, which I answered with full disclosure.

I'd grown accustomed to lesbians rejecting me either for being bi or being poly, so her first email was a surprise. In defiance of stereotype, our relationship developed slowly, and didn't follow the usual trajectory to cohabitation. Over time, a friendly synergy developed between S and T, and we started to discuss the three of us sharing a home.

The hurdles to doing that in Banff felt formidable. I was also feeling isolated there, both as a polyamorous queer and as a writer. So I instigated a move to Vancouver. We talked about it in *Star Trek* terms. S would stay on board ship while T and I formed a landing party to see if Vancouver was habitable. If not, he'd beam us back up. We collectively took a gigantic leap of faith, which spoke volumes about our confidence in our positive, functional dynamic and personal adaptability. We might have underestimated the enormity of the challenge ahead of us. But this essay is already overflowing, so I'll leave that for another handbag.

Five years, nine months and sixteen days into our relationship, T and I got the keys to our East Van basement suite with terrazzo flooring. She started working right away, while I went back to my place with S in Banff to finish out my work contract. After that, the plan was for me to live in Vancouver most of the time until we knew if the move was going to stick.

She couldn't know whether I would manage to live away from my beloved mountains, or if I would then adapt to such an enormous change. She faced that uncertainty during the time she was on her own in a new city and plunged into a new, demanding career. While she waited, she made a desk for me out of cardboard, so sturdy it can support eighty pounds of books. Three months later, I stepped off the Greyhound bus into her arms and a panic attack.

Each morning, I would wake up with Anxiety pressed close, missing S and my mountain lifestyle, wondering when we would all be together again, whether the upheaval I was going through was worth it. And so many mornings, she held me while I cried. This is no small thing. Witnessing your love's pain at being apart from another love is not an experience we are raised to understand, let alone face day after day. On top of that, she was living with me being in a kind of emotional free fall. I had left my home in mid-life, was on a tight deadline for a project, had never lived in a city the size of Vancouver. Plus, I had left behind two spiritual communities. Most destabilizing was living apart from S for the first time in eighteen years. Would I manage to stick with it and stay? T faced that uncertainty, too. Even with a week of ten- or twelve-hour cooking shifts ahead of her, she would wake up and make us a scrumptious, unpredictable and creative dinner-for-breakfast every day. And when I fell in love again with another person, B, soon after my arrival, she adapted to that as well. We'll celebrate our ten-year anniversary soon. I received so much love. Real love. Not the fireworks-and-cotton-candy kind but the kind that humbles you. Not the kind where you show up only when you're free of doubts and your partner is fun, but the kind that makes you stronger and your life broader than you ever believed possible. If that's what it means to have a wife, then I have one.

During my first weeks in Vancouver, I often cried on the phone with S, wondering aloud if the change had been a mistake, if what we stood to gain outweighed what I'd left behind.

"It's too soon to tell," S would say.

How much strength it must have taken for him to say that! And so many times, when all he likely wanted for himself was to have me near again. I received love. Real love. Not the convenient, self-gratifying, easy pleasure sometimes mistaken for love, but the kind that launches adventures into inner space.

As I mentioned, I met B two weeks after I joined T in Vancouver. Again, it was terrible timing. But love chooses us, and its timing is rarely convenient. All we can do is recognize we're being given a gift, choose whether to receive it and then not screw it up.

Meeting B was like a scene from a romcom, something I had dismissed as silly since the dawn of AMT. I won't go into it here—there's only so much you can fit inside a wallet-on-a-string. Suffice to say, I accepted the gift, and so did B. We'll have been together four years soon.

To describe B as emotionally intrepid is an understatement. They found themselves in love with someone who had not one but two existing partners. And they repeatedly chose to live that out—despite being on a steep poly-amory learning curve, despite my being embroiled in a huge life transition involving massive adjustments in my love-scape. Despite being uncertain I would stay long-term, they consistently gave me their time and energy anyway. In our early days together, they would simply show up and drive me through the mist and rain to some magical spot. Together we meditated near cedars, trickling creeks or ocean waves. B understood and shared my need for the wild energy of nature, and brought me there to find strength, solace and ground-ing again and again. Were it not for B's love, nurturing, formidable tenacity and deep spiritual strength during the two years T, S and I were in transition between provinces, it's easy to imagine that I would have turned tail and fled back to my beloved, yet limiting, life in the mountains. And if that had hap-pened, two of my dreams would never have come true: a shared domestic life with T and S, and a published memoir. Despite B's own fear, frustration and struggle, they stuck with me. If that's what a spouse does, then I have one.

I woke up with S one morning, after two years of managing a long-distance relationship with him. Soon, we were going to be packing the U-Haul again, this time to move in together with T. I stroked his head, the head I have shaved monthly for so long, and I thought of T and my more recent love B, and the fact that I would not have any of them in my life if each of them hadn't loved me enough to fully accept who I am, despite the risks. I remembered all the tears I'd shed over other lost loves while S and T held me in their arms. I thought about how S was now willing to leave his life behind, this place he had lived more than half of his life, because he *loved* me, and he loved T like family, and wanted to be with me—with us. I marvelled at everything T and B were undertaking too—all in order to be with me. And I heard the old "I'm-not-worthy" litany begin inside me.

But this time, an inner voice challenged, "What if you *are* worthy?"

What if I am indeed worthy of this depth of love and devotion? What if I inspire it with my own love and devotion? What then? What would there be to do but *let it in*? Feel it. Treasure and cherish and bask and steep in it until I exude love to anyone in my presence. So that when my loves leave this world—and leave we must, some day—what's left behind, what persists, even if my "I" is cancelled out by grief, is love.

What if each and every human being on this planet is worthy of this qual-ity, this breadth of love? What if the only sacred words are the ones we shout as we let this brand of love in? Or are forced to let it go?

The essential components of a wedding: sacred words, one person officiating and others bearing witness to the love being declared. In my way of loving, unexpected moments have felt like weddings. Meals can feel like rituals and honeymoons may happen repeatedly and randomly. Almost anything meaningful to the lovers can be a symbol of union. A brass infinity symbol, or a flower sculpted from foraged scrap wire, or an oversized candy diamond ring. A heart of plastic or wood. Ammolite or a heavy metal tune. Frigid water. The scent of sage and smoke. Or simply the feeling of abiding within a circle of shared trust.

All of my partners will read this essay before it gets published. I'm daunted to face their possible reactions and can't help but wonder how each might feel to witness my words of love and devotion for the others.

Yet anything can be a ceremony. Even an essay.

# Bees of the Invisible

## KARA STANLEY

---

I should say off the top that I do not believe in true love, soulmates or the institution of marriage any more than I believe in rigidly defined notions of gender or the ridiculous dichotomy that situates types of women on extreme ends of a spectrum: Angel-in-the-house versus Madwoman-in-the-attic. Our human biology allows for a rainbow-tinted panorama of possibilities while cultural dictates and mores have, throughout history, endorsed some of these possibilities while at the same time restricting others. As Yuval Noah Harari says in his epic historical account entitled *Sapiens*: "Biology enables, Culture forbids."

So what do I believe in? Last year *Elle* magazine asked me to be a part of a panel of fourteen love experts, offering up "new ideas on love." I was honoured to be asked, also amazed and deeply out of my depth. "Do you think it would be okay if I just quoted Lou Reed's 'Some Kinda Love'?" I asked my husband, Simon. I knew the words off by heart, and sang the first verse, the one about no kinds of love being better than others, in a poor imitation of Lou's signature sing-song-y voice.

"*La-dee-ta-ta-ta*," Simon sang in response, finishing the musical phrase.

As a preteen I was told this fact: Canada geese mate for life. Geese couples have a song unique to them, the male singing his part, the female singing hers, a kind of call-and-response, or repetitive, soothing conversation. If a mate dies, the remaining partner continues to sing, not only their part but also the part of the partner, so the song lives on, whole and complete.

This fact came courtesy of a next-door neighbour, one with a penchant for tall tales, excessive drinking and, worst of all, bagpipe playing. I do not know if this fact is accurate, but honestly it doesn't matter, because, true or not, the faithful geese with their chinstrap heads and graceless honks are central to the story I do believe in.

I believe in reciprocal love, call-and-response love, love that is a multifaceted mirror, one that reflects the thousand-and-one angles of the vast unknown, as well as something singular, familiar and richly *known*. I believe that love is a song we should sing loud enough throughout our lives that it has the potential to thrum and echo long after we have died.

It is thanks to these two musically themed threads—Lou Reed's "Some Kinda Love" and the enduring love song of Canada geese—that I can, without feeling too much the hypocrite, announce that I do not believe in the institution of marriage in an opening paragraph and then, in the next breath, introduce my husband. These two things are equally true: I never wanted to get married. I have been married, most happily, for more than half of my life.

The relative success of a marriage, like most things in life, resides in finding the delicate balance between truth and fiction.

Starry-eyed fantasies of perfect harmony are bound to weaken a marriage. And so I will note right here that Simon is loud and I am quiet, and this sometimes creates friction. Also, it drives Simon crazy that I habitually forget to tighten lids. How is it, he asks, that I can be so ordered, even compulsive, in my daily pursuits and yet routinely replace the jam jar into the fridge with the lid simply resting on top? To this I would counter that it is outrageous that after twenty-five years together he still never fully cleans the crud out of the sink stopper at the end of the night. Also, the recycling! Would it be so hard for him to occasionally transfer some of the tin cans and milk cartons to the bins outside?

But our fictions are important to us. Throughout our years together Simon and I have engaged in a kind of mutual idealization. I am always certain there are at least one or two people eyeing him in a flirtatious manner; reliably he feels the same about me. It is a complimentary fiction we extend to one another and the spark of jealousy it creates is an important component in the health of our relationship. Anyone in a long-standing marriage knows that love and desire often have different aims. Love anchors us with kindness and respect, striving to create secure, stable, continuous relationships. Desire thrives on embracing the uncharted and the unknown. It involves relinquishing stability as we allow for an abandonment of the self—to the other, to one's bodily sensations, to the rhythms and surprises of shared physicality. Love requires a solid home, with strong foundations, good plumbing and preferably one of those leak-proof metal roofs, the kind that last forever. Desire lives in a sandcastle that nightly is washed away in the tide. In an uncertain universe, the secure, stable home is no more real or true than the sandcastle, and both abodes require mutually-agreed-upon fictions to sustain and inhabit.

It's summer. Simon is planting seeds and I am watering, dragging the green hose around the yard. It is slow work: the hose is heavy and insists on looping, then kinking every few feet, the water suddenly blocked, the nozzle spitting and spritzing cold water down my arm. "It's a lovely state of mind,"

Simon says as I pass by. "Planting seeds. Every time you poke a seed in the earth you can't help but send out a little prayer: There you go, guy. Go for it. Grow."

After a rainy June, July's sun is hot, brisk in its skipping glitter across the ocean's surface, languid and billowy under our cedar trees and on the porch by the flower box, where the white alyssum trails between red geraniums and dark purple petunias, perfuming the air with its warm honey-and-vanilla scent. The rapid-fire tweets, the trilling pulses and the bellowing barnyard squawks of the ever-present birdsong provide a wildtrack of background noise. Chico, our brown Lab, is attentively following the cartoonish antics of two feuding squirrels who, chittering madly, chase each other with precarious speed along the length of our backyard fence. Earlier, I caught Chico in the raised garden bed tugging at a snap-pea vine. It's hardly worth it to chastise him, the dog's a goat, an incorrigible, veggie-loving goat. In the fridge is a slab of wild salmon marinating in a garden-fresh pesto and when I'm done watering I'll pick a colander of spicy arugula, baby kale and buttery leaf lettuce for a dinner salad.

Simon is smiling even as he navigates his wheelchair over the unwinding hose, moving to the far side of the garden bed to continue poking seeds—swiss chard now—into the earth. *There you go, guy. Go for it. Grow.*

The whole scene—the birdsong, the sun, Simon planting seeds, the marinating salmon—it's pretty much my idea of earthly paradise.

Reading the above bucolic description of my summer ideal, you might find yourself seamlessly contributing your own salient details—the scratch of dry grass under bare feet, saliva-inducing billows of barbecue smoke, the chilling thrill of diving into a cool ocean under a hot sun, water cascading down the slope of your face as you surface—all sensory cues that will help us, together, create and share a familiar picture of a slow, sunny, summer day.

One detail—the wheelchair—might have been unexpected and might lead you to make assumptions. The author is an older woman, you might justifiably surmise, her husband even older, an invalid. If you are of one type of mind, you might immediately feel less interested in what is to come. Why not? The elderly and infirm are not particularly sexy. If you are of another type of mind, you might read on, intrigued that this seemingly elderly couple is, despite apparent disability, successfully living in their own home. We can learn, can we not, how to live well by paying attention to those who have done it before us?

But the wheelchair is misleading. Well into my forties, I am neither young nor old but solidly middle-aged, healthy and, for the most part, feeling stronger and fitter than at any other time in my life. Simon is a year younger than me. He uses a wheelchair because nine years ago he fell off an unsecured piece of scaffold; and when he fell, the breathtakingly fragile, soft and spongy brain and spinal cord encased in its also breathtakingly fragile home of bone were seriously injured—catastrophic was the word doctors most often used at the time. Young, and very strong, when the accident occurred, Simon made a recovery that seemed to us, his family, nothing short of miraculous. And so I wrote a book about it.

I wrote the book because it's what I do: I write. I write to know what I am thinking, what I am feeling, what I am wanting. I also wrote the book because Simon's approach to his recovery—his determination combined with his acceptance—both moved and inspired me. And, finally, I wrote the book because it was my way to take control (however illusory) over events that had spiralled way beyond my control. I wanted to provide a beginning, a middle and, most importantly, an end, to what was arguably the most difficult chapter in our life.

Simon helped with the book but his input was limited. This was not because he was uninterested, or unable, but because his recovery time was difficult and long, ongoing to this day, and he had more important things to attend to. It was my first book but the excitement of publication was vastly overshadowed by the mind-numbing anxiety Simon and I both felt at the thought of sharing the intricacies and intimacies of our private world with a public reading audience. What had I exposed Simon to? What had I exposed us to? The stress felt enormous.

We reminded each other that writing the book was an act of love, and in the aftermath of Simon's accident our love had deepened. Like love, the aim of the book was to anchor us back in a story that made sense as we attempted to regain stable footing while navigating a post-trauma world that routinely featured the destabilizing forces of chronic infection and illness, debilitating pain and complicating issues of mobility and accessibility. We worked hard to rebuild and re-inhabit that fictional leak-proof home. It was tough at times but even more difficult—in our generally unmoored, destabilized state—were the attempts to return to the shifting ground of our castle made of sand.

The book was released in early spring, and nothing cataclysmic happened. Some more time passed, and more people read the book, and still our small world did not dissolve or fracture under pressure. In fact, we experienced one of reality's surprising, paradoxical sleight of hands. Not only did our private world remain vigorously intact, it also sprouted new connections: changing, expanding and enlarging our shared mythology of two.

When I was twenty-one and pregnant with our son Eli, the thought of marriage, a public ceremony, with all its pomp and circumstance and its implied binding social contract, terrified me. Being with someone should be a choice, a private, personal, daily choice. Fuelled by the memories of poor examples of marriage my short lifetime had provided, I believed in that act of daily choosing with all the bloated righteousness only a twentysomething can muster. Simon lacked my fervour but still willingly agreed: we would write our own vows, create our own mutable, transformable idea of marriage.

I have the rough drafts and the final copies of our ceremonial vows in a file folder in my office. Despite the intention of vows that could and should be renewed daily, the language is of the embarrassing to-eternity-and-beyond sort, mine especially so. There are a lot of spirit animals stalking the phrases— hawks, wolves and eagles—and a lot of ecstatic universal mumbo-jumbo. My particular focus on choice is clearly summed up in my final statement: *I love you, Simon. And I choose to spend my living with you.*

Simon's rough notes demonstrate a more subtle understanding of the concept of choice and a vaguer notion of, well, something else. He writes:

—*choice is an act of mind*

—*that is just electrochemical*

—*so it is my essence that moves toward you*

Trust and faith, he also writes, shall flow through our minds and bodies and "usher out fear by the coattails," a turn of phrase I find particularly endearing. But it is his final vows that are my favourite, the ones I wish I had written: *Together we will grow old. Together we will cease making sense. Together we will spend a lifetime learning to be teachers and lovers and artists of understanding. This is the beginning of a great adventure.*

I mean, c'mon. Tell me I didn't get lucky in love.

I still believe in this need for daily choice, but it is the more muted, considered and nuanced belief of middle age. My life and Simon's life have so deeply intersected that to choose to leave the marriage, for example, would be like choosing to cut off a limb, or dig out a vital organ. Impossible. But who I am, what I will give freely, what I will surrender to and what I will be open to receive are all choices we make daily.

Since the book came out, we have been travelling across the country to give presentations at literary and music festivals, and for large conferences, often for audiences who are survivors of brain injury, or who are somehow involved as family members, caregivers, service providers or researchers. We take turns telling our story and I read a few passages from the book and Simon plays a few songs that have been important to him throughout his recovery. Often afterwards, people talk with us, discussing their observations or insights, or sharing their stories. Each of those interactions subtly influences our current remembering of Simon's accident. This is how memory works. Our memories are not static and unchanging but rather grow and accrue new meaning in a process I imagine similar to crystallization: each time we revisit a specific memory we respond to it anew, and each new response adds another layer of feeling, another level of meaning. A singular memory, a small moment in space and time—say, the moment in the middle of the night when I stood beside Simon's ICU bed, assuming the posture of an ancient shamanic healer by hovering my hands over his frantic, feverish skin, hoping and imagining with all the force of my being that somehow, through some magical resonance between his atomic structure and mine, I could keep him alive throughout the night—this memory initially constituted a brief and spontaneous symphony of neuronal activity in my brain. Unheeded, it would have disappeared, a song forgotten. But I have returned so many times to this moment that its brief blaze of electrochemical mind glow has solidified into something more closely resembling a diamond: multi-faceted, multi-layered, precious to behold.

So beautiful is this diamond it leads me to believe my own fictions: love brought Simon back from the brink of death. Audiences like this message. The statistics for marriages surviving post–brain injury are grim, too dismal to repeat here, and people respond warmly to an example of a love that can, seemingly, conquer anything. But this is a fiction. A lovely fiction, yes, and possibly a necessary one. Both Simon and I would contend even a *true* one, but a fiction nonetheless. Love was certainly important in Simon's recovery, even pivotal. But, of course, it was a team of neurosurgeons and spinal cord surgeons and trauma doctors and ICU nurses, along with Simon's own strong body, that got him through that long and treacherous night.

*Can I give you a hug?* This is the question I am most often asked after a presentation. Usually it is followed with a compliment, *The book meant so much to me—you guys are amazing.* While I couldn't be more proud, or humbled, or moved by the fact that people have connected with our story, these compliments always make me feel profoundly uncomfortable. What can we say? Simon and I usually respond with a spazzy dance of self-deprecation. *Well, Simon is amazing,* I might say. *Phffft,* Simon is likely to respond and then, because he—unlike me—can be funny to defuse awkward situations, will say something like, *There's artistry in writing a book. Any fool can fall from a ladder.*

The truth is I wrote the book precisely because I did not feel amazing. I wrote the book because when Simon was in ICU hovering between life and death and when we, his family, were tormented with the thought that death might be a preferable option to what lay ahead if he survived, I couldn't stop thinking about the geese. I knew that as a partner I had failed. After sixteen years of marriage I knew I could not carry on Simon's side of the song. In fact, without Simon I didn't even know my part. I hadn't learned what I needed to. I was unequal to the task of carrying him on, if he left us behind. If I got a second chance, I promised myself, I promised Simon, I promised the universe, I would try to do better.

We humans are storytellers and we work very hard, weaving webs and webs of narrative, to make our daily life orderly, predictable and secure. Life, on the other hand, does not. Life, being life, and with no seeming effort at all, consistently thwarts, confounds, distorts, disorients, shocks and surprises us. Life, a master rope-a-dope strategist, sits back as we strain and stress, as we aim and fall flat, as we make the same mistakes over and over again, letting us tire ourselves out with the work of living and achieving and making meaning until such time (and it comes for each and every one of us) when life throws a knockout punch that sends us reeling. For a brief moment the veil parts, and even though we are shaken, our bells rung, cartoonish Tweety birds darting around our de-equilibrized skull, we can see clearly that our lives are a series of evolving fictions and not, as we previously supposed, an inviolate text where childish notions of fair/not fair hold sway. We humans have architected some fabulous narratives around concepts such as self, true love, marriage, nationality, money and meaning—all elaborate stories we have been telling in order to convince ourselves that it is us, and not life, that is winning the fight.

These brief moments of veil-parting insight usually involve a brush with mortality, the potential death of a loved one, or of a relationship, or of the self, and they are terrifying enough to shake us out of either routine complacency or obsessive daily pursuits. And life is revealed, the ordinary transformed into the transcendent, the everyday into the elusive, and all our stories slip away: life vastly eclipsing the finite scope of words.

Seeds planted, garden watered, dinner prepped. The late summer afternoon slows almost to a standstill. Bees buzz in the large pink hydrangea that has, after a few years of faltering, come gloriously into bloom this year. "We are the bees of the invisible," Rilke wrote. "Our work is the continued conversation of the beloved visible and tangible world into the invisible vibrations and agitation of our own nature."

No longer so perpetually pummelled by the gales of trauma, or posttrauma complications, the idea of *home* has once again begun to resonate between me and Simon, between who we once were, who we are now and who, in the future, we aim to be, an idea strong enough that once again we are finding the courage to venture into unknown and uncharted territory. To flirt, suckle, pound, tease or otherwise embrace uncertainty with sweat-kissed skin and open palms, allowing that transformative energy of desire to undermine our daily stable structures long enough to experience an abandonment of self to the other.

We open a bottle of red wine and set the small bistro table on the front porch. Chico watches jealously from his bed in the rock garden (the cool corner where the vinca has grown riotous) as we eat the salmon and the salad greens. After the dishes and before we go to bed, we sit in the kitchen and sing songs. It's difficult for me to shut down the incessant narrative voice in my head—the one that plans, edits, organizes, cautions, criticizes and creates boundaries—so that I can abandon myself to the rhythm and the melody and just *be* in this moment. With Simon's help, I am doing a little better.

Haunted by the geese, in the years since Simon's accident I did the thing that scared me most: I took vocal lessons. I have spent hours on the piano plonking out notes and trying to sing them. It doesn't come easily to me, and I will never be a gifted vocalist, but I have worked hard enough that I am a stronger one. Tonight, after I take a sip of wine, I belt out a version of Dylan's "One More Cup of Coffee."

"Yeah!" Simon says. "That's the way to give it up. You sound like Patti Smith."

I *love* Patti Smith, have since I was a teenager, for many of the same reasons I love Lou Reed, and Simon's compliment gives me hope. While Patti is not a traditionally good vocalist, it seems reasonable to aspire to being, like her, an honest singer, a raw and committed one.

"What?!" Simon said, when he read the opening to this piece. "You don't believe in soulmates?"

"Soulmate, no. Good timing, yes," I said. "Just keep reading."

# Shorter Days

## LORRI NEILSEN GLENN

---

The two sit with a thermos of coffee, watch light awaken
on the water, think in wisps as birds to-and-fro between
rocks and seaweed beds before rising into gunnels of wind
above the shelter of the bay. The summer morning leans into
itself, a swishing in the birches, hissing surf beyond the hill:

this is how they talk. Other days, rare, are sharp-edged,
words hurled from a roiled sea that soon wash out with
the tide. At night by the fire, a thickened silence as they tend
debris, remnants of the old house tossed into the pile,
someone else's past becoming flankers and ash. The language

of bodies, what can be created in fading light. Lost: friends,
trappings, houses, follies. They have learned how small
they are under the stars. She watches smoke rise, thinks
how his hands and breath keep her whole, how still,
after forty years, how soft his hair.

Summer heat retreats; they wake to fog and drizzle, relief,
and he walks a pitchfork and wheelbarrow to the beach
to bring back a glistening mound of stringy seaweed.
The prairie crabapple has been skinned at the base—vole,
rabbit, some creature needing water or food. The tree her idea,

a reminder of wheat fields and a sky she could drown in,
of youth, the past a living presence. Together they'd dug
a hole for the sapling, steel blades hitting rock all afternoon—
persistence—and finally, the fragile thing upright, given over
to the Atlantic's fierce wind. Four decades of this, she thinks,

of planting, nudging things to life, feeding them, sating
a ravenous need to be productive, an urge deepening as the body's
strength begins to fade. Hands will always be story, working
the future. The dog sniffs at the bare trunk as they wrap burlap,
pile seaweed to protect the open wound from winter, chancing

soft roots will toughen, push aside rock, burrow.

# Passion

# Getting the Marriage into Bed

**MICHAEL CRUMMEY**

Unplug the insatiable telephone,
the apocalypse unfolding hourly
on the network news crawl.

Ignore the kitchen's Victorian factory
of filthy dishes, the laundry pile
suffocating a lost child in the basement.

Ignore the lost children.
Forget music and saffron and oysters,
put aside the clichéd, the quaint

rituals of wine and lingerie—
aphrodisiacs are for amateurs
with more time than common sense,

who've yet to learn bliss is stolen
from the world in small, piercing slivers.
Think of stealth as foreplay

in the prison yard of daily events,
sneak out of your clothes
as soon as the coast is clear—

the air-raid siren of a youngster
crying is about to rise
through the bedroom floor,

the weight of the Three Gorges reservoir
has altered the planet's rotation
by the same rate at which yesterday's

dishes are going septic in the sink—
be resolute. Bliss lives for bliss alone,
apply yourself to that ephemeral sliver.

You have less time than you think.

# Fireworks

## EVELYN LAU

We watch the fireworks from your balcony,
your husband with a circle of gold
on a tarnished chain round his neck,
your silk-shirted lover holding hands
with his wife, her face a dark jewel
turning in the lit-up night.
As the first fireworks ignite over English Bay,
reflect in the windows of a high-rise blocks away,
we wonder who's on the barge tonight,
if Jimmy Pattison is out on his yacht
with rich men and beautiful women,
dancing and drinking champagne,
if they lead better lives
than ours, and what we'd have to do
to get on board. You bring another beer
for your love, fingers touching and eyes gleaming
in a flash so black and hot I wonder
how your husband does not see,
how he can know the names
of all the bands on the eighties soundtrack
and not know he is losing his wife.
"Missing You" blares on the radio
as strangers clap and cheer
at the cookie-cutter heart traced for an instant
in the sky, then the weeping willows
weeping into the water.

# Lice

## MIRANDA PEARSON

───────────

Jealousy is not green,
jealousy is plum-coloured
and mostly mental.
Safe sex?
No such thing.
Even fantasy is unsafe.
Dark imaginings. Teeth.
Foam. Erotica. Images
you thought could never
threaten you, never prod
that dark place, that
plum inside.

Limbs heavy
with something that
could be flu, could be
longing, dull and vertiginous.
At home, shaking,
the wife-at-risk, you
carefully pick lice
from your son's scalp.
Holding his head
in a good light,
        just so.

# The Woman in This Poem

**BRONWEN WALLACE**

The woman in this poem
lives in the suburbs
with her husband and two children
each day she waits for the mail and
once a week receives
a letter from her lover
who lives in another city
writes of roses warm patches
of sunlight on his bed
*Come to me* he pleads
*I need you* and the woman
reaches for the phone
to dial the airport
she will leave this afternoon
her suitcase packed
with a few light clothes

But as she is dialing
the woman in this poem
remembers the pot roast
and the fact that it is Thursday
she thinks of how her husband's face
will look when he reads her note
his body curling sadly toward
the empty side of the bed

She stops dialing and begins
to chop onions for the pot roast
but behind her back the phone
shapes itself insistently
the number for airline reservations
chants in her head
in an hour her children will be

home from school and after that
her husband will arrive
to kiss the back of her neck
while she thickens the gravy
and she knows that
all through dinner
her mouth will laugh and chatter
while she walks with her lover
on a beach somewhere

She puts the onions in the pot
and turns toward the phone
but even as she reaches
she is thinking of
her daughter's piano lessons
her son's dental appointment

Her arms fall to her side
and as she stands there
in the middle of her spotless kitchen
we can see her growing
old like this
and wish for something   anything
to happen   we could have her go
mad perhaps and lock herself
in the closet crouch there
for days her dresses withering
around her like cast-off skins
or maybe she could take
to cruising the streets at night
in her husband's car
picking up teenage boys
and fucking them in the back seat
we can even imagine
finding her body
dumped in a ditch somewhere
on the edge of town

The woman in this poem offends us
with her useless phone and the persistent

smell of onions   we regard her as we do
the poorly calculated overdose
who lies in bed somewhere
not knowing how her life drips
though her drop by measured drop
we want to think of death
as something sudden
stroke or the leap
that carries us over the railing
of the bridge in one determined arc
the pistol aimed precisely
at the right part of the brain
we want to hate this woman

but mostly we hate knowing
that for us too it is
moments like this
our thoughts stiff fingers
tear at again and again
when we stop in the middle
of an ordinary day and
like the woman in this poem
begin to feel
our own deaths
rising slow within us

# In *Anna Karenina* Furs

## SUSAN OLDING

So cold, it hurt to breathe. The squeak and crunch of snow beneath my boots, a flicker of lights from across the frozen lake. I walked quickly, swinging my arms, my whole frame vibrating, struck like a crystal goblet and still ringing. The cold, I told myself. It's only the cold that makes me shiver.

It was mid-January, the night of my thirty-second birthday, in Kingston, Ontario, and I was on my way to my legal ethics professor's house for supper. My husband, also a student—I'll call him Arthur—was out of town, visiting his family. He hadn't seen them over the holiday, and I'd sent him off with my slightly grudging blessing. Later, I felt sorry for myself. I didn't want to be alone. So when my teacher, Mark—I called him that even then—stopped by to drop off some materials, I invited him for tea. We talked, and kept on talking, and eventually he suggested we continue the conversation over an evening meal.

Mark and his wife had separated a few years earlier, and she was living in their former home. He was renting a place from a colleague on sabbatical. The main rooms of the house were fronted with glass, and, as I approached it through the darkness, it glowed.

From the street, I could see Mark setting the table. I didn't find him handsome. Although he was tall and dark, he was thin and wore nerdy eye-glasses. But I liked the way he moved. There was something graceful in the way he held himself, something deft and alert in his attitude. I thought about my husband, who was also tall and thin, but who seemed so much heavier, somehow, with his big raw bones. All autumn and winter, he'd been sleeping ten hours a night or more, and still he was always tired.

Mark cooked salmon in stimpirata sauce with celery and capers. There was salad and a citrus tart. A crisp but oaky Chardonnay. Toward the end of the meal, his twelve-year-old daughter came home—he and his ex-wife were sharing custody—and told us about the movie she'd seen with her friends, her ringlets trembling as she laughed. Some wax from the candles dripped onto the cloth. I scraped it up and pressed it, warm, between two fingers. When I pulled them apart, the wax held the delicate imprint of their whorls.

I walked home through Breakwater Park under a bright moon, the snow glistening and my toes losing their feeling. I considered the evening. Nothing had happened. But in the night I dreamed of him, and when I woke I knew that everything had changed. *Nonsense*, I told myself. *It's not as if I've done anything. I don't even intend to do anything. I'm not some Anna Karenina.*

The story is familiar. Anna—the beautiful, lively wife of Alexei Karenin, a dry bureaucrat—falls in love with a dashing army officer named Vronsky, and the two begin an affair that becomes the talk of St. Petersburg. Anna's husband reacts badly. In desperation, Anna and Vronsky run away, first to Europe, and then to the Russian countryside. There, Anna, barred from polite society and tormented by guilt, becomes increasingly jealous and paranoid, imagining that Vronsky no longer loves her. They quarrel, and, in drug-induced confusion and despair, Anna throws herself beneath the wheels of a train.

But the novel begins with Anna's brother, the pathologically charming Stepan Oblonsky, and his long-suffering wife, Dolly. Throughout the novel, Oblonsky has several affairs. His behaviour wounds Dolly terribly, but she stays with him and continues to care for their children, finding small moments of joy in parenting. Meanwhile, no one thinks any the worse of her unfaithful husband. Unlike his sister—but like most other men of his time and class— Oblonsky does not pay a price.

I hated that double standard the first time I read the book. This was the seventies, during the height of second-wave feminism, and I was sixteen. The unfairness of Anna's situation tore through me like a knife. Why should she suffer and die while her brother went on guzzling champagne? What kind of society could condone that?

The answer was obvious: a hypocritical one. And I knew all about hypocrisy. In high school, a person had to live and breathe it, along with the chalk dust—especially in my school, peopled as it was with fundamentalist Christians. A trio of them, earnest and judgmental and deliberately unworldly, sat across from me in English class. Two boys and a girl, Armeda, the daughter of a minister. Pale and buxom, with downcast eyes, she wore low-cut peasant blouses and blushed at the resulting attention.

Naturally, the fundamentalists didn't warm to Anna. They saw her as selfish and sinful, and said as much. So it fell to me to defend her, and defend her I did, railing against her desiccated stick of a husband and the stupid social rules that constrained her choices.

It made for lively debate; our teacher was pleased. And so, as the year went on, I continued to support the cause of emotional and sexual freedom. In the process, I became more and more excited by novels in general, and by this one in particular. I also came to identify with Leo Tolstoy's heroine—though I was an unlikely Anna, lacking her grace, her charm or her ability to fascinate men. But none of that bothered me. After all, I was young. I had plenty of time to grow into the role.

We first see Anna on a train platform through Vronsky's eyes. Rich, beautiful, elegant: he notes these qualities dispassionately, as if ticking them off a list. But what strikes him most powerfully is her restrained animation, "as if a surplus of something so overflowed her being that it expressed itself beyond her will, now in the brightness of her glance, now in her smile." By the time Anna throws an arm around her brother, in a movement that surprises Vronsky with its "resoluteness and grace," he has fallen in love with her.

At age sixteen, so had I. How could anyone not love Anna, with her firm, light step, her warmth, her humour? She bewitches everyone from irritable old ladies, like Vronsky's mother, to irrepressible children, like her nephew Grisha; she touches everyone she meets with joy. She even saves her brother and Dolly's marriage.

What an irony, then, that she can't save her own. Kitty Shcherbatsky, Anna's protege and rival for Vronsky's love, recognizes the danger first. Watching Anna and Vronsky at a ball, she sees that they feel themselves alone in the midst of the crowd, sees how they mirror one another's expressions, and knows her own fate is sealed. She will never marry Vronsky.

It isn't until the next day that Anna can acknowledge her own change of heart. Feeling guilty for spoiling Kitty's pleasure at the party, she leaves Moscow earlier than planned. On the train, she intends to read, but she's agitated and unable to concentrate. With nerves as tight as winding strings, she doesn't want to follow "the reflections of other people's lives."

She wants to live for herself—imagine the hubris of that. Anna is apparently struck by the same thought, because the minute she owns her desire she's overcome by shame. Yet when she thinks of Vronsky, some inner voice tells her, "warm, very warm, hot!" and, overtaken by joy, she's forced to stifle a laugh. Minutes later, when she runs into Vronsky himself on the icy station platform, she knows without his saying so that he has followed her. Forget me, she tells him. But she cannot hide her delight.

I was terrified. There was no one nearby I could confide in. My friends were Arthur's friends—and I certainly couldn't tell Arthur. So, instead of talking, I wrote. In the margins of my notebooks. On loose scraps of paper. In a long computer document. In letters to a friend who lived in England. I didn't know yet if Mark shared my feelings. I hoped he did and hoped he did not. Maybe nothing would happen; maybe it would all blow over and things could go on as before. But the dark closed in when I imagined that.

Sometimes, as I bent over my scribbler, tears would fall and smear the ink on the page. Arthur had never been able to stand seeing me unhappy or angry; if he caught me that way, he'd rush to my side, his face buckled in an uxorious frown. "What's wrong, what's wrong, *ma chère*?" he'd cry, in an unconscious echo of Karenin's name for Anna. I shrugged him off. I'd never kept a secret from him before. But what could I possibly say? I told him I was working on my ethics assignment. My whole life had become an ethics assignment, and I was failing badly.

If you'd asked me, I'd have told you that Arthur and I were happily married. True, there were subjects we struggled to talk about. True, in the past I'd been depressed, and lately he seemed depressed himself. In fact, I couldn't remember the last time he'd really relaxed and had fun. But domestic life was good for us. With little money and a lot of ingenuity, we'd fixed up our apartment. And even if, as one friend said, our kitchen walls were the colour of an old whore's makeup, they still glowed in the candlelight. We talked about books and ideas and we rarely fought; how could we fight when he hated conflict? Our friends thought of us as the perfect couple. Yet here I was, overcome by feelings for someone else that I couldn't control and couldn't explain.

"Women tell me, 'I was lonely, not connected,' 'I don't feel close to my partner and I was taken for granted,'" a marriage therapist says in a WebMD article I discovered years later. These are the reasons women commonly give for their infidelity. Revenge for past wrongs and sexual boredom may also play a part. Yet, as a biological anthropologist explains in the same article, more than a third of unfaithful wives claim to have been happy or very happy in their marriages—at least until meeting their lovers. It's only after she's danced with Vronsky that Anna notices the ugliness of her husband's ears, with their cartilages propping up the rim of his black felt hat; it was only after spending time with Mark that Arthur's habit of quoting philosophers in the midst of our rare disagreements began to drive me crazy.

Women don't leap easily into affairs. That is certainly true for Anna, who tries, briefly, to avoid Vronsky altogether, rather than give in to her desires. It was also true of me. The change in my feelings seemed to come in an instant, and took me completely by surprise, but, like Anna, I struggled to do what was expected of me instead of what I wanted. Like Anna, I lost that struggle.

We didn't have sex. Not while I was his student. Not while Arthur still lived with me in the same house. But we flirted. We carried on. And we became the subject of gossip every bit as wild as the gossip that follows Anna and Vronsky.

Once, we travelled to Toronto to see an art exhibition. Somehow we persuaded ourselves that the trip would constitute research. We took the train and then walked to the gallery, where we ogled the sculptures by Lipchitz and Hepworth and I got in trouble with security for venturing to touch them. I had to do *something* with my hands. On the ride home, our arms briefly met and an electrical current made the fine hairs stand on end.

Spring came early that year and lasted an unusually long time. Bluebells and snowdrops gave way to daffodils and narcissus, and, when the narcissus faded, the lilac bloomed. Its fragrance filled me like never before. "I am amazed at the clairvoyance of people in love," says Vronsky's cousin, Princess Betsy. I was reminded of her observation whenever I'd go for a walk at the lakefront, lost in reverie, and then turn to see Mark coincidentally emerge from around a corner. Even the air felt alive. *Time stops running when he's near*, I wrote. *Everything is here. Everything is now. And now and now and now and now.*

Anna tells Karenin in the springtime. Vronsky has fallen in a horse-racing accident, she has made a public scene and she is pregnant with his child. The words come tumbling out. Likewise, I told Arthur in early April at a point of crisis. Our classes were about to end for the year. He had accepted a summer job in Toronto and I planned to stay and work in Kingston. I couldn't bear to part with so much dishonesty between us.

Of course, he already knew. He'd heard the rumours. He'd seen me talking with Mark in the university corridors and had noticed the brilliance of my smile. "You haven't smiled that way for years," he said, his own mouth a crumpled ruin.

We talked and wept and talked some more, more openly, more genuinely than we had talked in years, maybe more openly than ever. Our conversations filled me with fear and regret. He was a good man, a decent man, and he really wanted our marriage to work. Was it his fault that he couldn't deal with sadness or anger in himself or in others? Was it his fault that this urge had overcome me? When I thought of losing Arthur, my stomach lurched and sank. But when I thought of losing Mark, the light disappeared. For the next few months, I was always falling through darkness.

At sixteen, I idealized the character of Anna every bit as much as a new lover idealizes her beloved. To me, she was a romantic heroine, ruined not by any flaw in her own character but rather by the rigid conventions of her day. After all, why is she punished? For living honestly—for refusing to cloak her true feelings. Vivid, passionate Anna does not want to pretend; she wants to live.

If Anna was a figure of romance to me, she was also a sort of proto-feminist—the kind of woman who, in my own day, could have lived with any man she wanted. She wouldn't have been stuck with the vain and shallow Vronsky—or, even if she had chosen him, she could have left him when she realized her mistake. If she'd lived in 1970s Canada instead of 1870s Russia, she wouldn't have had to invest her whole identity in the role of mistress; instead, she could have pursued a career of her own. Intelligent, decisive, charming, she could have succeeded in any number of professions. Or so my thinking went.

I was fully persuaded that Tolstoy saw things as I did. Why else would he make Anna so attractive, with her musical laugh, her beguiling ringlets, the warmth and animation that always suffuses her face? Why else would he show Vronsky attempting to comb over his bald spot? And why else would Karenin talk with such affected irony? Never mind his unfortunate ears or his wide feet; no woman could stay married to a man so incapable of forthright speech, much less a woman as earnest and ardent as Anna.

My fundamentalist classmates saw things differently. For them, Anna was a harlot. Vronsky was not only arrogant and selfish, but a pig. Karenin was a decent man, mistaken in some of his decisions, perhaps, but deserving of respect and honour. And the true hero of the story was Tolstoy's stand-in, the landowner Levin, who, with his tendency to lecture others, his social awkwardness, his religiosity and his humourlessness, seemed to me remarkably like the Christians themselves. No wonder they took his part.

"If Levin's not the protagonist, why does the book end with him?" my classmates demanded. Anna doesn't even appear until chapter 18, and she is dead for the whole last section of the novel. "Why did Tolstoy kill her off if he approved of her?"

"Then why is it called *Anna Karenina*?" I countered.

When Anna and Vronsky finally run away, Anna feels "unpardonably happy" for a time. The memory of her husband's unhappiness does not poison her pleasure. On the one hand, this memory is "too terrible to think of." On the other, it is also the cause of her own joy, so she can't repent: "The memory of the evil done to her husband called up in her a feeling akin to revulsion and similar to that experienced by a drowning man who has torn away another man clinging to him. That man drowned. Of course it was bad, but it was the only salvation, and it was better not to remember those dreadful details."

So I tried to ignore Arthur's pain in the flush of my own first freedom. I dreamed I was standing on a ladder, working on a large painting. I painted a tree, which on its own grew branches and golden leaves. I painted mysterious sea creatures that took off in flight against the blue-grey sky. As I worked, it seemed to me that the piece lost its symmetry but gained significance, and I woke up smiling.

Walking through Breakwater Park from my place to Mark's, in sandals now instead of boots, I felt the wind tickling my knees, the sun warming my face and ruffling my hair. Mark had a silliness that Arthur lacked. In the long evening light, we'd turn up the music and dance; we'd spin out puns and ridiculous pet names and then laugh so hard it hurt. We stuffed ourselves with strawberries and homemade gelato. We drank a lot of wine. And then, of course, there was the sex. If I thought of Arthur, I pushed the thought away. *To flourish is to become dangerous*, I wrote in my journal, quoting Robert Frost. And then I quoted Melville: *The only real infidelity is for a live man to vote himself dead.*

In the fevered excitement of a new, illicit relationship, a woman rereads her marriage from a different perspective. Belatedly recognizing that Anna has closed her heart against him, Karenin tries to adopt the unfamiliar language of love. "If he hadn't heard there was such a thing as love, he would never have used the word," she thinks. "He doesn't even know what love is." Until this moment, though, she has not seemed to doubt his affection for her, and outwardly, at least, they appear to be a devoted couple. Similarly, I parsed Arthur's sentences, finding only evidence of our incompatibility, despite a history that included at least as much contentment as dissatisfaction.

When an adulterous woman rereads her marriage, she also rereads herself. Having prided herself on her virtue, Anna is shocked by her feelings for Vronsky and no longer knows who she is. "Am I myself, or someone else?" she asks. A hundred years later, faced with the same unexpected emotions, I found myself struggling with the same unanswerable question.

I hadn't considered *Anna Karenina* for many years, but suddenly I couldn't stop thinking about the book. Even its size and heft seemed to echo the mess I was in. And everywhere I went I caught glimpses of Anna. On train platforms, of course, but also at the bank, at the grocery store, even in the mirror. It bothered me to think that my life had become a nineteenth-century melodrama. Wasn't I supposed to be creating my own story? Wasn't I supposed to be unique? Still, I couldn't stop the comparisons. As the weeks went on, they only seemed more fitting.

The breakup of the Karenins' marriage is as wrenching as the breakup of Baltic ice. Anna nearly dies in childbirth, Vronsky shoots himself and Karenin alternates between rage and forgiveness. My own breakup led to similar heartache. Arthur, though he was in Toronto for the summer, didn't intend to give me up, so he tried, with increasing desperation, to woo me back. We talked on the phone late at night; we visited one another. But these visits were painful, and between our strained conversations, we stumbled around like air-raid survivors. In a photo taken at a friend's wedding that summer, we raise champagne flutes for the camera. My eyes are red and swollen, and Arthur's smile looks like the rictus of a corpse.

In August, I made my decision. Like Karenin, Arthur refused to accept it. He brought me flowers identical to our wedding bouquet and begged me to take him back. He called me a slut and a coward. He paced our apartment and wept and then he began to rage.

He ripped a lamp out of the wall; wires dangled from the outlet like entrails. So much for the man who couldn't express anger. He threw a chair. He cowered on our bed like a child. Then he threatened Mark's children. It must have been past midnight when he opened *Anatomy of the Human Body* to the venous system of the arm and started rooting through our kitchen drawers for a sharp knife. A *knife*.

Somehow, I got him to the hospital. "I need a rest," he told the doctors in a rare moment of understatement. While they questioned him, an intern wearing a cross on her neck fussed around me. "Are you *sure* you've tried everything to save your marriage?" she asked. "Couldn't you try again?" What could I do except shake my head? The doctors weren't happy with Arthur's condition, but the hospital had no spare beds. They sent him back to the apartment with me.

The worst of it was that I still loved him. And, although it scared me to admit it, I wasn't so sure I loved Mark. By now, I'd learned that he wasn't always the exquisitely perceptive and responsive person he had first seemed. He fell asleep too early. He obsessed about insignificant details. His teasing had an edge that could leave me close to tears. Not to mention the fact that it took him twenty minutes to comb his hair—longer than it took me to put on my makeup. Waiting for some space at the mirror one day, I couldn't help but think of Vronsky. And not in a good way.

By then, Mark was renting a different sabbatical house, a gloomy, low-ceilinged ranch, its cupboards stuffed with the pack-rat owner's possessions. Once, I counted: Twenty sets of dishes. Forty jars of marmalade. Thirty cans of clams. Four tubes of truffle paste. Truffle paste! And that was just in the kitchen. In the bedroom I found drawers full of Arrow shirts still in their cellophane wrappers, dozens of unworn McGregor socks, thirty packages of Jockey shorts. Where was the space for us in all of that? Where was the space for me?

I had dropped out of school. I couldn't find work. Because I was the guilty party, most of my friends had taken Arthur's side. Meanwhile, Mark had a job, an ex-wife and kids to keep him occupied. I spent a great deal of time alone. As winter came on and the giddy rush of new love evaporated, I began to mourn my marriage. *It was easier then. We were comfortable together*, I wrote in my journal. *Our breaks for tea, the gossip about friends … Here, I always feel jolted, on edge. I miss Arthur and miss my life with him. I miss feeling part of a community. Now I'm a pariah. Why did I do this? Why?* Tangled in a rust-coloured blanket on the long couch of that cavernous living room, I listened to the creaking and humming of a house that wasn't home. *He is good, incredibly good. Who am I, to wound such gentleness?*

Outside, October's leaves gave way to November's frost and then to the snow. Shielding my eyes from winter's glare, I wrote, and kept on writing, filling forty, fifty, sixty pages a week or more, until my journals bulged as full as the cupboards of that place. *Cramps, headache, itchy joints, and a feeling of irritation and anger. So isolated in this horrible house. I don't feel mistress of myself here. Mark has his job, his life—and I have nothing. He has his life plus me, and I have only myself.*

Now I dreamed of facing a Russian firing squad, wearing a dress of red. The authorities gave me a scythe, no bigger than a paring knife, but sharp, and commanded me to slice myself under the left breast and put myself to death.

At some point during that long winter, I picked up *Anna Karenina*. A nice fat novel to distract me from my woes, a book that Oprah's website would later call the Harlequin Romance of its day—it seemed like just what the doctor might have ordered. Besides, given how often I thought about it in those days, it would have been silly not to read it.

I dove into it headlong, neglecting my other duties, breaking only to fix snacks for myself or for Mark's daughter when she came home from school. Standing at the kitchen counter, squinting at the too-bright snow, I'd half listen to Zipporah's tales of teachers and cliques while another part of me perched on the edge of my seat at the Krasnoe-Selo races.

I loved the book, loved it even more than when I'd read it the first time. Coming to it as an adulterous adult, I read it with an almost predatory zeal. I was searching for ways to exculpate myself. I didn't find them. Instead, I located a knot of disquiet that no amount of wine could dispel. Tolstoy, with his incomparable ability to dramatize the feelings of his characters, could awaken empathy for anyone—even the reptilian Karenin. Karenin's false, mincing tone still annoyed me on my second reading, but now I saw what in my teens I could not allow myself to see: the hurt beneath his clipped and supercilious manners. The recognition stung me.

As for Anna herself, all her charm and pathos remained. Her attraction to Vronsky was an expression of her desire to become her most authentic self. How could I fail to respond to that? At the same time, I found her unsettling.

The way she gloried in Vronsky's submissiveness, "like the expression of an intelligent dog when it feels guilty." The way she seemed to exult whenever she was the centre of attention. The way she'd wilt or brood or wax paranoid at the least suggestion that Vronsky might take interest in anything else. Was this the kind of woman I'd want for a friend? Was this the kind of woman I wanted to be?

Not only did I wonder whether Tolstoy really approved of Anna, I wasn't so sure that I approved of her. Worse yet, I felt implicated. "Vengeance is mine; I will repay," goes the novel's epigraph. Did I seriously believe that I deserved to die for what I had done? Of course not. But I couldn't prevent the terrible dreams that followed me into sleep each night, and I couldn't·erase the image of Anna bowing her head on those merciless iron tracks.

Since the 1970s, two interpretations have dominated scholarship about *Anna Karenina*. Outnumbered in the classroom, I considered myself a maverick. But in fact I had adopted the majority reading of the book, which sees Anna as a force for life, a victim of her time and place. Meanwhile, my fundamentalist classmates represented the minority who are critical of Anna, often on religious grounds.

Perhaps this tension can be traced to Tolstoy's own ambivalence. As early as 1870, seven years before he published *Anna Karenina*, he confided to his wife that he wanted to portray a high-society woman who ruins herself yet remains sympathetic, deserving pity rather than scorn. But in his early versions of the manuscript, Anna was fat, ugly and vulgar, her lover was sweetly poetic and her husband was something of a saint. It's only as the novel developed that the husband became colder and more concerned with his social position, the lover lost his interest in poetry and Anna became charming and complex. By the time he finished the book, Tolstoy famously wrote that he had fallen in love with her.

Most commentators have taken this to mean that he would like readers to do the same. But Gary Saul Morson, professor of Slavic languages and literature at Northwestern University, doesn't think so. He claims that Anna's tragedy results not from the clash between her natural vitality and the unyielding dictates of her milieu, but from her excessive self-regard and her refusal to empathize with others.

The tip off is Anna's preoccupation with her looks. "It would be tedious to list all the references to Anna's energetic care of her appearance," Morson writes. "We repeatedly detect her before the mirror. She titillates men, even Levin, with the amazing portrait she places strategically so that they see it before she appears. Her servant is Annushka, her daughter is Annie, and when she takes an English girl under her protection, we learn that the girl's name is—Hannah; everywhere around Anna we find Anna. Tolstoy could hardly signal her narcissism more clearly."

After she runs away with Vronsky, Anna devotes her entire existence to seduction. Even the book's title telegraphs her personality disorder. After all, her story occupies less than a third of the novel. It could have borne any number of more representative names. But only Anna, of all the characters, would like to be the heroine of a novel. It is called after her, Morson argues, because that is what *she* would call it.

Years passed. The scandal died. Arthur moved forward into his own life; Mark and I stayed together. I worked, travelled, wrote. And I carted those old journals around with me through six or seven moves, eventually piling them in a plastic container under our bed.

I'd deliberately kept and stored them. But I didn't like to think of them, with their battered covers, twisted coil bindings, torn pages, fading ink. And I couldn't bear to read them. They were the record of a tumultuous time, and I didn't want to go back there. I didn't want to face the person I might have been.

So when the time came to re-examine this chapter of my life, I took it slowly. I dug the notebooks from under the bed and brought them to my study. Then I let them sit there for a few weeks, gathering dust, while I screwed up my courage. Finally, armed with a bottle of red wine and some dark chocolate, I got to work.

As I had feared, the journals were boring and repetitive. At first, I wrote of my confusion. *What am I feeling? What is going on?* Then, when I'd finally acknowledged it to myself, the entries betrayed a note of terror—*What am I doing?*—and denial—*I'm not doing anything!*

There were horrible passages about the disintegration of my marriage—acutely painful to read even after so many years. Rare moments of insight (*I'm tired of the self I am in that relationship more than I'm tired of him; and of course with a new person I'm still creating the self I am there …*) alternated with blame and self-justification (*Oh, now he wants to listen! … But what about all the times I caught him checking his watch when I was trying to talk?*) and self-recrimination (*I've ruined everything. I've failed at everything*). Mixed in with these were incoherent exclamations of pleasure and joy. And then page after page of what even the most charitable person could only call complaint. It was all, and only, about me.

Armeda, the minister's daughter, hardly ever spoke in class, and when she did she blushed. Usually she took the boys' line, often finding better evidence than they did for their conclusions. With her demure expression, hyperfeminine wardrobe and tendency to fade into the background, she reminded me of Kitty, the ingenue. Or sometimes of the wan, overlooked and overworked Dolly.

Armeda seemed to sense this resemblance herself, but, rather than chafing against it, as I would have done, she embraced it. Dolly, after all, loved her children, and showed a Christian spirit of forgiveness; Kitty, meanwhile, gave Levin the practical ballast he required to pursue his iconoclastic dreams. These, she said, should be a woman's aims.

At sixteen, service to a man or one's children did not strike me as significant goals. I wanted to do something more. I wanted to write; I was learning that then, from my passion for the books we were reading. Of course, I had no idea what this meant. In real life, I'd never met a writer. I knew only what the culture taught me: Writers aren't conventional. Writers are exciting and special. Writers are a bit like Anna.

In the years since, I've come to recognize that "exciting" doesn't always mean "good." Sometimes it just means "self-absorbed." Once, I had dreamed of becoming Anna; now I feared I really had. On the evidence of those journals, I stood convicted.

There's a quiz you can take on the internet: "Which *Anna Karenina* character are you?" Naturally, I had to try it. It presents a series of questions to which you give a yes/no/either answer. Then you rate the answer's importance to you on a sliding scale. The direction of some of these questions seems obvious: "Would you hurt someone you care about to get what you want?" Others are more obscure, the answers applicable to several of the characters: "Is love important?" And some are simply difficult to answer: "Are you often confused?" How often is "often"? The question itself confused me.

Still, I did my best and pressed the button to get my result. It shocked me: Kitty Alexandrovna Shcherbatsky. Anna's protege, Dolly's little sister. *Kitty.* How could this be? It didn't make sense.

Searching my conscience and aiming for scrupulous honesty, I took the test again. The result was the same. There couldn't be any doubt. According to the test, I most resembled the character who "goes from being a naive child who loves carelessly ... to a mature adult with a level head. She grows mentally very much, and is on the road to true wisdom." Next closest to me was Dolly, who is "mainly concerned with her children, and is very caring and nurturing. She is close with family and is very reliable." Then the awkward landowner Levin, "who believes in hard work ... and spends much of his time pondering and on his own." "Sensuous and rebellious" Anna, who thrives on excitement and deceives others, came a distant fourth.

I anticipated a romantic idyll when I ran away with Mark. Reality turned out different. Our relationship took work. We were trying, really trying, to be honest with one another. We were fumbling to express our real feelings. If he did or said something that displeased me, I thought it over, and then spoke with him about it. If our positions were reversed, he did the same. And we didn't assume—as Arthur and I had—that we should always agree. Talking could be awkward. It could be painful. But I felt myself stretching to meet an unexpected challenge.

These changes were reflected in my journals. As the months went on, I wrote about Mark's children and the delicate business of how to relate to them. More and more I seemed conscious of the gravity of my new role. And a year into our relationship—around the time that I reread *Anna Karenina*—I noticed a kind of shift. Instead of dwelling on my regrets and fears and petty annoyances, I began to write about what I saw on the street or overheard in the café. I began to look out as well as in.

This didn't happen by accident. It was deliberate. Every day, I instructed myself to look and describe. Every day, I tried to experiment with form. Gradually, poems began to take shape. Sketches and short stories. Analyses of the books that I'd been reading. I had no one to show these to, no guides or mentors. So I worked in silence and alone. Draft after draft. Beginning after botched beginning.

Perhaps that test was right after all. Perhaps I most resembled Kitty. Her marriage to Levin is a little bit like my relationship to Mark. At age sixteen, I'd barely noticed their story. I skimmed the Levin sections, with their endless detail about farming, eager to get to the juicy stuff about Anna and Vronsky. I should have paid more attention. Kitty and Levin quarrel frequently in their early months together—not because they are fundamentally unsuited but because, as Tolstoy puts it, they don't yet know what matters most to the other. They need to learn that through open conversation. Their painful honesty sparks some conflagrations, but it also pays off; the longer they stay together, the closer they become. Day by day, they grow and mature and begin to feel confident—increasingly themselves and increasingly alive. In this, they are the opposite of Anna and Vronsky, who begin in passionate delight but eventually feel constrained by one another, and whose relationship ends in a misunderstanding so deep that it leads to death.

Rereading my journals, I saw this: when Mark and I started out, I may have acted and felt like Anna. But, as winter melted into spring, I cast off the mantle of her furs.

"Just as you'll never fall in love again the way you did the first time, you'll never read a great novel at 49 in the wholehearted way you would have read it at 20," novelist James Hynes writes in *Salon*, "if only because so much life, and so many books, have happened in the meantime." The same is true for the books of our own lives.

At sixteen, I saw Anna as a martyr to the cause of honesty and self-expression. She refuses to live for duty, refuses to deny her sensuality, refuses to maintain an image of propriety simply for the sake of convenience. Instead, she insists on taking a grand risk for a grand love. What self-respecting teenager wouldn't fall for that?

But, returning to the book as an adult, I noticed something different, or something more: Anna is not as honest as she wants to believe. In order to justify her affair, she must first convince herself that her marriage is a loveless sham. And this takes an effort of will. Her famous observation about her husband's ugly ears seems spontaneous, and perhaps it is. But we also learn that, in the past, "whenever he went to bed five minutes later than usual she noticed it and asked him the reason," and that "every joy, every pleasure and pain that she felt she communicated to him at once." This doesn't sound like a terrible relationship. In fact, it sounds like a pretty good one. But, in light of her new attraction to Vronsky, Anna finds it wanting. So she rereads her past, looking for reasons to dislike the man she once loved. As her story goes on, she expresses her revulsion for Karenin in more and more exaggerated terms. Instead of taking responsibility for inflicting pain, she makes excuses.

When I began my affair, I did much the same thing. I looked for differences. He wants this; I want that; therefore, we don't belong together. "You were miserable in your marriage," one friend told me, trying to assuage my guilt. "You didn't belong together." People want to believe in the power of one true love. People want the simple story.

Unlike Anna, I couldn't buy it—or I couldn't buy it for long. True, Arthur and I had our problems—but I wasn't miserable. True, he wasn't perfect—but he wasn't horrible. I hurt him anyway to get what I wanted. Facing up to this uncomfortable truth about myself was one of the toughest things I've ever done.

In the end, I'm luckier than Anna. Her circumstances really did constrain her. Trapped in a society that refused to recognize women's sexual or emotional needs, she could leave one man for another, but she couldn't conceive of herself as an independent being. She couldn't take responsibility for herself. She couldn't change.

A century later, I enjoyed more freedom and more opportunity. That doesn't mean change was easy—my journals are proof. Still, I've kept them. I won't discard them. The obsession that drove my embarrassing self-analysis is the same obsession that drove those faltering poems and stories. They deserve a spot on my shelves.

"True life begins where the tiny bit begins," Tolstoy writes, in one of his late essays, "where what seems to us minute and infinitely small alterations take place. True life is not lived where great external changes take place—where people move about, clash, fight, and slay one another—it is lived only where these tiny, tiny, infinitesimally small changes occur." Art, he claims, is much the same. It begins in small alterations. Not in the flame of passion or talent, but in painstaking observation and application. In ongoing daily effort.

During that long winter of my affair, I felt humiliated and frightened, like Kitty after Vronsky spurns her; I felt awkward and riddled with self-doubt, like Levin when he makes a social faux pas. Still, I sat on the couch and wrote. At first, the work of change felt beyond me, as impossible as lifting my own weight. But I kept trying. In time, the effort felt almost effortless. In time, the effort felt like love.

# The Good Man

**CHRIS TARRY**

The divorce wrecks you. She gets the car, the condo, the dog. You get a Vancouver basement suite and that waitress you meet a week after your marriage falls apart. The sex is mind-boggling, the waitress does things you've only seen online, the kind of stuff your ex-wife never even considered, and for a hot second, it sustains you. But you know it will never last because she's got a kid, and you didn't sign up for that, not after what you've just been through.

You were eighteen when you met the ex-wife, married her at twenty-five because that's what good men do—they marry their girlfriend with love in their hearts and hope for the best. Now you're thirty-four and feeling like you've been living in a cave. Sure, the cave helped you build a career. Hot damn, you've already won two Juno Awards and when it comes to playing the bass, you've got it, kid. You are seriously the man.

So the next thing you know you're handing the keys to your Jeep over to a friend, packing for an extended trip to New York, and saying goodbye to the waitress and the kid at the airport like it's a scene from a movie, crying and carrying on. And you believe in the crying and carrying on because you honestly feel like you could love this waitress and maybe even the kid when you get back, because some part of you is still a husband, the good man, the guy who married the girlfriend he'd had since high school, and Jesus Christ, if anyone can make it work, you can. *You've got this*, you say to yourself.

You tell the waitress, "I'll only be gone for six months." You tell her, "I have to recharge my batteries." You tell her, "I'll call you every day." Three weeks after you get to New York, she has a foursome with a random girl and two of your best friends. She tells you this over the phone while you're in Times Square shopping for a Spider-Man action figure to send home to the kid. Sure, you broke up with her three days after arriving in New York, but you're a good man, it was the right thing to do, especially since New York has added you to the pantheon of check-out-the-new-hot-shit-bass-player-in-town. But how does someone you've known for less than a year take you down so hard? *Never again*, you say to yourself. You're in New York now, motherfucker! Just look at all the girls. You've got this. Buck up, mister! You will never speak to your two friends again. But you call the waitress every day, sobbing into the phone like a child until she takes you back.

This is how you are now. A real Slick Rick. You're one way with the waitress on the phone and another with the Brooklyn roommate you find on Craigslist that you're already sleeping with. All it takes is the first time she walks in and sees you cooking dinner for two. But you don't know any other way to cook. It's only ever been cooking for two. Your husband skills are mad sharp; all you have to do to look better than 90 percent of the dudes out there is peel garlic and toss a salad. The roommate (who's your age and has been laser-focused on marriage for a good two years) is helpless, especially when it comes to your badass cauliflower soup. "I've never had a guy make me soup before," she tells you.

You want to keep things open, you tell the roommate. You're fresh off a divorce, you're here to concentrate on music and that waitress in Vancouver is still messing with your brain. The roommate listens, nods her amazingly thick head of hair and pulls you into her bedroom for the fifth time that week. She will fall for you, and you will hurt her. This much you know already.

The waitress comes for a visit. You've spent two months trying to convince her, and she finally gets her hot self on a plane. Before you know it you're having makeup sex in your bedroom while the roommate watches *Jeopardy* on the couch. This is the kind of man you've become, someone hollowed out with an ice cream scoop and stuffed with whatever assholes are made of.

The waitress stays for a week. You start to remember how wild she is when you find her coked up in the bathroom of your local Brooklyn watering hole making out with another girl. "You want in on this?" she asks when you open the door. The two of them are pawing each other like they're filming a rock video, coke still on the back of the toilet in finely drawn lines. You step in, but those Brooklyn bathrooms are never big enough for threesomes. Eventually you leave them to it, sit at the bar with a Red Bull and vodka (your new favourite drink). When the bar closes, you continue the party back at your place. The roommate is in her bedroom when you come home. You can see the light on under her door. Have you always been like this and never known it? Giddy-up, you tell yourself, you deserve it.

When the waitress heads back to Canada, she tells you she loves you. You tell her you love her too. You will not see her again for years. When you run into her during a trip to Vancouver, the kid is with her. He looks like he's got an album ready to drop. When she asks him if he remembers you, he shrugs and stares off at God-knows-what. You'll have questions about yourself then too, mostly about how far one can fall and pick oneself up again. That even though you're doing much better, the fear of what you've become will be the same. Are you a good man? Can you love again? The waitress will invite you to dinner, and you will accept. You will meet her at one of Vancouver's hottest restaurants—grain-fed everything with sides of quinoa. While you tear into your designer salad, you will hear the waitress use the word "like" five times in the space of two sentences. You will wonder how you never noticed this before. You *are* changing, you will think to yourself. And after you don't take her back to your hotel when she offers up the goods, you will take this as a positive step. Good for you. You've come a long way, cool guy.

You start to see a few other girls, and the roommate has finally had enough. But what really does it are your mad feelings for this shapely girl you meet at a bar in the East Village. And because your selfishness is on warp-factor-ten you tell the roommate all about this new girl because boy, isn't it nice to have a friend you can confide in? You've only seen this new girl once, you tell the roommate, made out with her on Fourteenth Street while the whole world streamed by. The roommate looks at you like she can't believe you're telling her this. It's the end of the line for you, mister, pack up your shit and get out!

East Village Girl never calls, and the next thing you know you're living in a loft with two twenty-year-old girls in the fashionably young neighbourhood of Williamsburg, Brooklyn. You meet the new roommates on Craigslist, and the shit-box of a room they rent you smells like cat piss. The apartment gets broken into the first week you're there. At night you lie awake and try to forget that you once owned a home.

The old roommate is still in the picture. Your cauliflower soup is hard to kick. She's got a new job, a new car, and Jesus, she looks great, that figure of hers is like something from a TV show. She gives you a hand job in the passenger seat of her new car, and the only thing you can think of is how clean the interior looks. You're doing it again; you're messing with her and you know it. You're a sad sight. You haven't been to bed before 4:00 a.m. in three months. The new roommates know how to party and they think it's funny that your thirty-four-year-old ass likes to try and keep up. You're supposed to be taking a break. You're supposed to be recharging your batteries. You're supposed to be one of the world's top musicians and you haven't picked up your bass in months.

When your six months in New York are up, you take a part-time job bartending at one of Brooklyn's hippest clubs. Something inside tells you that you need to stay in NYC, and you're going to need some serious bank to do that. You think you were drinking before? You think 4:00 a.m. was serious party time, fun guy? Now that you're all cocktail-Tom-Cruise, try 7:00 a.m. for eight months straight. One night, after you finish locking up the bar, you have sex with a customer in the bathroom. "Are you always this crazy?" she asks you when it's over. "I used to be married," you tell her.

The first audition you miss, the one for that once-in-a-lifetime Broadway show, should be a sign. But you chalk it up to disgust for "that kind of music" while lifting a White Russian into the air and cheersing the bartender at your new favourite after-work dive.

You end up dating the girl from the bathroom. You think you have problems? She's drama poured into a pair of skinny jeans. But when it comes to sex, she makes the waitress look like *Romper Room*. Of course you can't commit. Of course you're emotionally unavailable. But even a pair of skinny jeans needs love, and for a minute you try, and it's the trying that makes things worse. It's the trying that leads her on. But it makes you feel less like the person you've become and more like the person you used to be. Trying was what you used to do best.

You make plans to take her to meet your parents, but break up with her two hours before leaving for the airport. When you arrive in Phoenix, your parents are surprised she's not with you. When she calls the house at 4:00 a.m. high on whatever pills she's mixed with her gin, your parents think you're on drugs too and sit you down for a serious talk.

When you get back to New York, Bathroom Girl stages a sit-in outside your apartment. Even your twenty-something roommates look at you like, *What the fuck?* After a yelling match that wakes the whole building, Bathroom Girl leaves, and you spend the next three weeks avoiding her phone calls. You cut her off like an amputation. She leaves messages saying how she wants to marry you. No fucking way, you're not going down that road again. The next time you see her will be in the organic chicken aisle at Whole Foods, and you will pretend not to recognize her. "I'm doing great," she'll say, and then forgive you when you stare at your shoes and timidly apologize for your behaviour. She is a good person. You've known this all along. She will smile, touch your shoulder and tell you about the passing of her mother, the mother you were too chickenshit to meet while you were dating. You will hug Bathroom Girl and say, "If you need a friend, here's my number." She will tell you thanks, give you a long hug back and then be out the door with a bag of organic greens under her arm.

After Bathroom Girl's sit-in, you purchase your own bong and put your dealer on speed dial. Your mother leaves messages on your answering machine that sound like self-help seminars. She's great in a crisis. Are you in crisis? Can you ever get back to the man you were?

You get a call to play with the top wedding band in New York. *This gig is yours*, you tell yourself, because of course, you're hot shit on that bass you haven't touched, and who else would they hire? This band is a-thousand-dollar-a-week busy, cash you could really use, and when they send you the music ahead of time, you think you can manage to get it together to check it out? *I'll sight-read the book*, you tell yourself, and go back to squeezing grapefruits for your own personal greyhound party. When you're onstage a week later, looking all Magnum PI in the tux you borrow from another bartender, the bandleader counts off "I Want You Back" by the Jacksons, and the sixteenth notes on the page run together like paint. When the guitar player who recommended you for the gig looks down at his feet and shakes his head, you try to pull it together, but the gig only gets worse. You used to be able to sight-read fly shit, you tell the bandleader just before he fires you on the first break. He moves the guitarist over to bass and sends you home. You sit on the subway wanting to cry into your hands. You wish you could go home, you wish you could go back to your old life, you wish you could crawl back into your cave and never come out again.

Your twenty-something roommates tell you they're worried about you. How do you like them apples? *They're* worried about *you*! Your parents come to visit, and you're such a mess that they leave early. "This is not the son we know," your mother tells you. When they leave, you sleep for three days, thankful they're gone. You start internet dating, because boy, aren't you a catch! On screen, you've got it together; you're like the internet version of your cauliflower soup. The fact that you still have a good head of hair is a plus. Pretty soon it's six months of dating three girls a week. Look at you, the king of New York. Well done. How about a little sleep? What, you find it hard to be alone? Better get used to it, mister. Nothing can save you now.

And this is where she finds you—run-through, unreachable, former musician. You're like a pile of leaves kicked, scattered and left to rot. You decide that the internet thing might have run its course, but what the hell, how about one more date? What do you have to lose? There's a button on the dating site that says, *Let us match you*. You click it, and the site goes all big-bucks-no-whammies. You don't know it, but the computer is in the process of deciding the rest of your life. When it stops, you look at who pops up on the screen, and Jesus, the girl has a smile so sweet it practically gives you diabetes. You decide right there, this girl, Michelle, will be your final internet date, because with the bartending gig, and the online Mr. Check-me-out, and the way your parents are avoiding your calls, you're starting to think it might be time to spend a night in. It's all about timing, you tell yourself, and your time to shape up needs to start now, buddy boy.

But you nearly forget about the date because you're still too busy not practising and being your bong's best friend. When you do remember, you rush to the café, and tell yourself on the way that you'll have a coffee, and that's it. In and out, mister, this shit is ending and it's ending now. But there's something about this girl. She doesn't make you nervous. She doesn't ask you for anything. And that smile, it's even sweeter in person. When you tell her about your ex-wife, she says, "Tell me more," like she actually means it. She is not jealous. She is confident in a way that inspires you to find that shred of dignity still left inside you. That person you try to talk sense into every night between the evening's tenth beer and the next morning's hair of the dog.

When you take her to meet your parents, you actually manage to get on the plane. What is it about this girl? Have you really changed? Is there still love in you? Don't count your chickens just yet.

She makes nice with your parents so quick it's like a Hallmark card. Your dad pulls you aside and tells you in no uncertain terms that if you don't marry this girl, you're a fucking idiot. Your father has never spoken to you this way, and he never will again. It's like he's been saving these words for a moment in your life when he really needs you to hear him. Michelle has this effect on people. You see it when you're out with friends. You see it in how she excels at her job. You see it in how she starts to expect the same from you. Responsibility, mister. You want your life back? You better be on your best behaviour.

Music starts to burn inside you again. You start practising, slowly and methodically like you used to do, and soon the gigs start trickling in. You say goodbye to the bartending job because Michelle says you don't need it, and you believe her. And guess what? You start writing. Writing! Holy shit, check you out. You wrote when you were a kid, but those were stories about spaceships and little green men. You write more stories about spaceships and little green men, because Michelle says, write what you know.

You feel something, a goodness in you, rising up, and you start to wonder if you could ever get married again. What about your insides dug out with that ice cream scoop? What about the asshole who's been filling in? Is he a part of you now? Who wants to marry that?

You're on tour in Austria and go ring shopping on your day off. You decide to buy something simple, something Michelle would love because she is elegant and direct, and hot damn, you're starting to feel love like nobody's business. But will she say yes? After everything you've done? After the man you've become? But you've still got a long way to go, buckaroo. It's one thing to think you want it, and another to know when it's right. Patience there, hombre, don't push this girl away. Hold on to the ring, hide it in a safe place, you're still not sure you've got this, you're still not sure you won't hurt this girl like all the rest. Besides, you've got some practising to do. Get back in that cave and make yourself comfortable, because years later, when your daughter takes her first kick at a soccer ball in the park, your wife, Michelle, will clap and lift her into the air. The ball will come to rest a short distance away and you will turn to retrieve it. But before you do, you will take stock of this moment, marvel at the man you've become, the musician you've always wanted to be. You will wonder if the asshole is still in you somewhere, and push the thought away as far as you can. Congratulations, you're here, you're having a moment, and hey, moments are wonderful things, are they not? If you don't manage to fuck this up, the happiness might actually last. "I've got this," you say to your family, and turn to retrieve the ball.

# My Last Erotic Poem

## LORNA CROZIER

Who wants to hear about
two old farts getting it on
in the back seat of a Buick,
in the garden shed among vermiculite,
in the kitchen where we should be drinking
Ovaltine and saying no? Who wants to hear
about twenty-six years of screwing,
our once-not-unattractive flesh
now loose as unbaked pizza dough
hanging between two hands before it's tossed?

Who wants to hear about two old lovers
slapping together like water hitting mud,
hair where there shouldn't be
and little where there should,
my bunioned foot sliding
up your bony calf, your calloused hands
sinking in the quickslide of my belly,
our faithless bums crepey, collapsed?

We have to wear our glasses to see down there!

When you whisper what you want I can't hear,
but do it anyway, and somehow get it right. Face it,
some nights we'd rather eat a Häagen-Dazs ice cream bar
or watch a movie starring Nick Nolte who looks worse than us.
Some nights we'd rather stroke the cats.

Who wants to know when we get it going
we're revved up, like the first time—honest—
like the first time, if only we could remember it,
our old bodies doing what you know
bodies do, worn and beautiful and shameless.

# Struggles

# The Time of Useful Truths

**ROB TAYLOR**

Ten years ago you fell for me because I told the truth.
Today truths trip me up at every turn, the only one
that matters long ago laid out and analyzed—
the tenor of its words, how *love* and *very*
vibrate in the caverns of our mouths and lungs
and ricochet through the resonant depths.

And yet here we're obsessed with tinny questions:
Do these jeans fit? Was that steak overcooked?
When the vacation, first house, first child?
What sex? What name? What if? And if? And later still?
And would you? How could you? Lie.

We lie. Beside each other, on the bed,
another shouting match flared out and tossed aside,
we sense the time of useful truths has passed us by,
left us but this one that comes in our shared silence—
at first it is the subtlest sound, then grows—
a decade's echo filling us with answers.

# Cooking Class & Marriage Lessons

## JANE SILCOTT

A friend invites you to a cooking class. You agree because she's a good friend, a dear friend, but truly, you'd rather do long division in your head. You'd rather do push-ups or side planks or both. You'd rather lie on train tracks and die romantically, a train filled with oversized industrial stoves and sautéed duck breasts rolling over you, then serving you up, still warm with morel sauce on the side.

Your husband makes you sit in the front row. Your husband becomes the guy in the class who makes jokes out loud, so the chef starts using his name and you realize you've married the class clown. How can you have been married so long and not known that? As the chef lays his equipment out in front of him and begins to talk, the two of you look at one another, "She should be here." *She* is your daughter. *She*, who watches cooking shows to relax, who gets in the kitchen and immediately becomes a young woman full of certainty, a young woman who can command you to sit down and stay out of her way, and you always do, feeling proud and surprised and yes, a little hurt, all at once.

You watch the chef with his whites on, his large frame, belly firm but round, filled with excellently cooked and loved foods, and hands—deft, accomplished, certain—moving above the counter, reflected in the angled mirrors above, so you get a bird's-eye view. You will tell this to your daughter later, all agog. "Mirrors!" you will say, "like on TV!" She will look at you, in that tired way that your worldly, near-grown children have. "Mum, we have those at school." How could mirrors be in your child's east-side school when the music programs were cut? You will think of your own cooking classes at school, long ago in another city, another neighbourhood, the class taught by a woman who seemed more impressed by the laundry equipment than the stoves. A woman who would bring her dirty clothes to school and wash while she taught. The only thing you learned in her classes was to clean up as you cooked.

When the chef talks about his wet hand and his dry hand—the hand that handled the meat and the hand that didn't—you steal a look at your husband to see if he is paying attention. He is, and when the chef does something remarkable and memorable, one of those little tricks you can take home and teach to your daughter, you look at one another again and know you are both aching in the same way.

Meanwhile, the chef goes on. You wonder when it can be over and when you can have your wine back. The chef has made everyone put their glasses on the island, an island half the size of your house and almost as far away. He said it was because he didn't want anyone to knock a glass over accidentally but you think he doesn't want twenty inebriated adults playing with knives and fire.

After you sit through the lesson about duck with morel sauce and blinis, a lesson that's flown through your head so quickly it might have been quantum physics or gene splicing, you and the woman next to you confess to one another that you hate cooking. You decide this woman might be your new best friend and then wonder if it was destiny or survival that inspired you to marry a man who can turn on the giant fire-breathing stove without pause and pour half of Italy's supply of olive oil in a pan, then watch as it spreads, looking the happiest he's been all day.

"That's too much oil," you tell him. "The duck is going to swim again."

"It's olive oil," he says. "It's good."

You turn away after telling him his love of oil is what's made you fat, and he lies one of his marriage-saving lies, and you mix milk into the bowl for the blinis, which you've learned are just potato pancakes with an exotic name.

A moment later, he holds one of the ingredient containers filled with brown liquid above the pan. "Are we supposed to put all this in?"

"Yes," you say, annoyed because hadn't the chef said everything was premeasured?

"It seems like an awful lot," he adds.

"Just put it in," you bark, wondering if the edge in your voice comes from the military ancestors lining up in the back of your head, or your mother who was always good with commands.

A second later you both look at the tray and recognize a third container with white, creamy liquid that you were supposed to have used. And so what had you put in with the duck? The water from the morels. Water that had been used to reconstitute the mushrooms that are notoriously difficult to clean.

"Never mind," you say, "it's just a bit of dirt. The liquid will boil off."

Your husband is silent. Stone silent. The kind of silence you have learned to recognize after many years of marriage that it's best to leave him alone in. You turn back to your duck.

The chef arrives at your station when you are slicing the meat. You think you're doing fine, but he says, "How 'bout I do that for you?" and takes the knife from your hand. You suppress a small but familiar feeling of dismay—you've lived a life of people taking food preparation tasks away from you—and watch as perfect medallions of meat fall from the knife. "Voila," he says.

And "Voila," you and your husband repeat as you walk to the dining area. You're smiling now, thinking (again) how clever you were to marry a man who loves you anyway. Then the two of you savour your meal, chewing the wood chips with your morels as if they were there on purpose.

# White Night

## MAUREEN SCOTT HARRIS

---

A white night in the spare room
wind tossing the house, roiling
the cedars. Shadows riot
across the white blind. You're
in the dark, on the other side
of the wall, snoring. Is this
what marriage comes to?
Sleepless, I consider the yin
and the yang, their apparently
endless flow, their yearning
exchange. But if they fall still?
Stagnation is another form
of transformation. Form  fall
I decant the alphabet: fault  fear
female  frenzy  fester  failure
oh fie and fly! I fear my brain
is failing. I'm tired of the foolish
romp of words. The one I'm after
is always absinthe. *Absent*  advent
ancient  antsy  aimless  anguish—
My soul grows mute, slips into
the slough where even snoring
is stopped. Suffer the night
thoughts to gather their small
nipping selves and crawl under
my quilt. November's sad and
dreary ache, the turn to winter.
New moon no moon, shadow
play in the street light's spot light.
The ghosts of this year's dead
parade across the blind. I doze
and wake doze and wake, mark
the red-eyed clock's slender leaps

towards morning. Leaps  leans
leaves  learns  lurks  longs
loves— The lotus is said to prefer
stagnant water. Rooted in murk
it raises its astounding leaves like
wings above the pond's surface,
flowers rising on thick stems to
unfurl and catch the light. You're
snoring again. Are you my anchor
or tether? Tether  tender  taut
tight  tame  time— This night
may never end. The steady repeat
and return of your breath sounding
between a wheeze and a groan
strike the exact tones of my old
arguments with myself: to go out
or stay in? to speak or be silent?
Restive, resentful, woeful, weary,
I recite while the night grows pale.

# This Is a Love Story

## MICHELLE KAESER

---

1.

"A story has no beginning or end: arbitrarily one chooses that moment of experience from which to look back or from which to look ahead." So begins Graham Greene's classic novel, *The End of the Affair*, a sort of interfaith love story between a believer and a non-believer. It ends, inasmuch as stories ever end, in heartache and hate. But stories are mutable, they can change entirely when we shift our perspectives, even just a few degrees.

My current story, another love story, is also scarred by different understandings of faith. By the clash of ideas that rips through love like lightning. But since this is a love story and since we arbitrarily choose a moment from which to view any story, we might as well jump right into this one mid-love:

Into the middle of things then, into the heat and sweat of bodies intertwined. The action of the moment is familiar enough, though the setting for it might come as a surprise. We're here in a church, a small sleepy church tucked away in the woods, on a sofa that has been moved into the nave. Positioned on my back and peeking over my lover's rocking shoulder, I have an unobstructed view of the cross above the altar. It's a simple wooden cross and it hangs noticeably off-centre, a peculiarity of interior design which none of this church's parishioners seem able to explain.

It's a strange business, this having sex in a church. Strange for me because I'm not religious. I'm anti-religious. I hate the whole idea of religion. There's a distinct weirdness about drawing forth a climax inside a building and beneath iconography that typically draw forth only an eye roll, maybe an exasperated shrug. But perhaps it's stranger still for my partner in this love story, who is religious, devotedly so, who attends Mass regularly, who organizes weekly outreach activities, who is a parishioner in high standing at this church, which is why he has keys to the church and why we ended up here on the sofa one evening, no one else around, in holy congress, taking turns orgasming beneath the cross that hangs noticeably askew.

## 2.

But no, no, no, this is not the best place to start the story after all. It's too pleasurable, too blissful; it augurs the wrong thing entirely. Interfaith romances don't tend toward the blissful. Smart people know to avoid them. They understand the frustrations and resentments that arise when you and your lover cannot agree on the fundamentals of the human condition, the both dull and sharp pain that comes from constantly smashing your head against the wall of your lover's perception of the universe.

The grand affair at the centre of Graham Greene's novel doesn't start out as an interfaith concern. When Greene's lovers take up with one another, they are a pair of non-believers. And so they are, in some measure, compatible. It's only after one of them has "caught belief like a disease" that things between them fall spectacularly apart. Of course they do. Faith, unless it's shared, is toxic.

So let's restart our love story at a different moment, at the introduction of the toxin. Let's start like this instead:

I've moved into a new apartment in a new city. My next-door neighbour is a handsome man in a dishevelled sort of way, with overgrown hair and a small collection of old T-shirts that show their wear. He has a broad face and perfect eyebrows. On my first day in this new city, this new neighbour invites me over for dinner. He's new here too, it turns out, and our nerves about being alone in a new city are easily pacified with a home-cooked meal and one, then another, round of very pleasant sex.

These two rounds are followed a few days later by another two rounds. And again a few days after that. And on and on until a few weeks pass and we have ourselves a beautiful budding romance.

It comes as a surprise, the revelation of his Christianity. One of those loopy surprises that bounce their way into a romance, as you begin to uncover the dissonance between the imagined version of the new mate—the illusory mate—and the mate as he actually is.

It happens during a discussion about dinner plans. He declines an invitation; he already has other plans, he says.

"Ah, okay," I say. But then I add, casually, "Where are you going?" I'm curious about him, about what he does, about who he is. There's a natural instinct in these early weeks to dig and prod and pry—at least a little. Decorous prying.

"Oh, well … uh …"

"You don't want to say?"

"It's just … promise you won't make fun of me."

"Of course I won't," I say, alarmed.

"It's just a dinner with a … uh … a church group. It's no big deal."

And so the toxin slips in. We've been punctured.

A thousand questions pop up all at once. I want to ask: What kind of church group? What kind of church? Catholic? Unitarian? Something more fringe—born again, Mormon, jw? Do you believe in Sin? In Heaven and Hell? Do you believe in angels? In saints? In miracles? In demons? In exorcisms? In damnation? Am I damned? For what do you pray? For whom? How often? Define your faith. Explain yourself.

"Oh," I say. "Okay."


# 3.

I'm as consumed by the search for meaning in life as anyone. I think about it always, when depressed, when delighted, when nervous, but I've never been able to get a firm handle on any meaning or purpose or point. Humanity's greatest minds have been wrestling with the problem since forever, and although they have conjured up whole, beautifully articulated philosophies, the fundamental question persists.

With religion, of course, the answer comes easily. Without, it's more problematic. Camus describes the leap of faith as "philosophical suicide." It's intellectually disappointing. Which makes this whole romance disappointing. Or it would be disappointing if I thought the romance would last. But there must be a shelf life to casual flings like this one. So I bury the problem of religion beneath the certainty that the affair will come to its own graceful end soon enough.


# 4.

But the weeks turn into months and the simple lust turns into a more complicated infatuation. The problem of religion is there every Saturday night when he won't sleep over because it might affect his attendance at Sunday morning Mass. It's there every Sunday evening when he cuts short our afternoon dates to ensure his prompt arrival at church group. It's there whenever I reproach him, or when anyone does, it's in the bowed head, the shame that I'm beginning to recognize is ubiquitous and awfully close to self-loathing.

Turns out he's Anglican. My first (hopeful) thought is that this is strictly cultural, a hereditary hangover. But when I trace his upbringing, there's not much religious activity there—he's not even sure he was baptized. So this is a conscious, reasoned, adult decision. Which is more complicated.

"So you believe in God? The literal Christian God?" I ask in bed one night. "You just accept He exists?"

"I believe in some notion of divinity, yes."

This is how he answers everything. Never quite direct. Always qualified. So it's hard to get a read on the nuances of his faith.

"Why, what do you believe?" he asks, shifting the focus off himself, another evasive manoeuvre.

"Nothing really."

"So what do you think is the point of things?"

"There is no point, I guess," I say. It's an unhappy confession and one he wordlessly alludes to whenever I, in various states of existential contemplation, announce some version of: "I'm sad." It's then that he looks at me with the particular pity the religious reserve for those who just haven't found the right path.

And yet he's private about his faith, reluctant to direct me toward this path. But now I've turned my attention to it, I want to know everything. I pester him for months, until finally, and irritably, he says, "Look, if you're so curious, why don't you just come to Mass one week."

"I'm not curious *about* Mass. I'm curious about why *you* go."

"You sure about that?"

A ridiculous question. Of course I'm sure. All of my curiosities at this point centre on him. Because I'm starting to realize that our little tale of neighbourly comforts is transforming into a story of proper love.

## 5.

How easy it is to coerce the events of our lives into a story. It happens without thought, an instinct. As things between us deepen, I massage every shared moment into a narrative, more robust, more suited to our intensifying situation. What might have been an offhand remark, a forgotten conversation, an unimportant fuck, a meaningless glance, now gathers weight as each becomes a plot point in a grander story, a love story.

## 6.

Perhaps this is yet a better place to start the story. Because here, at Sunday Mass, we've arrived at what must be an almost universal experience: doing something you don't want to because you are infatuated. It's a hallmark of fresh love.

Throughout the service, I study my neighbour (now boyfriend?) in his various acts of worship. He sings during the hymns—quietly, as though he's embarrassed, which embarrasses me too. His enunciation shifts slightly when he's reciting from the holy books. It turns performative when he recites the Apostles' Creed—the broad-strokes outline of the whole magical story of Jesus. In sharp clear notes, he affirms his belief in the more preposterous, also, I suppose, most fundamental, points of Christian faith.

"You really believe those things?" I ask (demand) after the service. "You believe in the virgin birth. You believe in the resurrection. Literally?"

"Nobody believes these things literally," he says, which is news to me, and possibly to a substantial faction of the Anglican order. "The creed itself isn't important. It's the story of Jesus that's instructive. That's what I like. But it's just a story."

## 7.

Stories all have the same shape. The story of Jesus is shaped just like a thousand stories that came before it and have come since. Legends, myths, fairy tales, histories, love stories, they all bend into the classic narrative shape as they work the random events of life into a meaningful arc. Stories offer a solution to the chaos that defines the world. But stories are illusions.

## 8.

Time passes—months and years—and now we have fallen terrifically in love. We spend nights burrowing into each other, working out new configurations of limbs and torsos as we sleep, finding new ways to hold each other. We stay in bed late into the mornings, murmuring loving nonsense to each other, and when we finally rise we're surprised to realize that hours have passed. We test out terms of endearment, dozens of them, maybe hundreds, because no name, no single word seems able to contain the totality of all this affection.

At a neighbourhood bar, over sips of Jameson, our fingers mingle on the tabletop and we tilt our heads toward each other because each inch of distance between us seems like too much. We exist in our own world, from which we peek out at everyone else. Beside us is another couple, their manner less relaxed than our own; they force out stiff laughter and shift around on their chairs. It looks like a first date, probably an internet date.

"You think you could ever do that?" I ask. "Online date? If we weren't together?" It's amusing to conjure up the image of him, of either of us, on a string of first dates. Neither of us particularly likes meeting people. We're not good at small talk, or polite nods, or making friendly noises.

"But we are together," he says.

I imagine for a moment that we aren't. It's too painful to imagine us breaking up, so I imagine instead that one of us is dead. "But suppose something happened to me. If I died, say."

I think of both of our deaths often. Mine, because it's been a preoccupation since childhood. His, because it would be so unbearable that there's a thrill in emerging from these reflections and knowing he's here and alive and with me. He enjoys discussions of death far less. He thinks they're morbid.

"Oh baby," he says, "if something happened to you, I'd probably just join the monastery." He says this with a grin, like maybe he's just teasing. A compliment wrapped in a joke? A loving remark about my irreplaceability.

"But seriously."

"I am serious. This is it for me," he says and squeezes my knuckles between his own. A foggy delight spreads through my head. I'm so easily flattered by him. So eager to believe I'm the object of his love. We lean in a further inch and sip from our glasses of Jameson, the whiskey making us feel warm and close.

"Okay, but come on," I say. "Let's say I get hit by a truck on the walk home."

"Yeah, I'm telling you, I think it would mean the monastery for me."

It's an easy joke to play into. He already lives a life of relative austerity. He's still in the same worn T-shirts he was wearing years ago. His electronics are all ancient hand-me-downs. He buys food and drink, but he doesn't buy *things*. A few weeks earlier, I suggested he get a haircut, pointing out that it had been over two years, and he replied with that same mocking grin: "Long hair was good enough for the prophet."

I decide to play along for a moment. "Oh yeah, what monastery? Where will you go?"

"There's a little place about an hour from here, actually. Just outside the city. I've looked it up a few times. They farm their own food. Looks pretty nice."

I am less flattered.

I feel less like the object of his great love and more like an obstacle to a much greater love. I'm standing in the way of divine plans; I'm some kind of temptress, a siren keeping him from his duties and destiny. I wonder, for the first time, as we sit here with our foreheads hovering inches from each other, if he resents me, resents having fallen in love with me.

I take a big gulp of my whiskey to quell the tears burning up the backs of my eyes. The whiskey makes me cold and numb.

# 9.

The church looms, casting a longer shadow every year. After three years, he becomes a chaplain at a university. He assumes the leadership of a homeless ministry. He attends the synod as the lay representative of his parish. He observes the Lenten fast, giving up meat first, then alcohol as well. How long, I wonder, before he sacrifices sex in this effort to feel closer to his imagined God?

It's all leading in the same direction with him, but still somehow it feels like a sucker punch from behind when, five years into our love story, he floats the priesthood as a viable option.

He says it in passing at first, so I ignore it. And I ignore it again and again over the next few months whenever he drops a word about it. But one day I find a prospectus for a seminary among the papers on his desk, and a few weeks later, he announces that he'll be attending an information session at the school.

"Just to see," he says. "To get a better idea."

"Mm-hmm."

"What? You don't want me to go?" he asks.

"Of course not."

"What's the big deal? It's not like it's a celibate priesthood."

He aims at levity because he doesn't want to fight. I don't either, but what else is there to do? In real time I'm watching him move further and further away from me. How is it possible to be a supportive mate to someone whose entire life and livelihood orbit around an institution you disdain?

The seminary visit (blessedly?) doesn't go very well—the curriculum too ecumenical for his tastes. "A lot of postmodern academic bullshit," he says. And some conversations with local priests drill home the reality that job prospects in the Anglican priesthood are grim these days. These obstacles slow his movement down this career path, but it's not over. It's always in my mind now: will he leave me for the priesthood? Will he choose God over me?

I don't know how else to view this but as competition.

## 10.

"Do you love me?" I ask after sex one night, in soft light, our bodies humming with the lingering notes of our efforts. It was tender tonight, a slow crescendo, a gentle coaxing forth of pleasure. His hands held my face throughout, held me so close it seemed as though the only air I drew in came straight from his strained exhalations.

"More than anything," he says, his eyes resting closed.

"More than God?"

He cracks an eye open and smiles; he thinks I'm being playful. "More than anything corporeal."

Jealousy is always a sinkhole. But there's something especially excruciating about being jealous of something that doesn't exist. You're fighting a mist. Like Caligula waging war on Neptune, sending his army into the sea, a legion of ferocious soldiers all stabbing stupidly at the water. It's ridiculous to be jealous of phantoms. It almost makes you want to believe, just so there's an actual object for your jealousy. And your anger. And your hatred. The hero of Graham Greene's novel, a staunch non-believer, rants at the God that parted him from his lover: "I hate You, God, I hate You as though You existed."

## 11.

All stories demand a reversal of fortunes. There's always a fall. Or a rise. Our great heroes forever journey from either a high point to a low point, or a low point to a high point. From exultant love to crushing loneliness—or vice versa. This is how stories work. This simple movement across fortunes forms their familiar shape.

## 12.

Nobody is at their best when they're jealous. I am at my worst. I go on the attack. I make snide remarks about Jesus and religion and its adherents. Every day I challenge him about his faith and demand he untangle theological knots that have been worked at for centuries.

"Look," he finally says to me, his tone almost mean. "You believe in progress, don't you? In the idea of progress?"

"I don't know, I guess. In theory."

"As a race, we've progressed, haven't we? Morally? We're not watching gladiatorial bouts anymore. We denounce slavery. And torture. More or less. More than we used to."

"So what?"

"So we're progressing. And if we're progressing, then we must be progressing toward something. Some notion of morality and goodness, right?"

"And that's God?"

"That's what I believe."

"I don't know if I do believe in progress," I say. "Aren't we all just as shitty as ever."

"You don't really think that. Even you can't be that bleak."


## 13.

This is not our only fight. We begin to fight a lot. About everything. The more fervent his belief in order and meaning, the more mine falls apart. For every step he takes in one direction, I take a step in the other, desperate to drag him back. This period coincides with a fresh bout of existential torment for me—another stretch of anguish over the lack of purpose in life. I succumb to a vague spiralling depression, which my boyfriend attributes to grave ideological errors, and which I attribute to intellectual honesty, and which a psychiatrist attributes to a chemical imbalance.

"What's the point of anything?" I wail. "Does anything matter? Why bother? The world is shit."

He's lost compassion for this avenue of thought. "These are the problems of teenagers," he says to me. "This is the psychology of a teenager."

Maybe. Maybe it really is more sophisticated to believe in leaps of magic.


## 14.

Everything is tinged by God. Does my boyfriend look so peaceful when he sleeps because he has God? Does he take long walks because he wants time to contemplate God? When one afternoon we try to break up but can't figure out how to do it and have sex instead, does he look at me then, as he's ramming into me, with such horrified guilt, because he fears he's failed God?

# 15.

Our love story has reached a familiar point in its arc, the crucial part of any story: the ignoble crash into heartbreak and misery. We're headed for the rock-bottom, all-is-lost, dark-night-of-the-soul, *Why-hast-thou-forsaken-me-Lord?* moment. This narrative shape is so familiar that if you chart the arcs of thousands of stories, you'll find it over and over again with very little variation. Some researchers did exactly this: Andrew Reagan from the University of Vermont and his team analyzed over a thousand stories—they input story data into a computer and had the computer generate narrative patterns. They found that the overwhelming majority of stories conform to one of six well-known emotional arcs. The six patterns are graphed according to the happiness level of the protagonist:

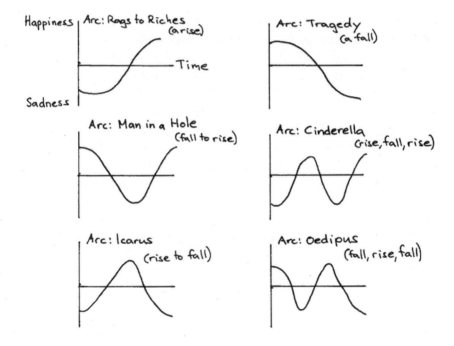

In each arc, we can see the reversal of fortune that defines any story—the moment when the curve crosses the x-axis. Sometimes there's one reversal, sometimes two or even three. The researchers draw distinctions along these lines, the number and direction of the reversals, but to me these distinctions are trivial. There's no difference in the fundamental shapes at play here. There's always a simple curve, bobbing up and down, forever oscillating between good fortune and bad, happiness and despair. It's only our perspective that creates the illusion of differences—our arbitrary selection of the start and end points. A more simplified graph of all possible emotional arcs, over all of time, might just look like this:

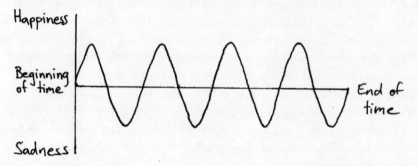

Pick any point on the curve to start your story! Pick a point to end it! You have now picked out one of the six classic tropes. With the story of Jesus we start somewhere below average on the happiness axis (born into poverty, under threat of state-sanctioned infanticide, etc.); then we rise and crest (with a triumphal entry into Jerusalem). But then down we go again, all the way to gruesome death. The big finale, another rise (Christ has risen!) carries us straight to the top. Classic Cinderella trope. Fortunately for Jesus, his curve ends on the upswing—his story kicks out when he's right at the top.

When we want a happy ending, we exit the story at the top of the curve. When we want a tragedy, we hang on till we hit the bottom. We impose these beginnings and ends to stories: "one chooses that moment of experience from which to look ahead or from which to look back," as Greene writes. But the archetypal shape of a story, that soothing shape that we seem to understand intuitively, it bounces on and on, like a sine wave through eternity.

## 16.

For now, though, in this current story, we're down in the trough of the curve. We have crashed hard and headfirst into the very bottom: the breakup. Of course there's a breakup. How else could things go? The toxin weakens the relationships at the joints until it collapses. We have fallen apart over religious differences.

But it's not me who finally decides these differences are overwhelming. He's the one who leaves. The faithful dispense with the faithless. Isn't that how it goes? It's certainly how things shake out in Greene's novel—the faithless hero abandoned.

My boyfriend lists dozens of reasons to end it. Each I dismiss, for each I have a counter-argument. I'm so confident in the merits of my position, bolstered as it is by love, that at first I'm not even worried. It takes maybe an hour for me to notice his resolve; the moment I do I veer sharply toward the hysterical. I argue, bargain, cajole and guilt him, I do all the things people do when their hearts are splintering. I beg. I am literally on my knees, at his feet, clinging to his calves, pressing my weeping face into the side of his calf (these beloved calves! their strength and breadth! their short curls of hair!) and begging him not to leave. This is a profoundly humiliating experience. It's a clinic in humility. I am quickly made an expert in this virtue.

"I have to go," he keeps saying in a hundred different ways. But I keep holding on. I mash myself against him, into him, hoping to dissolve into him, so that I'll never again be susceptible to this threat.

It takes a very long time (hours maybe?), but at last he extricates himself from my hold. He's got his boots on, now his jacket, now he's out the door. What else is there to do but chase him down the street?

Out then into the cold night, a November night, bitter and rainy—a scene straight out of a story. When I catch up to him, his face is hard. But he's crying.

"What? What is it?" he screams at me.

"Just please. Please don't go."

He tilts his head back and groans at the sky. "I can't watch you live your life the way you do, don't you get that?"

"But you love me," I say. It seems like the simplest, stupidest platitude in the world, but I'm so intensely sure of its truth that it seems almost transcendent.

"Of course I do." His eyebrows, still perfect, are pitched up in distress. "But—"

"But what?"

"Your nihilism. This miserable emptiness all the time. It hurts my heart. It's too hard to watch."

Even as he says it, I think it's a silly thing to say. What emptiness? What part of me isn't filled to the brim with feeling? What tiny alcove isn't at this very moment overflowing with thick, burning, molten sadness?

At home I lie crumpled against the kitchen cupboards, writhing against the pain of this grief until I'm exhausted but still not empty of it.

## 17.

In *The Hitchhiker's Guide to the Galaxy*, Douglas Adams imagines the grim results of a confrontation with infinity. His Total Perspective Vortex is a machine that provides the user with an accurate sense of the infinite universe: "When you are put into the Vortex you are given just one momentary glimpse of the entire unimaginable infinity of creation, and somewhere in it there's a tiny little speck, a microscopic dot on a microscopic dot, which says, 'You are here.'" This device is a torture tool. It crushes the soul instantly.

Our minds are frail and finite; they aren't built to handle perfect understandings of infinity, or God, or nothingness, or meaninglessness. These ideas, in their fullness, are deadly. A real nihilist, with the courage of his convictions, wouldn't bother with the stuff of life, with feeding himself and sheltering himself and otherwise promoting his own survival. He'd sit quietly right where he was until he died. But even this is almost too academic a thought experiment. Because a true nihilist, one who could, for just a moment, behold the infinite meaninglessness of his existence, would immediately lose his mind.

I am not a nihilist. Nobody is. We all find or invent meaning somewhere. Nobody overrides that need and lives to tell the tale.

## 18.

In the mornings, I wake up with tears already spilling from my eyes. I wonder if I've been crying through the nights, through my sleep. I cry all the time. There are no moments of reprieve, no fractions of seconds even in the no man's land between sleep and awake when I am able to forget that he's left me. And now every story of a silly heartbroken woman carelessly casting her life away makes perfect sense to me. Poor Anna Karenina, splattered out on the train track; or Dido, embracing the hot relief of that funeral pyre; or Medea with her demented revenge; or deranged Miss Havisham in her wedding dress, living in the squalor of her own decay. All very reasonable figures suddenly.

This sadness is just too big to handle. I don't know what to do with it, how to hold it, but I can see that without some method of containment, the sadness will destroy me. So I do what people always do. I put it where we contain all of our sufferings: into a story.

The great magic of a story is in how it connects one episode to another, one event to another, linking lives and experiences. The cumulative mass of all these connections makes the story seem important. On its own, tethered to nothing, heartache is just distilled pain. But woven through the tapestry of a love story, that pain turns into a necessary part of the whole. It's a requirement of growth and progress and redemption. It's part of the life story, which is part of the greater human story, which is everything.

Does this sound almost religious? Maybe. Maybe thinking in terms of stories is fundamentally religious. But we're all hard-wired to think this way— or we've evolved to think this way, as we evolve any survival mechanism. Stories protect us from the threat of meaninglessness; they keep us from killing ourselves in fits of despair.

I follow stories everywhere; I conjure them up all the time. In heartbreak, I cling to whatever story allows me to believe there's some value to enduring hardship, some growth to realize on the other side. In this way, I suppose I'm saved by stories. As my boyfriend—*ex*-boyfriend (oof, how that little *ex* smarts)—is saved by his Christianity. Adhering to story isn't so different from adhering to religion. Both are illusions designed to preserve the spirit. The only difference is that in one the illusion is prefabricated. In the other, the illusion is yours to design and create.

In this sense then, I guess I'm religious after all. Maybe it's incompatible with human existence not to be at least a little bit religious.

## 19.

So here's yet one last way to start this story. Let's start further back this time, much further back on the curve. Let's start years and years ago.

He and I first meet as kids, way back when. The twists of life throw us together in a high school English class and straight away he's my favourite. A few weeks into the school year, on my birthday, he presents me with a treasured gift: a bottle of Jameson whiskey, half-empty and stolen from his father's liquor cabinet. I have my first high school crush.

As the high school years progress, I see him only occasionally, passing by in the halls flanked by friends, or later a girlfriend, and I assume I've dropped off his radar.

After graduation, our paths pull us to different universities in different cities. But every now and then these paths intersect. One afternoon I bump into him on the street of my small university town. There's an instant flutter of excitement at the sight of him, then a thud of disappointment when I learn he's visiting a girlfriend.

A few years later I attend a show at an IMAX theatre, where I discover he now works. I haven't thought of him since I last saw him on the street, but when he looks up from his book to take my ticket, my belly twists into an exclamation mark. He barely looks at me. I watch the movie, return home and spend the next week plotting a return to the theatre, which for one failure of courage or another, I never see through.

More years pass and I move out of province. The decision to relocate (clear across the country to a city where I know nobody) comes with little thought, almost as a whim. It's so simple a decision, it's like I'm not really making it myself, but rather like I'm being tugged along, pulled by gentle but insistent currents.

On my first evening in this new city, walking through my new neighbourhood, ready for all things new, for new adventures with new people, I turn a corner and there he is. He takes a step toward me, his smile warm and familiar. "Oh hey there," he says and his perfect eyebrows lift up with mild surprise.

Once we discover we're neighbours, he quickly invites me to dinner. And so it happens that exactly ten years after we first meet, after the first adolescent stirrings of love, he is lying in my bed, tracing a thumb up and down my spine, kissing my shoulders and saying, "It's so strange how things work out. I was always really sweet on you in high school."

How, when I remember it like that, can this affair seem anything less than fated?

## 20.

Every good love story has a third act. After desperate, broken-hearted months of separation and silence, text messages resume. Then emails, phone calls, tentative meetings and finally: reconciliation.

Oh what bliss! What indescribable happiness! What unexpected redemption of the love I thought was lost! Here it is again! Right here, all around us, filling us, subsuming us. It feels like salvation. The split now makes more sense than ever, because it's brought us here, to this new incarnation of us. We rebuild the relationship on the hard scars of our mistakes, and it's all the steadier for it. How silly it was to doubt our eventual reunion—the story always carries us to its destined end. And doesn't this seem like the right place to end it? Right on the upswing of the curve?

We move in together. We make promises to each other. We even discuss getting married—though we quickly abandon the idea (and never talk about it again) once we crash into an immediate problem. He refuses to treat marriage as anything but a sacrament; I refuse to kneel before a priest. It's an impasse.

I am learning to adopt a broader understanding of religion (so broad it encompasses the practices of virtually all of humanity), but there remain some traditions and rituals I can't stretch my mind to reach. The same religious differences that disrupted us before persist, but since we've made firm commitments to each other, we find ways to ignore these problems. We invent illusions to hold the relationship together. He tells himself my relentless interest in his religion means I'm seeking God in my own way. I tell myself that with enough persistence and logical reasoning, I will one day shake him of his Christianity. It's imperfect—on some level, of course, we both know we're lying to ourselves. But everyone lies to themselves. Because the lies that uplift us and give us hope and affirm our lives and allow us to love are better than the truths that condemn us to despair. That's faith.

## 21.

"Hey, hey, it's Jesus!" A stranger stops us on the street to announce this revelation. He's looking straight at my boyfriend, pointing at his chest. "Hey, it's Jesus!" he says.

Maybe it's my boyfriend's long hair and beard. Or the tattered bits of cloth that serve as his clothes. I don't know what about him triggers in this stranger the image of Jesus, but something does.

"Are you Jesus, man?" the guy asks, stepping right up to us. From this close, it's clear this guy is a little unhinged. His smile stretches far too wide; there's an obvious craziness in the eyes. Still, it's interesting, how just a slight derangement of the mind can cause someone to look at my old friend and see God. I don't see that. When I look at him I see a story, a love story.

I suppose in the end those are near enough the same thing.

# Sentry

## JULIANE OKOT BITEK

---

Let's not sit with young lovers
with their hands locked    intertwining fingers
she asleep
lipsticked mouth hanging open
her head on his chest
her fingernail polished black, varnish cracked
& he with his heavy eyelids—sleep or love   I don't know
his other hand on her thigh
his hair fallen over the side of his face
mud on the cuff of his jeans
& his shoes
& a slit in her skirt
& all of us on the bus to protect young love
whatever   whatever    whatever it will take

Let's not sit with sleeping lovers
we who have been
married & married
divorced & divorced
we remember that
we're sentry, we're sentry, we're sentry
we're watching for edges that will start to turn
we're watching for pages that will start to burn
we're keening for salt that will dry out the heart
we're sentry for young love
we're thirsty for young love
we're sentry so we watch & watch
& watch young lovers in love & sleep
& it's all we can drink

We watch & we drink them
we who have been
married & married
divorced & divorced
we who remember
but cannot sit with them

They're vulnerable   weak   stupid
falling asleep on the bus
with interlinked fingers & pinked lips
her mouth agape   his hair falling across his face
beautiful   lovely   shimmery
unaware of the ways that the peeling paint
will reveal a crack in the wall

Let's watch the young lovers
with the dew from their kisses
& broken nail polish
& muddy jeans
& metal-studded cuffs
we can only be sentry
we can only be sentry
we cannot sit beside them
with our wide-open cracked selves

# On Being a Couples Therapist

## TONI PIERONI

I never wanted to be a couples therapist. The odd time I would see a couple, I hated it. I couldn't stand watching them fight and argue in front of me. I felt so helpless and ineffectual. It brought up a lot of feelings about my own relationship, as well as old feelings from growing up in my family.

My parents didn't actively fight in front of us, so I didn't know there was anything wrong until I was in my late twenties after my dad died, when my mother told me what marriage was like for her. After falling in love hard and fast, they got married a few months later. She had no idea what she was getting herself into by marrying an Italian man who—she came to realize—expected her to be the proverbial "barefoot and pregnant" housewife while he worked, went out with his buddies and gambled at the horse track. I was conceived during their month-long honeymoon in California. When they returned home, reality set in and my mom said she felt like she was in jail. She was not allowed any money of her own. She had no car, few friends and no say in anything. If they fought, my dad wouldn't speak to her for a couple of weeks and she would do whatever it would take to win back his love. That was the emotional climate and marriage I was born into and marinated in.

My role with my mother was to be her "right hand," helping her raise the next five kids who came along. Later, in my early twenties, I was the person my parents turned to for advice and counsel. At the time I felt proud that I was needed. Two decades later, I went into therapy to free myself from feeling responsible for their happiness.

When I'm sitting with an unhappy couple, I feel pulled into that role—that it is somehow up to me to save them, fix them, get them shaped up and out the door. And when I can't, I feel like the worst therapist in the world. My solution until ten years ago was to avoid working with couples altogether. That, too, didn't feel particularly satisfying, though I justified it in a myriad of ways.

Maybe I didn't want to see couples fight because I was fighting with my own partner. Larry and I had been together about ten years at that point. We had fought for years about money. Financial security was hugely important to me. Larry had struggled for years to get a new career off the ground. He said he wanted the same things as me, but it wasn't happening. I flip-flopped between trying to be supportive and getting frustrated by the ways in which he held himself back: expecting things to come to him, not being aggressive enough. I'd given up hope and I couldn't live with it anymore. We went into therapy.

Maureen's waiting room was small and long, almost more hallway than room, and we sat on a bench that occupied most of one wall. It was uncomfortable, one of those straight-back things that doesn't fit the contours of anyone's back. There was a small table at one end with a water pitcher with a lid on it. The lid looked like an afterthought, not really belonging to the pitcher—just something stuck on top to keep dust and bugs out. I filled a disposable glass and held it in my lap, waiting. Across from us were hooks to hang our coats and behind the door was a bulletin board with all kinds of things stuck to it with push-pins. I went over for a look. It held a hodgepodge of articles about relationships and posters for workshops.

Finally, a door opened and Maureen came out to lead us into her office. She was shorter than I expected, with grey wavy hair just covering her ears. I had never met her before, though I had heard about her for years. She had been one of the best-known therapists in Vancouver when trauma and sexual abuse became a big focus in the psychotherapy world. What I didn't know was that she also specialized in couples therapy. It helped me feel better about the whole thing. I had made up my mind that I was ending our relationship, so it felt like walking to the end of the plank as we walked toward her open door. I was really nervous, but also relieved.

Her office was spacious. One whole wall was filled with shelves that held books, art supplies and the odd curio. She directed us to sit in two wingback chairs in the centre of the room and pulled her rolling desk chair toward us. She smiled calmly and asked why we were there and how she could help. It was strange to be on the receiving end of the questions. At that point I'd been a therapist for about fifteen years and I asked those questions all the time. It made me appreciate what it was like for my own clients when they first sat with me. But how could I even begin to answer when I could feel the years of pain and frustration behind the dam, ready to burst? Therapy is not for the faint of heart!

"I'm not here to make this relationship work," I told her. "I'm here to end it. I can't do this anymore, but I want us to be complete and we can't seem to do that on our own."

"Okay," she said and turned to Larry. "And why are you here?"

"I want to try and make it work," he said.

I could feel my internal eye roll—yeah, sure, but you don't do what it takes to make it work.

Maureen seemed unfazed, like she'd heard this many times before. She asked us to turn our chairs toward each other. "I'm going to teach you something called the Dialogue," she said, explaining that it was a way of communicating in which one person speaks, and the other person mirrors back whatever is said. She told us it was developed by Harville Hendrix, the American psychotherapist who developed Imago Couples Therapy. I was familiar with Hendrix's ideas, having read his book *Getting the Love You Want* fifteen years earlier. Maureen explained that it was a way of keeping things safe between us, so that each person felt heard and understood. She turned to me and told me to tell Larry about my feelings, but to do it without attacking or blaming him. She said I should speak with statements that began with "I" and not with "you." Larry and I both knew this of course. We had taken courses at the Justice Institute in conflict resolution and had learned what they called "active listening" skills. (We teach this to our clients and never practise it ourselves!) She told Larry that he was to reflect back what he heard me say. Then he was to ask me two questions: Did I get it? And is there more?

"I just can't do this anymore," I said. "I feel so helpless. Nothing I say or do makes any difference to you. You make decisions that make no sense to me, that won't bring in any money, and it just doesn't feel like you care. I'm sick of hearing myself fight and complain. I know it just makes things worse between us. I'm just done with this."

Larry mirrored back everything I said pretty much word for word. Maureen wanted him to do it that way, so I knew he was hearing exactly what I was saying. He then asked if he had gotten it and if there was more. Of course there was more.

"I'm terrified of being poor and struggling with money like my parents did their whole lives," I said. My mother had poured everything into me, to get an education, to be self-reliant so that I would never end up in the position she was—totally dependent on a man and without any freedom or means of her own. I didn't need someone to look after me, I told him, but I certainly hadn't signed on for taking care of someone else financially. "I love so much about you but I just can't do this anymore."

Larry mirrored my words again and we kept going like this until I had nothing more to say. But it was the next step in the dialogue that I found the most powerful. Maureen asked Larry to tell me how what I said made sense. This is called the validation part of the process.

"I know you are afraid that nothing will change and that you will end up poor and having to look after me," he told me. "I can totally understand how frustrating this has been for you and that you feel hopeless about it."

It's not like I hadn't said those things to him before and hadn't heard those words back from him, though in different ways. But this time I felt like he really heard me and he wasn't defensive. Something shifted between us and we decided we would come back for another session. Then it would be Larry's turn to speak.

Larry and I continued to see Maureen for another six months or so. We used the dialogue at home whenever we had a difficult conversation and it got us around the land mines we would typically set off with each other. Still, we nearly stepped on them a couple of times during that six months and at one point almost ended things again. But we pulled ourselves back by repeating our lines back to one another and really trying to understand each other.

Sometime during those six months Maureen told me that there was going to be training in couples therapy and I decided to jump in.

There were about twenty of us around the outer edges of a small conference room at the Sylvia Hotel. Our trainer's name was also Maureen, a woman from Toronto who had been a faculty member for the Imago Institute for many years. She asked us to begin by going around the circle telling our relationship history: most were stories of heartbreak and divorce. It was a great leveller—as none of us was a star in the relationship department, we didn't need to pretend that we had it all together.

We were introduced to Hendrix's theory—that we are unconsciously attracted to people who carry some traits of our parents that have hurt or even traumatized us in the past. The therapy is to help couples become aware of the triggers in their relationship that have roots in their respective histories, and then teach them the tools and skills to respond differently. We would meet like this three times over the next year. In between modules, we were expected to take on couples as clients and to videotape sessions that we would show to the group for feedback.

I began to assist couples, and though I was really nervous, I believed in the process. Many of the couples I saw had similar experiences to Larry's and mine at the beginning; they felt heard by their partner in a new way and left my office feeling hopeful. It didn't always last, though. Hearing and understanding are important, but couples also have to change. That is where things can get bogged down. For example, when one person agrees to changing some behavioural pattern but never follows through, then gets mad at their partner for getting mad at them. And then gets mad at me if I press in to find out more about what's getting in the way. Or when one person continues to express contempt and then is mad when their partner doesn't want to have sex with them. There were times when I felt pushed to my limit, like when a woman wouldn't stop screaming at her husband and I couldn't get her to stop. They never came back.

There was one time when I thought it could go that way, and then something else happened: His face was red. His jaw was clenched and his fury spilled out, even though his wife was terrified of his anger. She shut down and withdrew, mostly into self-pity. He was contemptuous of me and my attempts to hold him in the dialogue structure and lashed out when I attempted to intervene. I was scared of him, too, and backed off, just like she did. But, more than fear, I felt helpless. My mind was scrambling, looking for something from my bag of therapy tricks that might salvage the session, which felt at that point like a race car careening toward a crash. I knew that underneath his rage was grief. And I knew that some of his dreams about his marriage were dying before his eyes. He had believed she would always be the way she was when they first met—crazy about him, attentive, listening to him endlessly when he talked about his work, seeing his flaws as amusing, thinking he was funny. But after their first child was born she had turned her attention toward their baby with an intensity and focus that left him feeling alone. When he complained, she went silent and withdrew. Over time, this cycle escalated and he railed against her. He was drowning in loneliness. It wasn't supposed to go this way. His marriage had become his parents' marriage, and he hated her for it.

Eventually I noticed that though he was loud and fierce, he wasn't actually attacking her. He was trying to tell her how frustrated he was, and I saw her leaning in, attentive. When he had spent himself, I asked her to tell him what made sense about what she'd heard. I held my breath and crossed my fingers that my intuition was correct and she would be able to do this. Otherwise, he would blow again. But she pulled it off and this began their turn out of the skid. He visibly relaxed, and so did I. Disaster averted—this time at least.

Over the next few sessions, I guided them through a process of defining their goals and placing more attention on their own growth than on trying to change their partner. A number of months later, he was all smiles and tender with her, less self-absorbed and more curious. She was coming out of her turtle shell and engaging with him, talking more readily about her needs and wants, and not getting as scared when his emotions built. They could talk about things without fighting. They left their sessions holding hands.

That is why I am a couples therapist.

The success with this couple cheered me—it made up for my terror and emboldened me to continue, though it's still not easy. A few year ago, the journal *Psychotherapy Networker* was titled "Who's Afraid of Couples Therapy?" In the lead article, "Facing Our Fears," couples therapy trainers Ellyn Bader and Peter Pearson wrote: "Couples therapy can feel like piloting a helicopter into a hurricane." They add that most therapists are "unprepared for the degree of hostility, bitterness, distrust and occasional homicidal rage" they encounter. In fact, according to them, clinicians are resistant to doing couples therapy for a simple reason—it makes them too nervous. When I read that, it helped me feel better that it wasn't just my counter-transference issues from my own family. At a conference devoted to couples therapy, a presenter told the audience that a psychiatrist colleague of his said: "I work with paranoid schizophrenics. They aren't nearly as hard as couples."

One of the reasons couples therapy is so tough is that we learn about love from our families. And growing up in families is like living in a fishbowl. We do not distinguish the water we live in as being separate from ourselves—it's all one. The water is all the ways, for better or worse, that we experience love. Children (and fish) "learn" to speak the language of their parents by unconscious osmosis—it gets laid down in their implicit memory system. The same is true for the language of love. A child will "learn" that love means safety, protection, care, comfort, loyalty, etc. Or a child may learn that love is lonely, rejecting and isolating, suffocating and controlling, terrifying and chaotic, or a myriad of other configurations. It's all "water" to the child, and it is what they will unconsciously seek in the people they love. The science of how implicit memory gets laid down is beyond the scope of this writing. Suffice to say that there are no accidents when it comes to the mates we find.

It's been ten years since Larry and I first saw Maureen. We are still together. We even got married six years ago and recently celebrated the twenty-year anniversary since we met. We still struggle at times over money issues. In some ways the situation hasn't changed much, but *we* have. We talk to each other without fighting; we make requests of each other without complaining. I have learned how to get clearer about my own limits and express them without making him wrong. He has felt safer talking to me about some of his own vulnerabilities and struggles, just as I have learned to feel and show more compassion toward him.

For a number of years, a group of us from the initial training workshop continued in a supervision group to get help and feedback with more difficult situations, and I have gone on to do other training as well. At a recent session, I heard about a study done in the seventies in which young, unmarried people described their ideal marriage: equal parts commitment, intimacy and passion, with safety as its overarching principle. The second part of the study interviewed people in their sixties to see how many had achieved this ideal. Only 4 percent reported having done so. I find that sad and shocking but also inspiring, and it's why I continue to do this challenging and rewarding work—to try to increase that percentage. I've grown a lot in my capacity to do so. I don't take it on personally as much when couples aren't doing well, and I've kept expanding my repertoire of tools to offer. Some couples still don't make it, but many do.

And sometimes I get to watch magic happen.

# Sonoma

**JANE MUNRO**

He totalled his blue truck—
slowly spun out on an icy bridge,
rammed it into a guardrail.

Climbed out unbruised.
Coal Creek. Middle of nowhere.
A passing couple brought him home.

Then three years
with letters from the Motor Vehicle Department
before he relinquished his licence.

Before we met, while driving cab,
he broke his neck. It rewelded
off-kilter: head stuck forward.

Six years later, it's that jut I suddenly see ahead.
It's late, but for once no mist or fog. And on all
the twists and turns of that coastal highway,

its bluffs and coves, I am following
the spitting image of him
in that battered Sonoma—

its peeling paint, cracked brake lens,
the slumped driver silhouetted by my lights—
only the two of us on the road.

# Warm Animal

**TANA RUNYAN**

This memory of yellow stone
stays with me till morning:
the buttery warmth of faraway walls,
sun rising like a broken yolk
above the mountains.

The vastness of memory lingers,
nestled in the heart's same soft hollow
where our fear of illness finally lies
down and sleeps like a fugitive deer.

I gather myself into our clean white sheets,
lavender drapes half-open
onto this day's cold pigeon-grey skies.
Relief is a slow turn onto my right hip
that does not yet ache.
His back is a warm animal
toward which I slowly nudge
my way forward.

# Third Sutra

**ANNE SIMPSON**

                                        Cut-paper blue, a slope, single tree,

plaid slippers on a tiled floor. A man
with a broken femur gets up, slides
a walker on tennis balls past the nursing station.

                               On the branches of the elm, party hats,
                                     doll-sized. Shaken

                                    in a northwest wind,
                                      shivered toss

of thoughts. She hasn't
visited for a week. No—eight
days. Can't be

right. Now she's here,
her walker's folded in the solarium.
Aluminum containers have been set out,
each cardboard lid tilted. The ginger beef
has leaked onto the fake wood, sticky
pool. He floats,

door to table. Balances on one foot—

                                            Dancer.

Should he kiss her?

# Partings

# Cleave

## RACHEL ROSE

Perhaps it was a mistake to buy you the ring
the week you asked for a separation. August swelled
with heat, loops of onion fell from my knife.
The children knew nothing of such sorrow.
My face streaked with sudden rain,
I served them lies:
*No, loves, it's the onions—she'll be home late.*
We touched each other
like curators in a museum of bone shards.
I separated our clothes. As I burned
in the guest room beside my stacks of poetry,
the ring kept its golden eye
open in the socket of its hinged box. It winked at me,
kept me from sleep.

Our country forbade us from vows,
then gave us permission to marry
but not divorce. I couldn't catch up
to history.

What would we have worn to the ceremony?
Everything that happened was brutally private.
I paid for the loop of gold
that let me dream of a different ending,
a ring that owed me wishes
which will be one wish spoken twice:
*Don't cleave.*
A ring that turns into a keyhole
that opens the door back to enchantment,
but your fingers refused the tradition.
Cleave: I cling. You unstring.
You sever. You halve. You rend.
I clasp. I cherish. I ring—

Once two girls castled themselves in a tower
and wrote their own story
but you were also the joker
who became the squire
who became the knave
while I was the milkmaid
who became the lady of bridges,
the princess of crows,
embroidering hausfrau: how
did our legend fail?

I return the fool's
gold untried: we are gathered today
to divide, dearly beloved, to witness
your great loneliness unmarry
my veiled pride.

# The Manual of Marriage Failures

**EUFEMIA FANTETTI**

---

**1. Follow instructions.** From fairy tales, you learn salvation is possible in the form of a charming man who is willing to battle and slay a wicked beast. From the *Sweet Dreams* novel series you read as a teenager, you believe it is possible to be loved for who you are: an only child, bookworm, fashion misfit, social moth drawn to situations where you easily get burned. From Hollywood, you grasp that relationships often involve heart-melting lines and perfect white teeth. From your Roman Catholic upbringing, you discover that every bad deed since Eve listened to the serpent is your fault.

**2. Heed warnings.** Your parents had a Molotov cocktail marriage—misery, martyrdom and madness left unattended for lengthy periods. A situation that resulted in radiation poisoning for the nuclear family. You hid in a bedroom closet from a violent mother and fantasized about escaping on *The Love Boat*. You grew accustomed to volatile tempers and were ashamed of your parents. Their savage quarrels (complete with choking, biting, kicking, jeering and yelling) led you to reject your heritage. Translation: you erroneously fused being Italian with hostile intent, noxious violence and brute force. Your mom proposes marrying you off to her nephew after you turn fourteen. Your father supports you in pursuing an education and gives you the opportunity he never had. Your mother rages: no one wants a smart wife. Then she switches tactics and cries while you pack for university three thousand miles away.

**3. Form attachments.** You fail classes at school but find love in the company of a kind, blue-eyed boy. His exotic Canadian family introduce you to yams, Brussels sprouts and turkey. He is sweet-hearted and sporadically snarky—reducing your confidence with a condescending remark. In time, he grows lax in attention to a degree that friends assume you are no longer together. You confide in a customer-friend who eats regularly at the sushi restaurant on Yates Street where you waitress six days a week. He always orders the special, a California roll and Ebi Sunomono salad. The two of you commiserate over your failing relationships. You tell him about your frustrations—five years of diminishing affection. He tells you his long-term relationship is ending because he found out his girlfriend cheated on him.

**4. Avoid overexposure.** The attraction you feel for the customer-friend is not physical, and his desire makes you anxious. He's a few years older, heavy-set and bearded. You are a not-that-tall, not-that-short, frizzy-haired immigrant's kid from Toronto who fiercely wants a secure home. He's a journalist. You dream of being a writer. You are not familiar with standard social conventions and think nothing of being vulnerable or exposing humiliating family secrets. You reveal too much information about your psychotic mother, the police visits to the house, your passive father—this intimate knowledge of your inner turmoil and central trauma confuses him. The assumption: if you can bare your soul over such private anguish, nudity must not be an issue.

**5. Proceed with installation.** You break up with your neglectful boyfriend and begin dating the attentive journalist. After seven months, you move in with him. You hide this living-together arrangement from your father until he calls one morning at six and your fellow groggily answers the phone. You snap awake and apologize for the deception. Your dad surprises you by saying he will sleep better knowing someone expects you home every night. At the crossroads of your late twenties, an intersection of guilt and failure, you remember your father's advice about choosing a spouse you could talk to because attraction will fade. You figure you're safe, hypnotized by the myth that Anglos are the essence of politeness, cool-as-a-cucumber civility, and born wordsmiths. Coitus is not so compatible this time but you're considerate of each other and hug all the time. There is no romantic proposal or engagement ring: when he points to a wedding date on the calendar, you agree if he gets his taxes filed first—he hasn't done them for a few years. The journalist self-medicates with pot and alcohol; you self-sedate by ignoring reality—a survival skill you've inherited from your father and honed.

**6. Assemble with care.** The dowry your mother began amassing for five-year-old you—full of embroidered bed linens, tablecloths, espresso cup sets, silverware and ten thousand doilies that reek of mothballs—is useless. This collection of material assets is no measure of your real worth but a reminder that marriage was a refuge for your female ancestors, protection against conquerors, marauding bandits, random men and poverty. Their families had to entice—essentially purchase—a husband with land, livestock or lucre. Love was not a factor. This millennia-old pattern of misogyny, your true inheritance, taught you women were worthless without a mate. Compile the elements of an unhappy marriage: unrealistic expectations, unhealthy codependence and an uneasiness with being alone. Invite all your friends to the wedding at the Hotel Vancouver. Your gown is white even though you have been living together for three years. Your father takes a pretend vacation to visit you on the West Coast to be there for the celebration; you never tell your mother—you want to be surrounded by family and friends who adore you, people who truly care for you and want to see you happy. Still, this is not the marriage of true minds but a match between a misfit and a curmudgeon. Your fiancé's father is an aging scholar and Lothario; his mother is prisoner to a devastating disease that has left her a human husk in a care home. You voice a concern to your intended about your combined motherless states as the possible basis of your emotional bond.

**7. Prepare for power surges.** Less than six weeks after the wedding, you arrive home exhausted from work as a cog in the wheel of a giant bookstore chain. He is cooking pork chops. You carp and complain about his failure to check whether your soon-to-arrive dinner guests have any food allergies or aversions. You simply can't believe he didn't bother to confirm. He comes at you in a rage. You put your palms up and back away. He grabs your hands and bends them slightly backward, hissing "I hate you" through a clenched jaw. You suspect this is true: his eyes are dark and unforgiving—like being stared at by a shark or your mother. You hold your breath. He returns to cooking. You walk over and punch him hard in the upper arm. He ignores you. You're shaking with fear and fury—you deceived yourself, imagining physical clashes were only the realm of Southern Italians. You head into the bedroom and call your guests to cancel. You leave the apartment and sit in the stairwell leading up to the roof for an hour, making sure your breath is barely audible. Afraid any noise will give away your location, you freeze like you did when you were a kid hiding from your raging mother. This is how animals in the wild remain invisible—no movement. You are in a state of panic. You married your childhood ally: chaos.

**8. Ensure regular maintenance.** Your ardour is tepid. Use shower gels. Buy bubble baths. Light candles. Pluck, shave, moisturize. He notes your weight gain; you alternate between fasting and stuffing your face. When he notices your frayed underwear with the elastic showing through, your tendency to wear the same plaid flannel shirt over and over (the one your friend calls "lesbian chic"), your lack of effort—admit defeat. Numbness, depression and exhaustion are your true companions in this relationship. You assumed a lack of desire was part of the married package. Your parents were chosen for each other by their parents—so you have no idea what a loving relationship looks like, sounds like, *is* like.

**9. Caution: dangerous voltage.** You put on a brave face after he calls you a psycho bitch. His words are similar to the way your mother spoke when she called you a gypsy whore and a filthy slut. He slams doors and cupboards, breaks the teapot lid and throws a shoe at your head. Familiarity has bred low self-esteem. Focus on tenderness. The compliments he pays and the encouragement he offers about your writing when you are racked with doubt. The time you had strep throat and he stayed up all night reading an entire book to you. Outside of a kindergarten circle, no one has ever read to you before.

**10. Avoid overloading.** Develop a crush on someone you work with that indicates how disenchanted you are with your husband. You can't afford to go out for dinner or enjoy yourselves on your meagre bookstore income. Your father has been helping you pay rent. Your husband's wealthy dad contributes nothing. Money matters create tension: bickering, frustration, the classic fight-flight-freeze sequence. The husband dreams every month that your marriage won't last. You have one recurring dream—a nightmare that haunts your adult life—you never left your claustrophobic childhood home.

**11. Beware of polarization.** When your husband realizes you won't stay to fix what you deem as broken beyond repair, he lashes out and calls you an evil cunt. The discussions are suffocating. Blame is frequently tossed around, occasionally hurled, each disagreement dissolves into an absurd circus act, juggling petty grievances and major grudges. You are told you are cold, uncaring, and at fault for more than you think or are willing to accept. The arguments scorch your insides. You leave after fifteen months of marriage. Friends help you move out, carting boxes of books and the futon sofa that will be your new bed. You suppress your sobs until the end of the day when dusk falls across the city. Alone in your new apartment, you fall asleep in a state of total exhaustion. There are a few failed attempts at friendship, at recovering what was lost in the day-to-day despair and multiple misunderstandings, then a final parting of ways.

**12. Replacement parts.** Five years later, your second wedding dress is ivory. Husband-to-be number two is an old crush, a friendly face from the theatre community you have drifted away from. He is an actor/director who puts on plays, runs a company and acts like a man in love. He gazes into your eyes for an embarrassing amount of time and you are desperate to believe this means you've been seen. You want to make this work. You overlook his disinterest and mistake his narcissism for charisma. You try to bury the shame about your first failed marriage and ignore multiple blinking red lights: Husband Two rarely carries cash, charges every purchase to credit and is drowning in debt. He has lavish tastes influenced by his extravagant mother. This guy doesn't want you, doesn't admire you—not like your first husband did. He discourages you from going back to school to study writing. He needs someone responsible to pay for the rented roof over his head. For a year you flirt with the idea of having a child. He's not serious about having a baby, yet he imagines he'll be a great father. After visiting a counsellor together, Husband Deuce tells you in eerily similar phrasing used by Husband One that he "puts up with you." You worry this marriage was built on his ego-driven manipulation of events to suit his purposes and your intense divorce-guilt. Three years after exchanging vows you are coping with a schizophrenic mother, a suicidal father and an absent, expensive husband. When he threatens you in embarrassingly clichéd speech: "You walk out that door, this marriage is over," shrug. Find a new apartment, suggest he try paying his own bills, and begin the relationship autopsy.

**13. Service and warranty.** In your occasional dreams about your exes, you keep saying, "No, this is over. We're finished." You don't want to ever go through another breakup. The mornings afterward, you stretch out, star-fishing across the bed before getting up to make coffee. Count yourself lucky, in another time you would have been burned at the stake. For being single or single-minded, for having an opinion, for demanding fair treatment, for refusing to be taken for granted. There will be days when loneliness overwhelms you. There will be months of serene solitude. There will be years of healing. Give yourself time. Consider a cat-husband. Remember there is random love in the universe. Make your goal the extension of kindness to everyone. Smile at strangers. Learn to say "I love you" in multiple languages. Let the world in all its glory confirm your wonder and affection for life. Singledom is not leprosy. Solitude can comfort. That ache you feel in the pound of flesh around your heart is the source of the original injury. Cut your incurable mom out of your life. Palm to chest, soothe the wound. Wear your heart wherever you want—sleeve, skirt, suspenders. Save yourself: in this fantasy, you are not only the princess, but also the knight, the dragon and a freaking unicorn too.

# A Tree House of One's Own

## ELLEN MCGINN

The first time I saw the tree house my friend Linda accompanied me. She was the one who'd heard through her network of children's writers that two rooms and a bath on the top floor of an old house near the University of British Columbia campus would soon be for rent. It was a bright spring morning; the trees full of birdsong, flower boxes brimful of red tulips. We were shown up a steep wooden set of stairs on the outside of the house. At the top to the right of a worn wooden porch with rickety rails was a door with green trim around a thick rectangular pane of glass. Peering through I saw a shadowed space, sparsely furnished, with walls an even neutral colour. We stepped inside. The trees crowded around the windows, a wall of green. "I'll take it," I said, without hesitating, already thinking of colours to paint the walls. My new landlady explained that a Russian doing post-doctoral work in particle physics would soon be moving out and going back home. She said he spent most of his time at the university. I looked around at the few sticks of furniture, the unadorned walls, and figured it made sense that someone who spent their time smashing atoms would be a minimalist as far as decor went.

A couple of weeks later I stood outside the white picket fence of the house I'd lived in with my husband, Charles, my belongings packed into cardboard boxes (books) and a couple of suitcases. What surprised me was how little stuff I had that was mine. The furniture, the art on the walls, the *objets d'art* carefully placed on shelves and in niches—all these reflected Charles. They were his things. So when I left there was scarcely a ripple. Linda picked me up and helped me move my few possessions into my new home. When she left I closed the door and was alone.

I was fifty-three and had been married for fourteen years. I would stay in the tree house for six years.

The first couple of weeks in the tree house were busy and purposeful. I made lists of practical needs: broom, hammer, dish soap, coffee maker, desk, light bulbs. The many windows needed curtains, thick curtains to block the black night that stared in at me. I found heavy white folds of material traced with patterns of white thread. They reminded me of my First Communion dress. I had them made to fit the windows. It was my major expense. Otherwise Linda and I trawled thrift stores. I felt like I had in my twenties when I thought of myself as an artist, a bohemian living on an edge. Not married. Not in my fifties. The most fun was finding the art to put on the newly painted walls, and the *tchotchkes*—Linda's word from her Ukrainian ancestry—the baubles and knick-knacks that provide a cheerful clutter on windowsills and countertops. Thrift stores were mines of art and *tchotchkes*. Once I dropped all pretensions of taste or sophistication—would Charles ever allow this thing into our home?—and found that anything with hearts, angels or flowers made me happy, decorating became simple. Thrift stores are chockablock with hearts, angels and flowers. And with no one else's taste to consult, the tree house began to reflect just me and me alone. Walking up the flight of wooden steps, putting my key in the lock, opening the door and stepping inside gave me a solace that I hadn't felt since I was sixteen years old and my parents had allowed me to decorate my attic bedroom all of my own choosing. I had picked wallpaper with pink roses, and a fluffy heart-shaped rug.

When all this happened, fifteen years ago now, I chose to tell my husband point-blank that I was having an affair. In retrospect, I would advise against such a move, based as it was on a moral righteousness around honesty somehow absolving me of all wrong, and transparency being healthier than deception for all concerned, especially me. He collapsed. He broke down and cried his eyes out. In my best Nurse Nancy manner, I tried to console him. Again, I advise against offering a hug directly after delivering a mortal blow. Understand that you are really not nice. Not remotely nice. At all. Who would want to be?

The first month, in my memory now, seemed to be about basking in the contented glow of my efforts to make the tree house mine. Staking out the territory of two rooms and a bath. Settling back in the old rocking chair I'd found. Waiting in dreamy anticipation for my lover to come knocking at my door. I imagined welcoming his visits with glad abandon. Then watching him go away. I covered the door glass with a yellow curtain. I made a lemon pie. I have no recollection of an inner voice commenting that I had fashioned a love nest. None at all. And if I had I would have been surprised. Possibly indignant. I'd read enough stories about women who left their marriages to lounge on silken pillows awaiting their lovers. Who bought pink satin nightgowns at the Bay and massage oil called Love Honey. I knew it always ended in tears. Or worse. Under trains. Here I sat in the waiting, the light so thin that I thought it would snap. The lemon pie untouched. Then darkness and the faint sound of traffic. A white sound. A wavelength that cancels itself.

Nothing went according to the dream. Everything fell apart surprisingly fast, and I was left alone with feelings of loss on all sides: my marriage hanging by a thread, the affair ending. And then I thought, no, actually, *I* left. I moved into two rooms and a bath. Put up white curtains, and sat in a rocking chair with my feet on a red velvet footstool staring into this place where no one came but me.

Time passed in the ritual of the opening of all my thick white curtains one by one in the mornings, behind them the day's edge, and then the drawing of each and every one of them against the night. I felt safe. I was enclosed. I had a green bowl full of pears and oranges, and a bunch of bananas with a sticker on them that said they were organic. What did that mean exactly? That an organic banana was a good banana and a non-organic one was bad? I considered my marriage. Was it good or bad? If I no longer had a marriage, if my lover would never call, and my father dead this one year past, how would I begin again? Where was that, the beginning place?

So there were, in the beginning, days of standing, arms crossed, of staring out the many windows, of long pauses best left unrecorded. I navigated through two rooms and a bath, through solitude and silence. I imagined myself in terms of an empty space and thought of fans opening and closing the way they do in long slow Noh plays where the actors move ritualistically at slug speed. During this time there was a war. Bush gave a final ultimatum to Iraq to say when he would begin the bombing—tomorrow, or the next day, or five minutes after I'd heard his speech on the CBC news. A thin white mist fell in long straight lines from the alder trees. I thought an angel would look like that: long and thin and spidery, made of straight lines and mist. I stood outside as if on a shore and looked into a blank expanse—on one side here I was; on the other, there I was not; nor was there anything at all, which gave the emptiness a neutrality. I felt compelled to stand like someone contemplating a departure—watching the sky, watching the way the wind blew. I needed a map and the geometric compass of an angel. I dreamt of a lioness that leapt into the sea. I needed her, too. As well as the baby spiders that hatched in the pot of purple sage on the tree house porch railing. They threw out threads into nothing and crawled toward something, impelled by their spider blood. A clump of yellow points heading out. I watched them—golden dots with tiny moving parts casting themselves out into space on silken threads—my heroes.

For six years I wrote in journals, a lifeline of words flung onto the blank expanse of the page; a white emptiness that I needed to make marks on, like footprints I could look back upon for traces of myself. If I kept moving forward word by word, page by page, journal by journal, I thought I would finally arrive at the end. I would walk down the slope of a steep hill through a leafy forest and come to the sea where there was a town, and I would move there and be at home.

I took notes on the world I inhabited, noticing what I noticed—weather systems, the muffled rhythm of days and nights, a siren. Here it comes. There it goes. What is that called? A red shift. Faraway, then close. The pleasure of pink spring trees outside my windows. Horses in the news. Mustangs rescued from the Bush government that would like to turn them into horse-meat. The slow slide of light, and darkness coming up through the trees. Everything moving.

Friends and family saw me as "cocooning," which was more polite than leaving my marriage and shutting myself away in the tree house, and which also promised a transformation. After a year and a day in my drab cocoon I would emerge—far more appealing, way more fun, easier to get along with, someone who would keep up their end of a conversation. For a while I was asked kindly, and with curiosity, if I was writing, and if I was, what exactly was I writing about? And for a while I would say that, yes, I was writing, which always perked people right up. That's good, they'd say. And they would wait expectantly to hear what I was working on, so I'd tell them about a poem or story that I was in the process of creating—but never quite finishing—just to appear actively engaged and productive. Time passed and the questions stopped. I think friends began to see through my evasive strategies. Tactfully, they dropped the subject of my artistic output. Nobody ever used the word "failure," but I felt like one. I felt unclean with failure. I'd failed at Marriage, failed at Being an Artist. I shut the door on both, sat in the rocking chair, rested my feet on the red velvet footstool and put the whole mess of myself into the journals where I felt as hidden and safe as I did behind the thick white curtains. Crafty old guilt sidled in close insinuating that journal writing wasn't real writing, that it was commonly known to be the refuge of women pretending to be writers, too cowardly to face the real world, too timid to risk the slings and arrows of outrageous fortune. Shame followed, sticky as mucilage. I wrung Guilt's skinny old neck. Peeled off Shame and watched as it shrivelled into a dried turd. I flushed it down the toilet.

I did go out, out into the days, if only, at first, to replenish my supplies of toilet paper, wine and Cheezies. Eventually I ventured farther. To Halifax to look after my dying mother, then to Antarctica with Charles to look for her because I'd dreamt that she was there sitting under a striped beach umbrella, then to the Arctic with eighty-two teenagers and a team of scientists (Students on Ice, a Canadian organization that takes high school students on science expeditions to the polar regions, and whose outlook on the world I found bracing and courageous). And every time I went out I returned, thankful to be putting my key in the lock, to be opening the door to my tree house, to be welcomed back home.

I finally returned to my marriage. I did. I went back to him. We had not parted in a black cloud of acrimony and rage. We had not stomped away, swatting recriminations at each other. The situation would have been clearer if we had, divorce a satisfactory end to it all. No, we withdrew in a fog of sadness. Poker-faced with resignation. I had shut the door of my tree house. I had needed to know myself as separate from him—not that I went there aware of such a purpose. We had an orange cat with whom we shared visiting rights—Gibson, a.k.a. Buster—whom we both adored. A badass cat. Neither of us knew which way either of us would go. We spoke on the phone. Those early conversations were painful, full of ringing silences, abrupt goodbyes. I would hang up relieved to be without him, without the weight of his despair, the dark moods when depression bit into him cold and awful. At least alone I began to feel less lonely.

We had always had a strong emotional affinity, and that continued to play out in both of our concerns that the other was, despite the ongoing separation, still okay. The finality of divorce had never been mentioned.

He turned up one night when I had a cold, with takeout Szechwan. In hindsight I see it was the careful beginning of an attempt to build bridges. As he opened cardboard containers and dished out the chili prawns, the green spicy beans, the rice, I told him about my recent dream of tigers, and that he'd been in the dream, too. He looked pleased.

"Neutrally," I said, making a point. "You were there neutrally."

He nodded, sagely accepting his role in my dream. They were, after all, my tigers and they were lying in the middle of the road. "How are you?" he asked.

That was a kind question. I told him about the prophecy of fires again in the Interior, of summer and the dry dead pines; that I had recently read that scientists only knew 5 percent of the universe and this made room for the tigers in the middle of the road. I told him I didn't know how to fit back into the world, and that I didn't know if I'd ever have sex again.

One night after too much wine back in the old apartment we wrestled in bed together—naked, no holds barred. We wanted to beat each other up. No surrender. It's a wonder we didn't hurt each other, but we didn't. I fell off the bed a couple of times. Yelled, ground my teeth and yelled some more. Kicked and shoved. Finally, we stopped, exhausted. We slept well, an untroubled, blissful sleep. At least I did. The next day I drove back to the tree house. I dreamt that Charles asked me, "Where are you now with G?" The man who was my lover. "He is," I said, "a faraway geography." It was the best I could do.

That time when I went back to Halifax to look after my mother before she died, I'd found I needed a break after a month or so. My mother was getting concerned for me, which struck me as all wrong since I was supposed to be caring for her. Charles called and invited me to meet him in New York for three days. Both my mother and I were relieved to have me go away for a bit. It was winter. Central Park glamorous in the snow, bedecked with orange bunting installed by Christo. I lit candles in our hotel bathroom. My hair caught on fire as I leaned over the sink to reach for the soap. I heard Charles shout, "What's burning in there?" In the mirror I saw a woman with flames fanning around her head and for an astonished second was reminded of a surrealist painting I was sure I'd seen of a woman with hair ablaze. Then Charles was throwing a towel over my head, shouting at me to back away from the candles. Both of us became very excitable. The bathroom smelled of singed hair and I had a new frizzy look. We sat on the edge of the tub. I had a bath running.

"Are you okay?"

"Yeah. Thanks. Does my hair look okay?"

"Pretty much. You just have to burn the other side to make it look even."

Then we climbed into the tub.

Around my third year in the tree house, we decided to spend the summer together on Saturna Island. We are part of a long-standing land collective there, and had built a small house years earlier. I sublet my tree house with reluctance. The thought of anyone else living in my two rooms and a bath filled me with deep unease. In June I went over to Saturna with a pound and a half of halibut cheeks, a classy citron tart, yellow beans and a crusty loaf of sourdough. What made the summer living together possible was the "fence" I put up for myself. Between 9:00 a.m. and 1:00 p.m. was my time to be alone, come what may. Guests, visits to the general store, potlucks, salmon barbecues, blackberry picking—all that could happen after 1:00 p.m. I'd need a project since I couldn't sit behind my own fence and stare at the walls for four hours. I could do that, but I'd rather not do that every single day. So this became the time to plan, to take a look at what was seen from the corner of my eye, gather notes, sharpen pencils, observe and imagine as I sat in the happy sunshine among the bees, birds and flowers all busy busy buzzing, blooming, whirring, humming. Charles commented on my "interiority," which probably set back the date of my return for another couple of years. On the other hand there was a night when neither of us could sleep and we decided on a walk. Shuffled out in our slippers and dressing gowns, up to the road. Darkness sank to the ends of all we could see, though we had a flashlight so that we would not fall. There was a marvel of stars. We lay down on the road. It was almost morning. At 3:30 a.m. on our backs on the road with the sound of water near we were beside the stars, both of us. I remember this, remember thinking, I am married to you here. To you.

It is difficult to say what brought us back together. The other day I asked Charles if he had any recollection of a turning point.

"Yup." He looked up from the renovation he was drafting for clients. "I told you you could have a tree house on the island above the workshop I was designing for myself. Two rooms and a bath. All yours."

"I thought it was that walk on the beach at Jericho."

"Yeah? Maybe."

"We agreed that we needed to have a talk."

"We had fish and chips."

"I told you that we still seemed to be married, and you said, yes, you thought so, too."

"Well, there you have it."

My last night at the tree house, Linda brought over champagne and sushi. We had a picnic. And the next morning as I sat on the floor saying a final goodbye to the place that had sheltered me for six years, I went from room to room, which did not take long, into all the corners in a gesture of gathering the self whom I could not bear to leave behind, the one I had come to know in my time there alone. Aloud I said, "Come with me. Please come with me. I cannot leave without you." Then I shut the door behind me once and for all and left with her. As I walked down the steep wooden steps with my suitcase I met a young woman coming up. She told me she would soon be moving into the place upstairs. I wished her luck.

"You'll need curtains," I said.

# La Cumparsita

**KAREN SHKLANKA**

By the time her husband stomped off
the dance floor, halfway through the song,
she was thin, with sorry hands.
Their dogs never got along.
She'd started to flinch
when he raised his voice.
There was the condom he put in her wallet
as a going-away gift; the birthday dinner
he made to entice her home, uneaten.
She wrote him a postcard
from Seville, said she had fallen in love
with the city of flamenco.
She was really saying:
*Now I can dance alone.*

# The Good Wife

## SAMRA ZAFAR

When I was a kid, my only goal was to get a good education. I dreamed of attending Harvard or Stanford, and planned to become a doctor one day. I was the eldest of four daughters in a Pakistani Muslim family. We lived in Ruwais, a small town in the United Arab Emirates, where my father worked in an oil plant and my mother was a teacher. At school, I always stood out among the girls in my class—I was brash, clever, outspoken. I took pride in acing every test. When I brought home top marks, my father would celebrate by handing out sweets.

One day, when I was in grade ten, I was in my bedroom doing math homework. My mother walked in. She told me I'd received a marriage proposal. I laughed. "Mom, what are you talking about?" She didn't crack a smile, and I realized she was serious. "I'm only sixteen," I said. "I'm not ready for marriage." She told me that I was lucky. The offer came from a nice man who lived in Canada. He was twenty-eight years old and worked in IT. His sister was a friend of hers. The woman thought I'd make a perfect match for her brother—I was very tall, and he was six foot two.

"They're going to look so great together in pictures," she had said to my mother.

For weeks, I pleaded with my mom not to make me go through with it. I'd sit at the foot of her bed, begging. She would tell me it was for my own good and that a future in Canada would give me opportunities I wouldn't have here at home. She assured me that she'd spoken to his family about my desire to continue my education. "You can go to school in Canada. And we don't have to worry about you being alone," she said. The next thing I knew, his parents were measuring my wrist for wedding bangles. The date was set for five months later, July 1999.

My friends would talk about their own dream weddings—the gowns they would wear, how they planned to be dutiful wives and homemakers. When I told them about my doubts, they thought I was crazy, a fool, that Allah would punish me for being ungrateful. Marriage was their ultimate goal in life. But I didn't want it. I just didn't know how to get away.

For the next few months, I had recurring nightmares about my impending marriage. In my dreams, I was trapped inside a house, watching from the window as students made their way along the sidewalk to school. I'd wake up sweating and scared in the middle of the night. My mother would try to calm me down, telling me I was being hysterical. One night, when I woke up screaming, she decided to do something about it. She phoned my future husband in Canada and allowed me to speak to him for the first time. All I knew about him were those few details my mom had shared with me the night he proposed.

When I picked up the phone, I was meek. I had only one question, "Will you let me go to school?"

He reassured me, "Yeah, yeah, I'll let you go to school. Don't worry."

The first time I saw him was on July 22, 1999, the day before the wedding, at his family's home in Karachi. As we sat sipping tea, I snuck furtive glances at the man who was going to be my husband. I felt dwarfed by him.

The next day we were at my grandfather's house for the wedding. As my mother adjusted my gown, I pulled back. I told her I wanted to run away.

"Don't be silly," she said. "All the guests are here."

Someone put the marriage licence in front of me. I was told to sign it, and I did. Later we held a celebration at a high-end restaurant in the city. Strings of lights and red ribbons decorated the room, and two hundred of our parents' friends came. There were piles of food, and everybody laughed and sang and danced long into the night. I wore a long red lehenga sari. I was told to sit there quietly and look down at my hands, playing the demure bride.

This was the first of two ceremonies—we had to make it official so that my husband could apply for my sponsorship in Canada. The second ceremony was still months away, as was my wedding night. In the meantime, I continued to live with my parents and attend school. My new husband stayed in Pakistan for a month. We saw each other a few times, but never for long and usually with others around. One evening, we went to Pizza Hut with his older brother and his brother's wife. It was my first date, and I was so shy that I barely spoke. We talked regularly online, over MSN Messenger and occasionally on the phone. Slowly, I grew more comfortable with the marriage. Nothing about him struck me as special. He wasn't smart or funny or warm, but he was a normal enough guy. He told me how pleased he was that his wife was so smart. He suggested university programs I should consider in Canada. He agreed to wait to have kids until I finished school. He said all the right things.

When my immigration papers came through in August 2000, we both flew to Abu Dhabi for our second, smaller celebration. After it was over, we slept together for the first time. I was petrified. I knew nothing about sex or birth control and neither did he. My aunt had told me about ovulation, explaining that I couldn't get pregnant if I had sex on certain days of the month. I thought our wedding night was one of those days. I'd never even seen a condom before.

Later that week, we flew to Canada and I moved into his two-bedroom condo in Mississauga. I missed my parents, my friends, my school. I was so unhappy that I stopped eating, and I spent most of my days watching TV while my husband was at work. I stopped getting my period right away. At first I thought it was because of the move, the abrupt change in environment. But a month passed, then another. I was getting sick every morning. My nausea was so severe that I was afraid to go outside in case I fainted. Finally I told my husband that I needed to see a doctor. I sat in the doctor's office, listening to him ask me if I understood what being pregnant meant. All I knew was that it meant I couldn't go to school. *This can't be happening*, I thought. *This isn't happening.* I was only seventeen.

During the first few months of my pregnancy, my husband was kind and thoughtful. He took late-night trips to the grocery store to satisfy my cravings. He'd call a couple of times a day from work to ask how I was feeling, and every night we cooked dinner together. I discovered an adult learning centre near our condo and enrolled in an ESL course. I thought our marriage was going well. Then, two months before our daughter was born, he told me his parents would be moving to Canada and staying with us. He had planned for them to live with us all along, but this was the first I'd heard of it. We moved out of the master bedroom into the smaller one so his parents would be more comfortable.

Everything changed when they arrived. My husband and I stopped spending time alone together. His mother got upset when he paid attention to me, so he didn't show me any affection. When I would ask if I could call my parents in Ruwais, he or his mother would tell me we couldn't afford international calls.

In May 2001, I gave birth to our daughter. When we returned from the hospital, my husband slept on the couch while I stayed with the baby in the second bedroom. I'd never felt so alone. I fantasized about stealing money from my husband's wallet and taking a cab to the airport, calling my parents and asking them to buy me a plane ticket home. But I didn't want to leave my daughter behind.

When she was a few months old, we bought a four-bedroom house in Streetsville with his parents. I was rarely allowed to leave. I never had a penny to my name. My mother-in-law gave me her cast-off clothing to wear. I didn't have a cellphone. I wasn't allowed to go to the grocery store on my own. If I didn't iron my husband's shirts or make his lunch or finish my chores, he and my in-laws told me that I was a bad wife who couldn't keep my family happy.

I walked on eggshells all the time. If I asked my husband something, he would reply, "Bitch, get out of here."

Two years in, the abuse got physical. He would grab my wrist and shove me around. I'd be sitting on the couch and he'd slap me upside the head, or grab me so hard on my upper arms that my skin would bruise. Once he tossed a glass of water in my face; I slipped on the floor and threw out my back. Another time he punched a hole in the wall next to my head and told me, "Next time, it's going to be you." On one occasion, he picked up a knife and said he was going to kill me and then himself.

I was having suicidal thoughts all the time. I was convinced my life was over. One time, I took a razor blade into the shower and thought about cutting myself, stopping only when I heard my baby cry. I believed my unhappiness was my fault—that the secret to perfect wifehood was eluding me. If I'd just done the dishes better, been quieter, anticipated that he wanted a cup of coffee or a glass of water, then none of this would have happened.

When my daughter turned three, I learned about a parent drop-in centre called Ontario Early Years, funded by the Ministry of Education. Located in a Streetsville strip mall, the space was bright and cheerful. My daughter would make crafts or play with Play-Doh, and the parents would gather in a song circle with their children and recite nursery rhymes. My husband took my daughter and me there a couple of times. Eventually, he let me walk over on my own. I looked forward to those two afternoons a week, when I'd be allowed to step outside by myself without fear, when I'd feel fresh air on my face.

The woman who ran the centre was Pakistani, and she recognized some of the signs of abuse even before I knew what to call it. She saw how jittery I would get if the sessions were running long, or how I'd have to ask permission from my husband if there were any changes to the schedule. She let me use the phone to call my parents. I tearfully told my father what was happening, that I felt imprisoned and helpless. He was horrified, but advised me to wait until I got my Canadian citizenship. "That way you won't risk losing your daughter," he said. And so I waited another year. Throughout this period, I resumed my education, taking high school courses by correspondence. I applied to university several times. I was always accepted but my husband would never pay the tuition.

In 2005 I told my husband that I wanted to go home to visit my family for four months. It had been five years since I'd last seen them. When he told me he didn't have the money, my father sent plane tickets for me and my daughter, who was four by then. On my way to the airport, I asked my husband for $10 to buy myself a coffee and my daughter a snack.

"Bitch, go ask your father for that too," he told me, as he dropped me off at Pearson.

When my parents picked me up at the airport, they almost didn't recognize me. I'd lost so much weight I looked skeletal. My family were shocked. The bright, confident girl they knew had been replaced with a skittish, scared young woman. It took a couple of months for me to realize I could go to the mall on my own, or to the grocery store. These were small triumphs, but they helped build up my confidence. By the end of my visit, I was resolved not to go back to Canada. As soon as I delivered the news to my husband over the phone, he unleashed a flood of apologies. He told me he'd never hurt me again. He promised we'd move out of the house, that we'd live alone together like we used to.

He wore me down. In August 2005, I returned to Canada. We moved into a new apartment, and my husband was paying both his parents' mortgage and our rent, leaving little money for anything else. At first, he was kind again. But within a few months, I got pregnant with our second daughter, and the abuse resumed. I needed an escape plan, so I began tutoring and babysitting children in our apartment building, slowly saving money for five months until I had enough for my daughter and me to fly to Karachi, where my sister was getting married. This time I wasn't coming back.

My father had been diagnosed with kidney failure before I'd arrived in December, and over the next few months I watched helplessly as his condition deteriorated. One day, I sat with him in the ICU.

"Papa, if something happens to you, what am I going to do?" I asked him.

"Realize the strength you have inside of you," he told me. "Go back to Canada and find a way to get out of your marriage." He died two days later.

My husband arrived in Karachi that week for the funeral. Sex was the first thing he wanted. It wasn't until he'd finished that he asked me how I was feeling. I said I was fine, got up and walked to the bathroom. I turned on the shower so he wouldn't hear me cry.

When I asked my mother what to do, she told me I should go back with him. After all, she had two more daughters to marry off, she said, and she didn't have the money to support me. I couldn't work. I had no education or experience. And I was pregnant. Resigned and defeated, I went back with him. While I'd been away, he'd moved back into his parents' house. This time I got a small room in the basement, with bare walls and a little window in the corner. My daughter slept in her crib in the room next door. In June 2006, I gave birth to my second daughter. I was miserable.

And yet my father's words had ignited something in me. I knew I was smart, and I knew the only way out was through school. I studied in my room every night, finishing the last course I needed for my GED, a grade-thirteen economics credit. A few months after my younger daughter was born, I earned my diploma and decided to apply to university again. I knew my husband would never let me leave the house to earn money for tuition, so I resurrected my babysitting service, telling him I was earning money for the family. I co-opted my mother-in-law with the promise that she'd earn easy money taking care of kids, and my husband even let me buy a van to drive my charges around. I was making between $2,000 and $3,000 every month, and though I had to turn over my earnings to my husband, I managed to sock away a few hundred dollars here and there. It took me two years to save enough for one year of school. In 2008, I applied to the University of Toronto's economics program. I was accepted. Nothing was going to stop me from going.

"Who's going to pay for your tuition?" my husband asked.

"I am," I responded.

My in-laws were so angry about my decision that no one in the house spoke to me for six months. I didn't care. This was my chance to get out. It had taken me nearly ten years, but I'd gone from victim to survivor.

My first day of school in September 2008 was one of the best of my life. I got to school fifteen minutes before my class started and walked through the Kaneff Centre at U of T Mississauga. After everything I'd been through, I'd finally achieved my dream. I sat in the hall, tears running down my cheeks. *If only my father could have seen this*, I thought.

I thrived in my new environment. I aced every class and other students gravitated toward me, asking to study or socialize. My success changed my thinking. If I was the scum on the bottom of my husband's shoe, like I'd been told all these years, why were my marks so high? Why did classmates want to be my friend? I could feel vestiges of confidence I hadn't had in years. One day in October I was walking to the campus bookstore to buy textbooks. Just around the corner, outside the health and counselling centre, a flyer on a bulletin board caught my eye. On it was a list of questions. "Do you feel intimidated? Do you feel like you don't have a voice? Do you feel like you've lost your identity?" As my eyes ran down the list, my brain screamed over and over again: *yes, yes, yes.* "Come in and make an appointment," the poster read. I opened the door and walked inside.

A few days later, I sat across from a counsellor, describing what was going on at home.

"I don't know what to do," I told her. "I'm trying to keep my husband happy and I'm still not good enough. He keeps telling me I'm worthless. All I want to do is fix it."

She grabbed my hand. "It's not your fault," she said.

It was the first time anyone had said that to me. As I continued my counselling, I realized that what had happened to me was wrong. My agency had been stripped away. I learned about the cycle of abuse that characterizes so many unhealthy relationships.

Our marriage was becoming more toxic every day. He once bought me a cellphone as a present, but installed spyware on it so he could monitor my calls. He kicked me in the stomach. He kept threatening to kill me. A year after I started counselling, I told him I wanted a divorce.

"What are you talking about?" he asked me. "I love you. I can't live without you."

One January night in 2011, he picked a fight. I wasn't doing enough housework, he said. As he loomed over me, tightening his fist, I picked up my phone.

"If you touch me, I'm going to call 911," I shouted.

And then he spat out the word divorce, in Urdu, three times: *talaq, talaq, talaq*. According to some Islamic scholars, uttering those words means the marriage is over.

I thought I'd be thrilled when he left, but I was terrified. I'd never lived on my own, and I was bracing myself for the shame I believed I would bring to my family. He sold our house out from under me, leaving me and the kids with three weeks to pack up. We had nowhere to go. I even registered at a couple of shelters, expecting to be homeless. One day, I was at the U of T tuition office, and a woman overheard me lamenting my situation. She suggested I look into campus housing; luckily, the university had one family unit left. Two days later, I had the keys to my very own shabby three-bedroom townhouse.

I couldn't afford movers. I packed all my belongings into garbage bags and made ten trips back and forth every day for five days, in the van I used to drive the kids who attended my home daycare. I used my last hundred dollars to pay a couple of students to help me move my furniture. I was relieved not to be out on the streets. I slept in one room with my youngest daughter. My eldest had the second bedroom, with enough space just for a single bed. I rented out the third room to a Pakistani student who watched my girls while I worked in the evenings. It was tiny, but it was ours. That year, I juggled five jobs to stay afloat. I worked as a TA, a researcher with the City of Mississauga and a student mentor. I did night shifts at the student information centre on campus. I even ran a small catering business out of my apartment.

One day it dawned on me that my husband was a man willing to put his own kids out on the street to teach me a lesson. I drove to the police station and reported everything. I gave a three-hour-long videotaped statement, offering as much detail as I could about the decade of abuse I'd endured. The officer said he likely wouldn't be able to lay charges because there weren't any bruises on my body. But it didn't matter. Just telling the authorities was a huge relief. It was my way of acknowledging everything to myself, of finally saying it wasn't my fault—none of it was my fault.

The officers interviewed my doctor and counsellors, and two days later they arrested my husband for assault. He pleaded guilty. We finalized our divorce and he got joint custody. My older daughter refused to see him, but my younger daughter visited him every other week.

There were many times over the next year that I thought I'd made a mistake, that I couldn't do it on my own. I thought the shame would never go away. After my marriage ended, none of my old friends would speak to me. My mother refused to tell people back home. I had no family in Canada, no friends at school who knew what was going on. I was completely isolated. I'd always been told that women are responsible for upholding the family's honour. A woman living alone is a sin. A woman travelling alone is a sin. When everybody around you says you're in the wrong, that your dreams aren't valid, you start to believe that. And there were many times that I'd fall into those sinkholes.

Education was my only refuge from my dark thoughts. I focused all my energy on school. In my fourth year, I was promoted to head TA. I worked as a senior mentor for the school's first-year transition program. I carried an eight-course load and earned a 3.99 GPA. One day, I got an email from my department adviser. In it was a description of the university's highest honour, the John H. Moss Scholarship, a $16,000 award that's given to an outstanding student who intends to pursue graduate work—the Rhodes Scholarship of U of T. My adviser encouraged me to apply. No one from the Mississauga campus had ever won it, she said. The deadline was only a few days away, but she convinced me to hustle up the paperwork.

A few weeks later, I got an email saying that I was one of five finalists. I arrived for my interview on February 6, 2013. The committee ran through questions about my academic record and leadership experience. I'd written about my abusive marriage in my application, too, and at the end of the interview, the panel asked me how I go on after everything I've been through. My polish wore off in that moment. "Every day I feel like giving up," I told them. "But I don't want my daughters to grow up thinking that being abused is normal."

Forty-five minutes after my interview concluded, I got a phone call. John Rothschild, chair of the selection committee and the CEO of Prime Restaurants, was on the other end of the line with a few other panellists.

"Congratulations," they said. "You're our winner this year."

I couldn't believe it. I grabbed my daughters' hands and danced wildly around the house with them. I wanted to tell the whole world. Since then,

John has become a friend, a mentor and the closest thing I have to a father figure. He taught me how to believe in myself again. He says if I ever get married again, he wants to walk me down the aisle.

In September of that year, I started my master's in economics. By the time I graduated, I was surviving off the Ontario Student Assistance Program, and my debt load was piling up. I wanted to stop borrowing money as soon as possible, so I decided not to pursue a PhD. Instead, I accepted a job at the Royal Bank of Canada, where I work today as a commercial account manager.

Around the time of my graduation, I was named the top economics student at U of T. At the award ceremony, a journalist introduced herself to me (her daughter was in my class). I told her my story, and she published an article about it in a Pakistani newspaper. As my story circulated through the community, I received hundreds of messages from women all over the world trapped in forced marriages and looking for help. So many of them sounded just like me five years earlier, isolated and helpless. Women who show up at shelters or call assault hotlines or leave their homes find themselves completely alone. Without any help, they return to their abusers or fall into new relationships that are just as bad.

Once, while I was a TA at U of T, a father barged into my office yelling. "You're pushing my daughter to get her master's degree!"

I couldn't believe it. To me, it was natural to offer encouragement—his daughter was the top student in my class.

"She's supposed to marry a boy in Egypt. Stop poisoning her with your Canadian bullshit," he barked.

Years ago, a woman wrote to me asking if we could talk on Skype. She was a Canadian university graduate whose parents forced her into a marriage in Pakistan after she finished school. Brutally abused for three years, she returned to Canada to have her baby. She wanted to leave her marriage. After we finished talking, I drove to her house and encouraged her to do it.

"No one will ever love me again," she said.

Three years later, she graduated from a master's program and got a job working full-time in Toronto. I realized I couldn't stop abuse from happening. But I could offer friendship to women in similar positions to my own. I started a non-profit called Brave Beginnings that will help women rebuild their lives after escaping abusive relationships.

For the past three years, I've lived in a three-bedroom condo in Mississauga with my daughters, who are now fifteen and ten. I serve as an alumni governor at the University of Toronto, and I speak about my experience for organizations like Amnesty International. I'm happier than I ever imagined I could be. I want women to know that they deserve a life of respect, dignity and freedom—that it's never too late to speak up. It infuriates me that many women are expected to uphold their family's honour, yet they don't have any themselves.

Last April, I called my ex. I wanted to help him repair his relationship with our older daughter. It had been four years since we had spoken in person. I decided to meet with him. Despite everything, I believed that my girls deserved to have their father in their lives. I sat in a coffee shop at Eglinton and Creditview Road, desperately hoping that I was no longer scared of him.

I saw him walking across the parking lot and waited for an avalanche of fear to hit me. It never came. Sitting across from me, he was just another person. To my surprise, he apologized.

"I cannot believe after everything that you're still willing to help me repair my relationship with our kids," he said.

That day in the coffee shop, I finally felt free.

A few weeks ago, I lay in bed cuddling with my youngest daughter. Every night, we snuggle for ten minutes before she goes to bed, just the two of us, unpacking the day.

Out of the blue, she said, "Mom, I think Daddy's family picked you because you were only sixteen. They thought you were just going to do whatever they told you to do and they'd be able to make you into whoever they wanted you to be." And then she paused. "Man," she said. "They picked the wrong girl."

# As Women Scorned

**LAUREN MCKEON**

---

Last year, my husband abruptly left me for another woman—moving across the country and very publicly crafting a new life that didn't include me. Predictably, I was devastated.

He'd confessed he was in love with someone else the day after he'd returned from a too-long business trip. I've since tried to erase that scene from my mind, but it's stubbornly stuck, saved somewhere in the coils of my brain for whenever I want to recall it, which isn't often. Him, mostly naked because we've just had welcome-back sex, hugging a pillow I've had since university. His arms have always struck me as too short, like a T. Rex, pinned absurdly on a big, barrel-chested body. This is what I remember with Technicolor clarity: that his arms seemed all wrong. His face wasn't right either: pulled down at the corners, like a fish caught on a hook, an old woman's ear heavy with jewellery, a broken ventriloquist's puppet.

Surely, it couldn't have been him talking.

The next day, my body was the Grand Canyon, vast and hollowed out. My mind obsessed over a dead narrative: wife, mother. Me, who was never quite sure I wanted to be a wife. Me, who hadn't decided whether or not I wanted children. Me, undone. *With him gone, who am I? With him gone, I'll never have a baby. With him gone.* As if I'd wanted one. As if he was my only chance to become whatever I was supposed to be.

Maybe I wasn't the canyon. Maybe I was the hole in the sandbox from Robert Munsch's *Murmel, Murmel, Murmel*, only impossibly deeper and assuredly empty. No babies here. No story. No life. *Gone. Gone. Gone.* Maybe I was both. Or maybe I was a thunderstorm—loudly inconsolable, pelting tears, taking up more space than I ever had before.

The day after that one, I bought new pillows.

For a week, my parents and my friends watched as I pushed food around my plate, creating mountains and rivers and roads, a kid again. They brought me takeout, wine, water, chocolate, placed it before me, said nothing as it piled up like offerings before a terrible god, untouched. They nodded, satisfied, if I ate one bite. Their bodies made cradles, willing me to sleep. I started to imagine this would go on forever. That I would wake up every morning feeling more feelings than one person could possibly contain. That I would wake up feeling nothing for the rest of my life. That I would never pull my shit together. This was the new me—at least until I was ready for the prescribed haircut and killer makeover.

I mean, that's what happens in the movies.

Yet, there's something about a shocking and cruel separation that forces you to confront the ugliness of a marriage. I was, in those first weeks, desperate for my husband to stay, madly googling marriage crisis counsellors. I even cajoled him into calling one and booking an appointment. But as I stared at the step-by-step explainer of my upcoming session, thrumming with urgent hope that it would make him want me again, I started to wonder what my life would look like if I succeeded and saved my marriage. Would I be saving myself, too?

I'd forgiven him before. This was *never supposed to happen again* infinite times. I was so scared to confront it, the truth. If we worked through this latest infidelity, I knew the exquisite, loving calm would turn eventually, and all at once—another betrayal topsy-turvying my world, just like it had so many times before. And every time I forgave him, I ate the responsibility for my pain like a glutton, until it was all I could taste.

In the 1950s, a counsellor at the American Institute of Family Relations told a woman, after her husband had an affair, that it was her fault. Far from uncommon, this was accepted wisdom. "We have found in our experience," the counsellor admonished, "that when a husband leaves his home, he may be seeking refuge from an unpleasant environment." He (I'm just assuming the counsellor was a he) went on: "Could you have stressed your contribution to your marriage in such a manner to have belittled the part he has played and thus made him uncomfortable in his presence?" In other words: What have you done wrong? Half a century on, it's a question we're still supposed to ponder, possibly forever. How archaic.

How many ways would I have to contort to fit until nobody would ever recognize me, least of all myself? I was already like a wacky Picasso. Soon I wouldn't even resemble a person-shape. But here was my chance to stop it. It was terrible and difficult and I didn't want to confront it, but there it was: my divorce could save me.

I called off our marriage intervention. And suddenly my grief vaporized. Relief settled into place. I realized I was grieving something that didn't deserve much sadness. I was, if you look at it another way, crying over the death of that jerk-y uncle nobody really liked anyway. When somebody dies, we eulogize the good parts and forget the rest. It's what we're expected to do. But what happens when we flip the playbook? When we admit, yeah, dear ol' Uncle Bob was actually a dear ol' jackass? Like, good riddance, Bob. Good riddance, marriage.

The buoyancy was so alarming that I fearfully asked my therapist whether there was something wrong with me. I worried I'd misplaced my emotions without realizing it, like I was always doing with my house keys or my favourite red lipstick. Maybe I'd unintentionally killed them like every plant I'd ever owned. Ever. She looked at me, fretful, and wisely, gently suggested that maybe my marriage wasn't as happy as I'd always pretended.

After nearly eight years together, this last betrayal allowed me to finally excavate the truths of my relationship. Step by steady step, I began to shed my "wife" identity. Let me tell you, some days I wish I could have done it earlier, on my own. Most days, though, I'm just thankful that I did it at all. Because I realized I had that gnawing question all wrong. It wasn't, "With him gone, who am I?" But a small edit: "With him gone, who can I be?"

After the first month or so, I could honestly answer "I'm good" to anyone who asked, eyes full of concern like I'd explode on them in bitterness. But I didn't feel bitter. Instead, I felt happy. Shaky, sure. But hopeful. In charge. I wasn't putting on a brave face. I wasn't fakin' it 'til I was makin' it. For the first time in a very long time, I actually felt brave. Except, nobody believed me.

As women scorned, we're expected to follow a certain narrative when our husbands leave us, especially when they do so dramatically: despair, bitterness, obsessiveness, self-blame, loss of self worth, maybe drinking and one-night rebounds. Lots of ice cream. There are even rules about how long it should take us to get over divorce—and it's a depressingly long time, by the way. Experts say it takes about two years to recover from emotional trauma, such as a break-up or divorce. And it can take even more time to restructure our lives and be ready to date again. I've heard that we should cleave the length of our relationship in half; the result is an expected grieving period. It doesn't matter how wonderful or awful our marriages were: being un-wifed is supposed to be the worst thing that ever happened to us as adult women, and society expects us to act accordingly. If we don't, we're lying. We're cold. We're in denial. We're unnatural.

Nearly every single person I spoke to about my post-relationship optimism—from those who knew far too much detail about my dead marriage to those who knew nothing at all—would fix me with a judge's stare: *Are you sure? It's okay to be sad. YOUR MARRIAGE ENDED, FOR GOD'S SAKE!*

My grief never made them uncomfortable, but my happiness did. Everywhere I turned, people prodded me for signs of depression and anger, sure it must lurk somewhere inside me. If I seemed all right, they surmised, I was feigning it. My parents refused to take down my wedding photos, protesting that it was okay to remember how beautiful I looked on "my happy day."

When I hesitantly mentioned my therapist's push for me to move on, I was sure I'd swallowed a malfunctioning Babel fish—because everyone reacted as if I'd told them I wanted to buy a velour track suit and maybe go coffin shopping. *But you can't! It's too soon! The horror!* Even my lawyer seemed surprised that my only instructions were to untether me, ASAP.

The same week I signed my settlement papers, I watched my first divorce movie—a classic of the genre, *The First Wives Club*. I adore Goldie Hawn and Bette Midler. Ditto Diane Keaton. I aspire to pull off menswear as spectacularly as she does. But I absolutely hated the movie. It's all the acceptable women's divorce narratives tumbled into 103 minutes. The wives exact gleeful revenge and viewers are meant to believe it's fantasy fulfilment for every jilted woman.

We're sold a story of empowerment. Underneath, though, it's the same dynamics: women who are defined by their relationship to men. Their exes dictate their weaknesses, that's obvious, but also their strengths, less obvious. Interests, personalities, quirks—it's all based on how they interact, or not, with the dudes in their lives. Even Keaton's daughter, who is a lesbian, has only one motivation as a character: disgust for her philandering dad.

At the end of the movie, we're given some feminist scraps: the women blackmail their ex-hubbies into paying for an abused women's shelter. It's named after their friend who catapulted off her balcony when her own husband announced his decision to leave her for a younger woman (this is presented as a tragic but logical response to such news). Bread crumbs of freedom.

We also learn a bunch of other things we're supposed to be happy about. Midler's character is on her way to reconciling with her ex-husband, a man who left her for a young blonde, is a criminal and possesses no redeeming qualities whatsoever. Hawn's character is dating an unknown younger actor (oooh, stereotype reversal!) and has therefore, apparently, re-established her worth as an attractive commodity. Keaton fares the best of them all, I think. Once meek, she finds her voice, buys out her husband's company (for revenge, not because she wants a career) and finds independence doing ... well, I'm not sure what exactly. It's unclear. But something.

In the months following my separation, well-intentioned friends encouraged a single-gal lifestyle scripted by Hollywood. They wanted me to sleep my way through Toronto. Go out for cosmos. Debut bangs. Buy racy lingerie. Use physical reinvention and casual sex as a salve. Even people I didn't know very well seemed dismayed when I refused to google my erstwhile husband's new girlfriend. Confusion abounded that I knew nothing about her and didn't want to, not what she looked like, not even her name. Nobody believed that I didn't track his every move—that I'd let him slip away so easily, water off oil.

Of course, as they all knew, I'm a journalist. I could have found out. I don't think anybody would have been horrified if I'd actually done something truly alarming, like stalking them or wasting entire days bawling over their Facebook photos. When I shrugged off speculation on his new life, more than one friend called me "enlightened." But the looks on their faces said "sadly in denial." Or, perhaps, "batshit crazy." When I seemed too blasé, they peppered me with fear. I was newly home alone, but since my ex refused to turn in his house key to our rented apartment and I couldn't legally change the locks, I was advised to sleep with a chair wedged under my front door. If I didn't call a friend or family member every night to confirm my safety and general vitality, they phoned non-stop until I picked up. Once, buried under a deluge of deadlines, I forgot to answer a friend's text and received a panicked email asking if my phone had been "compromised."

I mean, sure, I could have done a lot of things. I could have plotted revenge, called in debts, driven him out of town, hacked his email. I could have told everyone every detail. I could have executed elaborate plans to win him back, professed love, performed grief as a spectacle. I could have gone to court, haggled over every penny, nailed him to the wall. I could have burned every picture, thrown out every knick-knack, left closets full of plaid shirts on the porch. Turned the debris of my marriage out for everybody to see. How exhausting.

I could have let it all consume me, made my divorce everything. I *could* have. It seemed to be what everyone expected: an unfurling of my sanity for the prescribed seventeen months and twenty-six days. But I didn't want to.

It's okay to be sad when a marriage ends. I'm not advocating that women embrace politeness, Stepford smiles and funhouse cheer. It's okay to be angry. We need more angry women. The world would be a better place, I think, if more women expressed their rage.

I was angry about so many things—just not the things everyone seemed to expect. I was angry that I had become so fearful. I was angry that I had fit myself into smaller and smaller boxes, until I had become a speck of a person. I was angry that it had been so easy to make me feel discarded. I was angry that it was so normal to meet women like me—women whose identities had become unmoored when their husbands traded in one life for another. I was angry that, as feminists, we'd won the right to divorce, but not the right to be happy about it. That, to move forward, everyone seemed to expect us to erase (or eviscerate) our exes, when really we just need to fill ourselves in.

I can think of a bazillion better things to do with my time than debating what my husband's affair says about my worth. It's time we start forging a new narrative that allows women to claim power over their identities, and their grief. I didn't initiate my divorce (though it's worth mentioning women initiate nearly 70 percent of divorces). It's true that I didn't want it. But as strange as it sounds to many people, I'm happy it happened. When my divorce papers arrive in the mail next year, I'll sign them with a champagne toast. I'm already dreaming about it—a moment that's Christmas and my birthday and the first day of spring, but somehow better. It could be a scene from a movie.

# Death

# Are You Still Married?

## LESLEY BUXTON

"Are you still married?" the customer asks.

I look up from her bill and glance toward my section on the patio, hoping to find an excuse to leave. Nobody needs me. I'm stuck.

This customer and I share an unwanted and one-sided intimacy. For the last months of my sixteen-year-old daughter India's life, this customer was our social worker. Her job was to navigate us through the medical system. She was neither exceptionally good at her job nor bad. This is the first time I've seen her since my daughter died ten months ago and I can't remember her name.

Finally I say, "Yes, we're very nice to each other."

"That's good. Most couples blame each other."

"But it's not his fault. Why would I blame him?"

"They just do," she says.

And with that she's gone, unaware of how her question will follow me all night long, as I refill water jugs, scrape plates and polish silverware. Later it will strike me as ironic that even this woman, who makes her living as a voice for the vulnerable, has no idea how to treat me.

This is not the only time I'll be asked this. In the months that follow I will grow to resent this question, even when it comes from a close friend. Often, I will have an urge to ask the question back as a kind of admonishment. Or, perhaps, if I'm honest, out of spite.

I never do. Partly as I don't have the energy, and partly as I understand that this question is simply a fumbling attempt at connection. A well-meaning but not necessarily well-thought-out effort to be empathetic. Even so, I find myself speculating about why people feel they can be so presumptuous. If I'd lost a leg, would they ask if I expected to lose the other?

When I say that my husband, Mark, and I are fine, the response is invariably the same: *Oh, you're so lucky to have each other.* At this point, I sometimes have to stifle a laugh. Usually I take a deep breath and clamp my mouth shut. Yeah, we're really lucky, I think, so bloody lucky. Clearly they aren't thinking about the fact our only child died of a neurodegenerative disease so rare that at present she's its only casualty.

I'm afraid eventually I won't be able to contain myself. I'll be transformed like the bitter sister in the fairy tale *Diamonds and Toads*, and all these pent-up thoughts will drop from my mouth in the shape of snakes. I don't want this to happen. I've seen enough of life's cruelties to know I don't want to perpetuate them.

Nobody ever asked if we were still married when Mark and I were caring full-time for a dying teenager—a time when we were sleep-deprived, financially strapped and terrified. During those months, the days were filled with appointments with a small army of medical professionals from the local provincial health organization, the CLSC, most of whom treated India as an illness rather than a teenage girl. The only exception was the massage therapist, whose arrival was always followed by laughter. In addition, India had two caregivers: one, we considered family and trusted implicitly; the other always made sure to feed us.

At night, alone, we lived under siege, taking turns sleeping in India's room, attempting to reassure her when the hallucinations took hold. When she'd wake up screaming, petrified of the giant cockroaches she believed were going to kill her.

As we adapted to the new realities of our lives, we developed an in-the-trenches kind of attitude. As the writer and Vietnam veteran Tim O'Brien wrote in *The Things They Carried*, "War is hell, but that's not the half of it, because war is also mystery and terror and adventure and courage and discovery and holiness and pity and despair and longing and love."

There were times I hated Mark. Nights, mostly, when it was my turn to stay with India, and I was so tired and anxious, I thought I'd vomit. When all I wanted was for him to rescue me. Rationally, I understood he couldn't. He was just as besieged. How could he not be? Watching our daughter suffer night after night was like watching her repeatedly be raped.

Our relationship changed; we became war comrades. In our moments alone, we shared cigarettes, Scotch, even laughter. But our jokes are different now. Cynical and dark, evidence of what we've lost. I never blamed Mark for what was happening. We shared an intrinsic, silent agreement that if either of us could take India's place, we would.

As a bereaved mother—particularly in a case like mine, where the facts were all over the local and national media—you become public property. A story. "Will they or won't they survive?" I imagine acquaintances asking each other over cups of coffee. As if suddenly my marital status has taken on the importance of the latest Hollywood breakup. Mostly this doesn't bother me. Grief has shifted my priorities. But it's odd to think the same people who wince when I say my daughter's name are comfortable asking about my marriage.

I suspect the interest in my love life stems from the common misconception that the death of a child frequently signals the death of a marriage, a notion that many a made-for-TV movie has nurtured. A 2006 survey conducted for the Compassionate Friends, a society devoted to the support of bereaved parents, "showed a divorce rate among bereaved parents of only 12 percent ... [and] suggests that the 70 percent, 80 percent, and 90 percent divorce rates often quoted as fact by professionals and in the media are completely inaccurate. The figures indicate that the death of a child actually appears to draw bereaved parents together as they travel life's grief journey."

Though I hate the term "grief journey" and the image it provokes, I admit Mark and I are so in sync in our grief that my bad days frequently shadow his. Still, I find statements like "You must be a comfort to each other" naive, merely proof of how misinformed our society is. It's beyond our capabilities to comfort each other. There's nothing I can say that will make it better and he knows it. Our emotions are exhausted. In order to survive we must portion out what remains frugally.

In the early months of grief, I would lie in bed next to Mark contemplating suicide, knowing he was doing the same. Sometimes I would sob and he would hold me. Sometimes it was the other way around.

During this period, I used to wish Mark had a lover. When I pictured her, she was a compilation of a Dutch nurse I'd known at summer camp and Uschi Digard, the Swedish star of Russ Meyer's soft-porn films. An earth goddess, with boundless empathy, a strong embrace and a raw sensuality. I didn't go so far as to envision them having sex. Though the idea of that wouldn't have bothered me. At fifty, I appreciate that people have sex for many different reasons, grief being one of them.

This surrogate lover would provide Mark with what I couldn't. Endless nurturing and energy. A warm place for him to lay his head. I'd never been good at those things to begin with, but now it was worse. I felt as if my heart had shrunk. It was like an old cashmere sweater accidentally thrown in the dryer, battered and small. And no amount of pulling would change that.

Recently I told Mark about this.

"I never wished you had a boyfriend," he said.

"I didn't think so," I said with a smile.

"But that's what I would have wanted then. Just to lie in bed and be held."

For a while I felt guilty about these thoughts. In retrospect I no longer do. I've learned enough about the character of grief to know it can't be trusted. It's as unpredictable as a teenage girl. One moment I can't figure out how I will survive the day without India, the next I'm daydreaming that I'm living in Mexico. Loss has trained me to look at people's intentions. When I imagined the surrogate lover I wasn't being cruel. I simply wanted Mark to have what he needed.

I love Mark, but there are days I'd like to run away. Watching him grieve hurts. It's like when India was learning to walk and she'd stumble and injure herself. As much as I wanted to protect her, I couldn't stop her from falling.

When I told my grief counsellor I wanted to run away, she said the feeling was probably linked to how I dealt with past traumas. Later she told me she imagined if I was alone, I might travel to the East, volunteer at an orphanage or school. She could see me mothering the children. She said she knew I'd been a good mother and that I still had a lot of love to give.

When she said this I believed her. In mothering my child I'd discovered the best of myself. I loved India in a way I'd never loved anyone else, fearlessly and without reservation. With her death, I'd lost the person I'd become because of her. I wondered if the urge to run was instinctual, an attempt at preserving that fraction of myself that remained.

Sometimes I allow myself to think what it would've been like if Mark or I had died instead. I've never wished it had been him over her. But if I did, I don't believe he would have blamed me. It would've been easier if it had been one of us. We've lived big lives: travelled, made art, loved, lost.

Now and then when I imagine Mark and India living without me, I see them driving on a long curving piece of highway. The windows are open and the music is blaring. India is singing or laughing, maybe at something I once said. In this scenario, they are moving forward. They are sad but intact.

There's a saying I keep coming across on the internet grief sites, and it's one of the few I believe: "When a parent dies, you lose your past; but when a child dies, you lose your future." I'm not sure of its origins. But I'm certain it's by a bereaved parent.

What that saying fails to mention, though, is that bereaved parents lose both the past and the future. Every good memory is enveloped in pain. I can't think about the day India was born without remembering the day she died. Even my wedding is shrouded. I was five months pregnant when we got married.

I no longer worry about the future. Like a reformed alcoholic craving a drink, I survive by breaking the hours into minutes and distracting myself with plans. A road trip with Mark, house hunting, a good movie.

While I was writing this, I worried that some of what I wrote might hurt Mark's feelings.

"Write it all down—everything," he said. "People need to know."

India looked like Mark. She had his dimples, green eyes and wide smile. Occasionally I find myself studying him in order to catch a glimpse of her.

This is not comforting. It's more a reminder of what was. One of the cruelties of my situation is that I still look for proof that it really happened. That I really did have a daughter who died. Mark is evidence of that chapter of my life. This links us. It's what stops me from running when it gets too hard. Like all lovers, I'd like to believe Mark and I will be together forever. But my personal history has demonstrated life is anything but predictable. Still, no matter what, I believe we are united in our burden. This story of grief we share.

# The End of a Marriage

## DONNA BESEL

---

I will never forget the howl.

My husband was supposed to pick up the kids. He was late. I called a friend and arranged for her to call my husband's sister and let her know that he had not showed up for his scheduled time with our children. I did not want to speak to anyone in his family; they had threatened to report me to the police if I contacted them. They did not want me telling them, or anyone else, that my husband had suffered a serious mental-health breakdown.

Despite the darkness, RCMP officers found him hanging in the warm-up shelter at the local cross-country ski trails. The female officer, a ringette team-mate of mine for several years, arrived at our home around 1:30 a.m. She explained the details and listened to me until my friend Jeanne arrived.

I could not stop crying. Jeanne sat holding my head in her lap. She stayed with me until my sister and her husband drove to our house, around 6:00 a.m. After they arrived, I faced the most difficult task in my life—telling my son and daughter that their father had killed himself.

Before Jeanne left, she said, "I'll need to do some body work with your kids."

About three weeks after the suicide, she brought her portable massage table to our house and set it up in the living room. She put a CD into the stereo. The repetitive notes of Pachelbel's Canon filled the air with bird calls and running water playing in the background. My son was nine years old. He had never had a massage, but I had been seeing Jeanne in her capacity as a professional masseuse for years. He agreed to the treatment.

We had no air conditioning so it was warm in the living room. I pulled down the window shades to block the morning heat. Then my fifteen-year-old daughter and I excused ourselves and went to the downstairs bedroom to give Jeanne privacy while she worked with my son. About twenty minutes later, we heard the howl, long and low and full of pain, like a wolf with its leg caught in a trap, trying to chew its own limb off. I could not believe a child of his age could utter such loud, primal sadness. My daughter and I did not know what to do. The howl continued. We decided to go upstairs. Treading as softly as possible, we went into the living room and watched.

Jeanne shook her head ever so slightly and kept her palms on my son. She held one hand under his neck, supporting his head, and the other on his chest. He was fully clothed. We sat down on the couch, in the darkened room, and waited for the howl to end.

I remember thinking, *If we all start to howl, we will never stop.*

Not wanting to break the outpouring of grief bursting from my son's small body, I sobbed quietly. Then my daughter started to cry; I held her in my arms.

If I am going to write about the end of the marriage, I need to write about its beginning. I met my future husband in high school. Until grade eight, I had attended a two-room school with the same teacher for seven years. Going to a bigger institution meant an hour-long ride on a tiny bus. I did not know anyone there except for the nine students from my isolated community, and two of those kids were my siblings.

The high school overwhelmed me, even though it had only two classes of each grade. After grade nine, students had to choose a track, either general studies or university entrance. My future husband and I scored well so we ended up in the same classes. He didn't talk much and he played lead guitar in a band. He stood out, as many of the guys in our high school were bikers and thugs. Almost every dance ended with a drunken fight. I got to know him better in grades eleven and twelve when our class participated in year-end canoe expeditions that I helped organize. I already had the idea in my head that the way a person handled a four-day canoe trip was a good gauge of character. On our first voyage, after a sunny start, the temperature dropped and it rained for three days, soaking tents, clothing and sleeping bags. My future husband did not whine or grumble.

On our second trip, I asked him to be my escort for grad. This momentous night did not go well, as I got quite drunk. And despite his role in the popular local band, he did not like to dance. After the rough start, we dated on and off through university, drifting apart when he was deep into his studies at law school. I took teacher training at a different university and then started working in a rural school.

After a few years teaching, I left my job to travel in Europe. When I returned, we got engaged. I knew my future husband had trouble with intimacy, but three factors influenced me. First, ever since I was six years old, my father told me that no man would want to marry me. I believe he did this because I fought back against his physical and sexual abuse. Second, I had ten siblings and we were always poor, especially after my mother died. My new stepmother insisted a lawyer was a good catch. Third, given my encounters with my predatory father, I liked that my future husband was not sexually aggressive. I thought that I had enough experience for both of us and could help him enjoy his body. But he never grew comfortable with sex. Many times, early in the marriage, I suggested counselling.

I got pregnant and, a few years later, got pregnant again. I thought I could handle his lack of interest and focus on the kids. When our daughter was six, we built our new home. I had thought about its layout for years, ever since we erected our first cottage, just eight hundred square feet in size. I designed the second house to accommodate the law office and supervised the build. It served our family well. We had a small beach on the river with a dock for swimming and boating. We had ten acres of pasture with a shed for our riding horses. I helped in the home-based business and did the yardwork. However, despite the beautiful setting and two healthy children and a growing practice, my husband remained stoic and silent, reluctant to express joy or interact with the kids.

Three years prior to my husband's mental-health crisis, our family faced a disturbing trauma. After disclosures from two of my sisters, the RCMP charged my father for the sexual assault of me and four sisters. My husband had experienced a similar dysfunctional family history. He had talked to me about also growing up in a home where there was physical abuse, alcoholism and plenty of denial. He told me that his father had sexually assaulted his two sisters and exposed himself to young girls, and that his family was scared that I might be able to have his father charged. We both knew that I could not report these crimes to the police. It would be hearsay.

Despite the mounting tensions, he supported me through the three and a half years and twenty-six court delays it took to bring my father to trial. Once again, I encouraged him to seek counselling for himself.

"We can't have both of us in crisis," he said.

In the summer before his death, his family persuaded him to pretend that he wanted to take our kids camping without me for the August long weekend. My daughter refused to go. She suspected it might end up a boring disaster. He never took holidays. In summers, he'd say, "I'm too busy." In winters, he'd say, "I'm not busy enough; we don't have money." I was the parent who organized family outings, and as the kids got older I had started taking them on longer vacations by myself, tired of waiting for my husband to clear his schedule. My son jumped at the invitation; he looked forward to time alone with his dad. My husband threw the camping gear into our van and raced out of our yard. Thirty minutes later, his brother showed up at our door. He did not accept my invitation to come inside for coffee. Instead, he handed me a fat legal envelope. Then he spun around on the sidewalk and peeled his truck out of our yard, just like my husband had done.

I had to read and reread the documents in the envelope a few times before I understood what they meant. My husband had filed for divorce and he expected me to show up in court two days after the long weekend. I found out later that he had dreamed up this plan in cahoots with several colleagues.

At that exact moment, our lives came untethered from so-called "normal" existence and entered the bizarre. Despite my shock and my daughter's distress, I started a frantic search for a family law specialist. I hesitated to ask attorneys I knew, fearing they might be colluding with my husband. From a fluke recommendation, I found one who agreed to work for me. Even though it was a holiday weekend, she could start right away. Four days later, we appeared before a judge.

My husband was not in the courtroom. He was requesting custody of the kids and my immediate exit from our home. It appeared that he envisioned returning from his "camping trip" and carrying on as if nothing had happened. My lawyer asked for more time to respond to the divorce petition's allegations. The judge agreed to allow her until August 20. This gave us a couple of weeks to prepare a rebuttal, but the judge refused to order my husband to bring our son home.

In the next two weeks, my lawyer managed to contact seven people who agreed to write affidavits attesting to my character and child-rearing abilities. During this time, I had a rotation of friends staying with me twenty-four hours a day. I don't remember sleeping.

Despite several attempts by my husband's relatives to get me arrested on various fabricated charges, I called my brother-in-law's house and asked them to tell me where my son was. They refused. I called the RCMP and told the officer about my husband taking our child under false pretenses.

"Well, a father can take his kid on a vacation," the officer said.

"That's what the judge told me. But I am worried about my husband's mental state. Our son needs to come home," I replied.

"Do you have a custody arrangement?"

"I thought I explained. He served me with divorce papers just a few days ago."

"We can't do anything. It's not kidnapping. You don't have an agreement."

Despite further entreaties, his position did not change. I wanted to go to my brother-in-law's house and yell at them. I wanted to break down the door and carry our son away. But I did not want to risk it. In another legal ploy, my husband had claimed that I planned to kill him and our children. He swore in his affidavit that dealing with childhood sexual abuse had made me dangerous and irrational. If I showed up at his brother's house and made a fuss, my husband would call the cops. And then he'd use my actions as proof in the looming legal conflict.

After a few days, my daughter called her grandmother.

"Oma, it's me," she said. "This situation isn't good for me, or my brother. Tell Dad to bring him home."

Her grandmother faked deafness. She asked again and again. "Who is calling?"

My daughter repeated her name and her reason for calling at least four times.

"I do not know any of these people," her grandmother said. Then she hung up.

Both of them had been speaking loudly; I overheard the entire conversation. My mind jumped to a vivid memory of a lesson from Sunday school, about Peter's three denials of Christ before the Romans crucified him.

The day after the August long weekend ended, clients started to show up. The first time, the visitor kept a finger on the office doorbell, determined to make someone appear. After a few minutes of buzzing, I went outside to greet them—a short, older woman, about sixty, and her tall husband. I'd seen them around town but didn't know their names.

"We came to see the lawyer," she said.

"He's not here."

"Where is he?" She assumed he had just stepped out. All of his clients knew he did not take holidays.

I hesitated. "I don't know."

They both stared for a half minute. "You don't?"

"That's right."

They got into their Audi and left. Like wildfire, stories about the runaway lawyer and the missing trust funds spread in our small community.

A couple of days later, one of the brother-in-law's sons drove into our yard in the Ford van that my husband had taken on his camping trip. The young man unlocked the office and started removing objects.

I came out of the house. "What are you doing?"

"My uncle needs this stuff," he said.

From what he was loading into the back of the van, it appeared that my husband planned to run his practice from a satellite location. I opened the rear door wider and lifted out a mechanic's tool box.

"I need this," I said. "He left me with the crappy car. It's falling apart."

He grabbed the box. Wrenches, ratchets and sockets spilled onto the parking lot. He knelt on the gravel and threw the tools back into the plastic case. It looked like he wanted to cry.

"Why are you doing this?" I asked.

"My dad told me to," he said, and then threw the box into the back and drove away.

The next day, my husband showed up and started loading objects into the van.

"Why are you doing this? When will you bring our son home?" I asked.

He stared at me. I had never seen such a flat, glazed expression. His eyes looked dead and vacant. He left without answering.

After this visit, I knew he must be staying at his brother's house. I dialed their number and the sister-in-law agreed to let me speak to our son.

He kept asking to come home. "I don't like Dad's brother yelling at me. His wife bosses me all the time. I don't know these people at all."

This was true; they rarely visited.

I cried and he cried. Someone grabbed the phone and hung up. The next day, I called again. The sister-in-law answered.

"This is not good. It's hurting both of them," I said.

"I agree. I have three kids."

"Okay, will you ask him to bring our son home? He's never been away for longer than an overnight sleepover."

"I can't."

"Why? It's your house, too."

"My husband said they have to stay with us."

"Can I speak to our son?"

"No, he cried too much the last time you talked to him." She hung up.

After this conversation, they did not answer my calls.

His family worked hard to slander me. Friends relayed what they'd heard: I stole my husband's money, abused our children, made false accusations about his mental state, had affairs with both men and women, slept all day and had never learned how to cook.

When my lawyer and I returned to court, in the third week of August, the judge instructed my husband to bring our son home, vacate the family dwelling and start paying spousal support. The judge also ordered my children to be questioned by the RCMP. My husband took our son to the local station. Another officer interviewed our daughter in our gazebo with a social worker present. She was a longtime friend. Both children refuted all allegations.

When the police dropped off our son late at night, I asked him about talking to the officers.

"They asked if you hurt me. I laughed and told them I had never even been spanked."

My husband had asked the judge to issue two restraining orders: I could not enter his office and I could not come near him. But the judge did not tell my husband to find a new place for his practice. This set up several logistical and emotional challenges. We never knew when he might appear. He started phoning our children and asking them to visit him in the office. They liked using his computer; it was the only one in our home. He also approached them at the bus pickup spot. Even on weekends, he returned to our home and went into his office and stayed late. Another problem, the small bathroom for his business was in the house. His clients rarely asked to use it. But, given the long hours he stayed in the office, he needed to go in there.

After a month, I asked my lawyer to help arrange a schedule for our children to be with their father. They did not like the randomness of his interactions. I had no idea where he was staying but this request meant he'd need to find a place to live.

"Having the office in our house is hard on everyone. And it's not good for his psychological health. Could you ask him to relocate?" I asked when we next appeared before the judge.

The judge looked at my husband, who had somehow mustered his calm, lawyer-face demeanour, and smiled. "Well, then you will settle sooner."

After this session, my husband began to stay in his office even later. At night, we often heard him crying. He started shoving contradictory notes under the door to his office. In some, he begged me to forgive so we could return to being married. In others, he threatened financial ruin: had I paid the car and house insurance, the hydro bill, the line of credit? Another concern: if the kids used the computer, when he was not there, they often ended up on sites he had not bothered to hide. During his long hours in his office, he was looking at porn. I called and told him this could not continue. He agreed to stop.

I wanted to be away from our house as much as possible so I took any substitute teaching job I could get. But on one day in the fall, I was home. As I was going out to clean up the garden, I heard him enter the small bathroom. After an hour or so, I rushed into the house to use this toilet; it was closer to the front door. He was still in there. The door bumped his knees; he reported me to the police for assault. Another day, he approached me when I was chopping wood. I threw the axe on the ground and ran.

Around Christmas, he started leaving suicide notes where I could find them. I contacted a friend to let his family know.

"They found out that he'd asked you to return to the marriage. They've stopped seeing him," she said.

I called the crisis line.

"The person with the suicidal ideations has to be the one to phone for help before we can intervene," the woman said.

I could not stop thinking one of us might discover his body at any moment. Several times, I spotted him, standing on the nearby bridge, gazing at the dark current where the ice never froze. One night, we came home late and found the van parked by our house. I looked into his office window. From the faint light of the moon, I saw him splayed on the floor, naked. I called his office and let the phone ring and ring. He got dressed and left.

In the next months, his actions grew more erratic. The kids dreaded their time with him and I dreaded seeing them go with him. He put off buying beds so they slept on mats. He did not know how to cook or what they liked to do. He often drove around with them for hours with no apparent destination, and then took them back to what they called "his smelly house." For ten months, he refused to move his office and refused to agree to a settlement. He kept writing suicide notes, begging for reconciliation and blaming me for his financial situation. On the long weekend in May, the kids found more pornographic websites on the computer.

I called him. "They can't keep seeing this shit. Those websites open up whenever they go on the computer."

"You're right," he said. "I'll take care of it."

These would be his last words. His phone was breaking up because he was on his way to the warm-up shelter.

On the morning after I told our kids about their father's death, members of his family appeared, accompanied by a young RCMP constable with a strong French accent. They entered the office and started rummaging through file cabinets and desks.

I invited the cop into our foyer. "You may not know this, but after a lawyer dies, the office can only be accessed by Law Society representatives. All files are confidential. My husband told me this many times."

He shrugged. "They have a key. They want to find his will."

"Last night, the female officer who informed me of his death locked up his office and reminded me to stay out."

The officer shrugged again.

"Please phone your superior," I said.

After this call, he attempted to remove my husband's relatives from the premises. They refused to leave until the executor, another lawyer, showed them the will. During the forty-minute wait, they stood in the yard and yelled and swore at me and the cop. My brother-in-law even tried to load up a fishing boat and some tools from the garage. I went back inside to comfort the kids; they were still crying. When the executor arrived with a copy of the will, he informed the relatives that our children were the sole beneficiaries.

After the suicide, I found out several disturbing facts. A couple of people took my husband to the hospital and tried to have him committed. I'm not sure who they were, but it was not his family. Right after he filed for divorce, he stopped seeing clients. His daybook had few appointments listed after that date. He applied for various jobs, some out of the province, but never accepted any of them. When the kids stayed over, he would let our daughter sleep late and our son watch cartoons while he would sit in a chair and sob.

Here's a short excerpt from one of his many suicide notes:

> I am hoping that my mind is sufficiently sound as I write this. How could I be when the situation is like it is? I continue to put you and our children through extreme stress. You deserve a better life; the children deserve a better life. You are entitled to one half of what we have. I know that. I can't deal with reality and get on with my life. It is not and has been not fair in any sense of the word. The best thing I ever did was to marry you. I will miss you so much— take good care of our precious children—I know you will.

As they say in recovery parlance, my children and I have "worked hard on our healing journey." At the time of the suicide, we lived an hour and half from the nearest city. At first, we visited a counsellor there, but the drive made it expensive and the timing made it difficult. After school, the kids needed to eat and we could not afford to keep dining out. Also, I could not expect counsellors to work late to accommodate our schedule.

A few months later, I arranged for a different counsellor to come to our house every couple of weeks. She picked up my son at school, and they walked and talked if the weather suited, and then she drove to our home and met with the whole family.

We joined support groups. My kids attended a once-a-week program for children who had lost a parent. It helped them, but they both noticed that other kids' parents died from cancer or car accidents or heart attacks. No suicides. The parents met while counsellors worked with the kids. In the adults' group, I also noticed that death from a physical ailment or accident was much more palatable than mental illness. After this experience, I joined a suicide bereavement support group. To this day, the facilitator remains a staunch ally.

Over the years, we had competent and caring counsellors. I spent thousands of dollars. My kids learned to talk about feelings. However, we could not overcome the torrent of aftershocks. My son, my daughter and I still struggle to get past the trauma.

And the howl goes on. We survived the suicide and now the pain is internalized. It is a low keening. It never goes away.

# Your Body Is a Lone Tree

## GINA LEOLA WOOLSEY

Imagine you're walking uphill to your chiropractic appointment and the entire right side of your body is complaining. *This is ridiculous*, you think, *I'm only forty-eight. I should still be able to walk up a bloody hill.*

You live in a glass and steel city by the sea. Mountains are visible from your living room wraparound windows. You have a fireplace, two bathrooms and a queen-sized bed. You've come so far.

The street you walk is lined with monumental deciduous trees. It's late November and the leaves form a kaleidoscope overhead. Tourists stand in the middle of the road, under the red-orange arch of branches, and point technology at this spectacle of nature. Cars move slowly. Drivers wait, displaying Canadian kindness, while the oblivious photographers shoot at time and light. A small traffic jam forms.

*Think of Thoreau*, you say to yourself. Imagine the cars are cows lowing in a field. A garbage truck is a horse-drawn carriage with a load of manure. There is still birdsong in your temperate climate. Low, fall sun shines in your eyes. Everything has a flare. It feels warm. This is the tonic.

A guy walking half a block behind hacks violently and spits on the sidewalk. You slip out of the wildness, back to worrying the bead of pain next to your spine. Try to logic out the knot under your right shoulder blade. *Did it start when he was diagnosed? No, it was long before that. When we moved in together, maybe?* Remember the spasm that exploded in your shoulder after a day of packing boxes. Your mother said the agony represented every other man you'd loved and left behind. She was wrong.

The knot is eleven years old now. The chiropractor drew up a four-month schedule of treatment over a year ago. You should have followed through, but there was always something else: school, business, illness. You remember the chiropractor holding the folder of papers with columns showing the percentages of your expected increase in pain-free mobility as a function of time. He didn't know about the ghost living under your shoulder blade when he populated your charts.

A year goes by so quickly. Weeks pass with the speed of days. It hits you only occasionally. You've become accustomed to existential despair piercing your everyday thoughts. You will be left alone. Your love will perform a heart-wrenching magic trick and disappear.

The speckled linoleum and calamine walls of institutional hallways bring tears to your eyes with little warning. After five years of regularly scheduled visits, you've developed environmental sensitivities.

"For how long?" You've managed this string of words at most appointments. The oncologists usually brushed it aside with a prognosis of double-digit years, or some form of data-poor ignorance. When they found the metastatic lesions in your husband's liver, the answer changed.

"On average, about a year."

Friends still insist on a miracle. It's exhausting. "We're all going to die," you assert, too loudly, when you're weary of the fallacy. *Please let it be painless*, is your mantra now.

*Think of Thoreau.* You wrench yourself from images of the end and throw back your head to see sky blue, hoping the tears will run back into your eye sockets. Light falls through black holes. Involuntary responses buck and you squint, spilling what you hoped to conceal.

Start again. Push everything down. Suffocate your guts. Your legs are heavy with the weight. Your feet are dead.

You're almost there. You have to pee. Two more blocks.

"Here for my weekly exorcism," you say to the chiropractor from your prone position. He chuckles. Your body is keeping secrets and you're here to root them out. Concentrate on relaxing. Replace obsessive thoughts of impending anguish with the practical truth of biology.

*"Every path but your own is the path of fate."*

The chiropractor explores your spine for hidden messages while your brain works on the nature of mortality. You've seen death before. Recounting the bodies is a talisman against the fear. Grandma's body looked tiny in the nursing home bed. On the final day of her life, she had looked like a bird embryo with her skeletal legs pulled up to her chest in fetal position. Her frail hand, with wax-paper skin showing blue veins, had gripped the rail of the bed, despite her unconscious state.

After she died and her body was stretched out under the sheet, only her nose and feet gave away her presence. You approached the bed to confirm, and your mother whipped back the cover, exposing dusty yellow skin, a gaping mouth. You felt relief. The pain was over.

"Turn over," the chiropractor says, then grasps your right foot with both of his hands. He gives the limb a sharp, short yank and the table drops away from the small of your back. Warmth washes through the sacroiliac joint and rushes down your leg to the cramp in your foot.

You remember interviewing a doctor in a morgue for a story you were writing. On the other side of a thick glass partition wall, a young man's body lay on an autopsy table. Death's presence was insistent and distracting. The body seemed to glow. You wanted to stare, but felt like a voyeur. The corpse was horribly beautiful, naked and contorted in rigor mortis on the silver platform. Blue eyes wide and glistening, crimson lips, the scruffy blond facial hair of a twentysomething male. His chest was open. The cut ends of white ribs jutted above the folds of dappled pink and rust-red flesh.

You looked away. Stainless steel fixtures lined the perimeter of the room—sinks, cadaver drawers, countertops. He had died in a single-vehicle accident. The body held the form of sitting behind the wheel. Fingertips and toes were missing. The skin faded from blush pink to bruised yellow at the extremities. You looked at the blue eyes again. The mouth open, the neck broken, like a bird felled by a pane of glass.

The chiropractor tells you your lower ribs have been pulled forward from shallow panic breathing. It happens when you sleep. He gently counsels you to allow for the natural space between exhale and the next, life-giving breath. You focus on the in and out, train your autopilot to be patient, but you know the problem is in your dreams. Breathing is a conscious act, but the heart has its own mind.

Stacked palms press and release the springy cage around your lungs. Heat climbs your neck and you drown in the visceral reaction. Tears-spit-snot erupt at the touch of a rib. Swallow and focus. Breathe. Pay this price to make the journey out of your head and back into your body. Answers are there, you're sure of it.

*Think of the forest.* Crowds of trees wave and rustle far overhead. They will always be wild. A lone tree on a city street is as wild as a tree lost among its kind on a mountainside. The river tumbles over rocks toward the ocean, roaring with the pleasure of the ride. Water and gravity push-pull the landscape. Their marriage creates a valley where life drinks, then washes away. A trail through the forest pulls you forward, unfurling toward a focal point, the family you will build together. *What ancient feet may have walked the same steps?* You were always headed here. This was always going to happen.

Someone laughs in the waiting room and pulls you back to your body and the memory of that broken boy. You left the autopsy suite in an altered state and stood with the pathologist for several minutes before the nurse entered. She unzipped a bag on the table to your left. You hadn't noticed the body in its thin, gauzy shroud. It did not glow or demand attention like the body of the young man with his vibrant, violent colours fighting against the blanching of death. The nurse used a dressmaker's cloth tape to measure the length of an arm, then let the pliable limb fall. It landed with a soft thump on the metal table. The deceased was dressed in a plaid shirt. The facial skin looked grey green, dusty and pale from where you stood, maybe six feet away. This man had lived to old age. Death felt at peace.

You turn over again, put your face in the paper-covered hole and lay your arms on the padded rests below. Relax. Breathe. One hand cups the ci vertebra at the base of your skull, his palm cradles your occiput. The other hand rests on your sacrum. He applies steady pressure and a slow, subtle untwisting of your spinal column. Untying. Unravelling. Relief.

The walk home is easier. Enjoy the fluidity of your joints, like the ache and pleasure of moving after long stillness. It's dark now. The leaf arch is a stained-glass ceiling, illuminated by the street lights above. Walk downhill, buoyant, like the water. From your vantage point, the sparkling city lies at your feet. The mountain range backdrop creates an ink-black line that slopes into the ocean.

You will be there at the end. You will wash him with love before and after. Embrace him even in death. Close the eyes that have watched you with awe and anticipation, their deep brown warmth fading away. Tie the mouth that consoled you in times of trouble and exalted you in triumph, the lips that kissed you softly. Fold the hands that were so warm, the arms that held you safe. The body is important and you won't forsake it, though fear clings to the back of your throat.

A car forces you to stop and wait while it speeds past your corner of the dark intersection. *Think of the Milky Way.* You look to the sky, hopeful. City lights obscure the universe. As a child, you lived in a town with one paved street. The edge of the galaxy had been a regular part of your nighttime world. It whispered *eternity* as a bedtime story. Insignificance felt like a precious truth. *"Heaven is under our feet as well as over our heads."* Go to the forest inside yourself. Find what you've buried there.

Your body is a lone tree and death is the sky of stars.

# Gifts

**ELISE PARTRIDGE**

*to Steve*

———————

Yes, there are souvenirs—
holiday photos
posed at the waterfall or lumpy
dolmens, a mussed
napkin with a chocolate blotch,
pink palm-tree keychain;
the race-day T-shirt; inevitable postcards:
gargoyles, pillars, groves,
Sea World with a draped walrus.

But words invaluable
as a monkish scrip
overlooked by Calvinists;
a detail that snagged
on a log in a stream;
scenes bubbling toward me
from reservoirs—
all my memory-skiff
offers, then sails back to mist,

will vanish. I leave
nothing of enviable worth;
no children; tureens of cracked
china (an aunt's).
Why shouldn't I drift off
like a lost balloon?
But you gave me another gift:
"I'll carry you in my heart
till my last day on earth."

# Celebration

# Valentine's Day

## BARRY DEMPSTER

To say, *I love you*, on Valentine's Day
is like leaping into the body wave
at a Blue Jays game or snapping a lighter
at a Springsteen concert. Safety in numbers,
economy-pack thrills. A whole day
to express your feelings, to tinker
with them in public like doodads.
Even engagement rings aren't out of place
at the greasy bottom of a Cracker Jack box.
Come on, be bold, get naked, candy
arrows quivering in your ass.

*I love you I love you I love you*, go
ballistic, say it until you get slapped.
Take her in your arms
and absolutely refuse to give her back.
Dip both hands in his pants and feel around
for pleased. This is a *Get Out of Jail Free*
day, a second toss of the dice. Some wild card
between Roll Santa in the Snow and
Hell, Let's Have a Party. Lust on one half
of the oyster shell, lifetime on the other,
one-liners swallowed whole.

It would be an honour to share
an orgasm with you, things you'd swear
weren't meant for twenty-first-century ears,
wish lists like badly translated de Sade.
For one day, you're legendary, heart
swelling purple, spelling out the syllables
of your most cherished fantasies. Go

ahead, arch that back, lift that breast,
Cupid with his gift bag spilling over.
One more time: *I love you*,
in oh so many crowded ways.

# On Anniversaries

## MANDY LEN CATRON

---

"Are you disappointed?" Mark asked as we heaped pineapple fried rice onto our plates. "Do you feel like this is not special enough?"

We sat at my kitchen table on a Sunday night eating Thai takeout. It was damp and cold on the evening of our first official anniversary, which meant that exactly twelve months earlier we'd decided to drop the pretense that our relationship was, primarily, a friendship. We deleted our OkCupid accounts.

Mark arrived in a properly ironed button-down but I was still wearing the T-shirt and leggings I'd put on for breakfast. I'd thought about changing before he arrived, but I hadn't actually done it.

"I guess I could've at least put on a pair of jeans," I said, reaching over him for the spring roll sauce.

"Nah," he said. "I still love you in yoga pants. I just feel like maybe I should've planned something nice."

"But why?" I pulled my knees to my chest and slid the plate toward me. "What's really the point of an anniversary anyway?" I asked. "To say we managed not to break up this year?"

"No. It's like: 'Hey, you're important to me. Let's celebrate this thing we created,'" he said.

It's not that I needed him to defend the idea of an anniversary to me, though I appreciated his willingness to do so. I spent the entirety of my last serious relationship advocating for special occasions: birthdays, holidays, anniversaries. Why couldn't we make a big deal out of things just this once, I asked. But my ex always resisted, sure that I was overly invested in occasions that had been manufactured by the greeting card industry.

Now I was the one avoiding the celebration and I wasn't sure why.

Maybe Mark and I had made a mistake choosing November 1 as the day of our anniversary. We'd spent the evening before on a brewery tour with friends. It's hard to fight the inertia of the growing dark and the Halloween hangover.

A year earlier, I'd gone straight from work to the dollar store across the street from my apartment where I bought a pair of Minnie Mouse ears. I threw on a polka-dot dress and painted my lips bright red. Ta-da: a costume. Mark showed up in a cowboy hat and a plaid shirt. I found two Pabst Blue

Ribbon beers languishing in the back of my refrigerator. "Where did these come from?" I asked.

"Let's take them," Mark said, and shoved them in his pockets as we left the house.

I'd known Mark a while—he was a student in a continuing studies class I taught a few years earlier—but we'd only recently started spending time together, going on hikes and to the climbing gym, grabbing coffee or walking my dog Roscoe. We had recently started kissing good night—just to sort of see how it felt—but we hadn't discussed its implications.

We headed to Commercial Drive for Vancouver's Parade of Lost Souls. We got cheap pizza and doused it with hot sauce and sat on the sidewalk to eat and admire the passing costumes.

"I've always loved Halloween," I said to Mark, "the way the regular world transforms for a night. It feels like anything could happen."

He wiped the grease off his hands with a napkin. "Maybe we should shotgun our beers," he said.

I laughed. But he was serious.

"Where?" I asked. "Here on the sidewalk?"

"What about under the SkyTrain?" he suggested, pointing to a shadowy area down the block.

"Okay. Why not?" I shrugged.

I hadn't shotgunned a beer since I was in college—over a decade earlier. Mark had never done it, but he liked the idea—and I liked that about him: his willingness to try. He would play any game, read any book, down any beer in any unseemly fashion.

"So you have to stab the bottom of the can with a key and poke a hole in it," I explained when we arrived at a poorly lit patch of grass. He readied his house keys. "Then you pop the top open and hold your mouth to the hole. It comes out fast so be ready."

Mark nodded and gave the can a stab but it didn't puncture. "Harder," I said. "Oh and watch out for my coat. I just got it back from the dry cleaners."

As I held a key to my can, I heard a crack and felt a wet spray on my hair and down my back.

"My coat!" I wailed, more amused than annoyed.

"Oh shit, I'm so sorry," Mark laughed and we downed our beers, then crushed the cans in the grass. (Before picking them up to recycle them, of course.)

The whole evening felt like that: effusive, giddy, like we were getting away with something.

Eventually we found friends and wandered along the parade route. When he reached over to hold my gloved hand, I felt like skipping. We went to a brewery and then out for late-night burgers. Somehow, sometime after midnight, everyone had gone and it was just the two of us at the back of a restaurant, glasses of bourbon icing on the table between us. He grabbed my hands and asked, in words I can no longer remember, about this, about us.

I admitted that I wasn't seeing anyone else. I had deleted my online dating profile. But still, I felt cautious. In the past I had always avoided dating friends. It just seemed that the stakes were too high. Because there would be no getting-to-know-you period; there would just be a relationship. And you had to be sure you wanted it—because if you didn't, you were suddenly left with nothing. It wasn't that I didn't want to start a relationship with Mark, it was just that being in an almost-relationship had its appeal—like a roller coaster's first slow crawl up the hill, simultaneously enthralling and safe. And, honestly, sometimes the anticipation is the best part of the whole ride.

But even I was getting tired of my curiosity.

"I totally love you," I confessed, "but I'm a little scared of the prospect of being *in love* with you." He squeezed my hands.

"I think I should write something about anniversaries," I told Mark the night of the Thai takeout the following November. "People don't really talk about how weird they are."

"Are you going to write about this?" he asked, glancing around at the Styrofoam containers of rice and curry, the paper napkins, the plastic bag.

"I think so," I said.

"Ugh." He slumped. "I knew I should've tried harder."

After dinner, we decided the evening felt too mundane, so I put on a dress and we headed down the street for cocktails and dessert.

It was a nice night. Still, I had never actually celebrated an anniversary before and I couldn't escape the feeling that there was something romantic I should be doing or saying. Over chocolate mousse I fretted that there was an appropriately sentimental note that the evening hadn't quite hit. I thought of that night on Commercial Drive the year before, a night which had felt so unpredictable, so full with possibility. Why couldn't we make this feel more like that?

Just a couple of months before our first anniversary Mark and I went on a road trip to California. I remember thinking, on the day we drove out of town, that by the end of it—after thirty days spent side by side in a car and a tent—we'd arrive back home in a state of total comfort, total ease together.

Instead, on our last night we stopped for enchiladas in Seattle and, somehow, by the time we crossed the border into Canada two hours later, we had broken up.

"I don't want to be in a relationship with someone who isn't sure what he wants," I said. I was thirty-four and worried about wasting time with a man who wasn't serious about me. On our first date, Mark admitted to having had a series of relationships that only lasted about a year. "Do that enough times and you realize the common denominator is you," he'd said. *Don't date this guy, Mandy*, I'd said to myself as I ordered a second and then a third beer. But I liked talking about books while we went climbing. I liked how all his friends seemed to admire him.

On our trip, though, I began to worry. Why was it we were spending every hour together but only feeling more distant as the trip wore on? I decided that if he had doubts, I wanted out. That night, I dropped him and all his gear in the alley behind his house. He stood awkwardly by the car as I pulled away.

It took me a week to realize that what I'd said wasn't true. I *did* want to be in a relationship with someone who wasn't sure about what he wanted—if that person was Mark. I wanted to be with Mark, doubts and all.

All of this was on my mind as we ate our Thai food a couple of months later: the tyranny of the timeline and all the risks involved in choosing to love someone. I wanted to say something meaningful about all this, but I couldn't figure out how.

Maybe I should've said something about how much I appreciate his willingness to try—how nice it is to spend my time with someone whose default response to my suggestions is an enthusiastic "Okay!" How this makes me feel brave when we're together. Or maybe I should've said something about how grateful I am for his unfailing kindness—even when we disagree, even when we almost break up. Knowing that he will be kind, that he is in fact kind to his core, is part of what has made the risk of love feel manageable to me. That's what I should've told him.

Instead we got into a debate about whether or not it's your job to make your partner happy.

"Definitely not," I said.

"But your happiness is important to me," he countered.

"I think our relationship is going well right now *because* I'm not trying to make you happy—because I've actually made a conscious effort to stop trying to please you."

I explained how I'd spent so much of my life trying to figure out what other people needed, what they wanted from me, who they wanted me to be. Especially when it comes to love.

"So much of the ritual of love is about pleasing," I said. "It's about performing the role of partner to someone else's exact specifications. I mean, isn't that why anniversaries are weird—because we are trying to perform the anniversary script? It's not like I don't want you to be happy. I do. I just don't want to lose myself in the process."

"I get what you're saying," he said. "But I still want you to be happy and I think I have some influence over that."

A friend of a friend is divorced and dating. Every time she hears about someone celebrating a milestone anniversary, she feels defeated. "I will never have that," she laments to my friend. She is nearing fifty and this has robbed her of hope. "Even if I met someone tomorrow, we would never get a fortieth anniversary."

At first I was puzzled by this, even a little annoyed. There are so many things a life can contain—who really needs a forty-year marriage? Isn't it the quality of the relationship—of all our relationships—that matters? If we are lucky, my best friend and I might make it to sixty years together. My sister and I could get to eighty! But what will these years mean if we haven't invested ourselves in them? And don't short relationships sometimes have profound impacts on our lives too: teachers and mentors, bunkmates at summer camps, flings in foreign countries, unexpected friendships that come and then go?

Part of my annoyance with anniversaries is the implication that it's the duration of a relationship that matters most. "How long have you guys been together?" we ask one another, as if a number tells us much at all about intimacy or investment. Mark and I have been together for three years now, and I sometimes worry that if we get married, which we consider from time to time, we will become counters, measuring our success in years: paper, cotton, leather, linen, wood, iron, wool. Will we make it to china? To silver? To ruby? I amuse myself imagining what sort of ruby I could possibly buy him. The internet suggests a vintage Bordeaux, or a cut-glass paperweight with a red heart inside. Are there glass-paperweight people inside us, just requiring a few more decades to emerge?

Yet surely it is no small feat to stay committed as the decades pile up. We act as if this is natural—that we should all desire one partner for all time and that that desire should be unwavering. But of course it isn't. Maybe there is value in the commitment itself, in sticking it out despite the worst of it. I have friends who almost ended relationships for any number of reasons—boredom, infidelity, everyday estrangement—but somehow, perhaps because of a fidelity to the institution itself, they stuck it out and are now glad they did.

My parents raised my sister and me to be the type of people who stuck things out. We were not allowed to quit sports teams mid-season or bail on a party we'd agreed to attend. We didn't play hooky from school or fake sick when we were well. I always thought that love went like this too. You dated around a bit and then you chose someone and you stuck it out—even it if was hard. Even *because* it was hard. Because the difficulty made it meaningful. Now that I am older, I'm less convinced that this kind of stubbornness always pays off.

But then I think of Mark, whom I already love so fiercely. And I think of all I know about him today that I didn't know a year ago, of all I might come to know in another three years—or in another thirty-seven, should we live that long.

Isn't there something kind of beautiful in the accumulation of that knowledge? Just this past summer, for example, I discovered that he'd never eaten corn nuts. Never even heard of them. He picked one up from a small dish on a restaurant table and popped it in his mouth. "What is this?" he marvelled, crunching it between his teeth and grabbing for another.

On her anniversary, my sister posted a series of wedding photos on Instagram. I responded with an eye-roll emoji.

Later she sent a link to a video of the ceremony to me and our mom and dad. "In case anyone wanted to watch!" she wrote, adding a laughing emoji. She knows she's ridiculous. She knows she sent us the video last year and the year before.

But I watch, every time. On the screen I see my hands fastening the back of her dress, adjusting her veil. I see my dad beaming as they walk, arm in arm, through the grass. I hear her voice crack with emotion as she begins her vows. And then I'm in tears at my desk, embarrassed by the fragility of my cynicism.

Of the two of us, I am the one who looks forward; I plan ahead and make to-do lists. But Casey is always looking back, remembering the past, celebrating it, making a big deal out of so many things because, to her, so many things are a big deal. She drinks the same wine out of the same glass every year on her birthday. She listens to the same songs in the same order (Willie Nelson, Kenny G, Nat King Cole) every Christmas morning. And she is always documenting these small traditions for me, sending pictures of the CD cases or the wine bottle or the many other rituals she's built into her life.

We don't fight often but when we do, this is what it's about. She wants to do things the way they've always been done. I want to try something new. She is a stick-it-out type. And so is her husband. They will have a ruby wedding and I will cry because it will be beautiful.

---

Now, Mark and I live together. My dog has become our dog. We own a car together and furniture. And we are about to sign a mortgage. When I bring up our anniversary, an embarrassed grin appears on Mark's face. He can't remember which day we celebrate it.

"It's in the fall ..." he says hesitantly, putting down his fork.

I smile.

"No, it is. It's in the fall." He picks up the fork again and stabs his salad, confident now.

"It's November 1." I remind him of the night on Commercial Drive, the parade, the PBRs.

"Oh yeah," he says fondly.

"Doesn't it bother you that I remember this stuff and you don't?" I ask. "It's not like I'm trying to do this record keeping. It's not like I'm more invested in this than you are—or maybe I am. I don't know. I just feel like years of gendered programming have made us like this."

He shrugs off this suggestion. He's just bad at dates, he says. But am I inherently good at dates? Or have I been raised to be attentive to them, as so many women are? The birthdates of friends from elementary school are still locked in my brain. I am a record keeper, a counter even if I don't want to be.

"The problem with anniversaries," Mark says, "is that you feel a lot of pressure to do things right."

"Pressure from whom?" I ask. "Me?"

"No. You know," he says, gesturing vaguely toward the window, "society."

He pulls out his phone and puts November 1 in his calendar. "Repeat yearly," he confirms as he adjusts the settings.

Even though he can't remember the day, the anniversary is important to him. Last year—our second anniversary—he bought me flowers and grabbed the check for our fancy French dinner.

I didn't want to be so pleased by such a conventional, gendered approach to anniversary celebration, but I was. If I'm honest, I was delighted.

I used to believe that romantic conventions were just poor substitutes for love, gestures that we offer in place of actual care or kindness. I guess I believed this because I had never received a bouquet of flowers, because I had seen too many movies where the smarmy husband hides his infidelity with roses.

But Mark's bouquet didn't feel like a substitute, it felt like a signifier, a sign that he was willing to make a big deal out of things. A reminder that love, when it's sincere, is a big deal. It's worth celebrating.

I must've taken twenty pictures of the flowers as they bloomed and then wilted, raining their petals all over the kitchen table.

I have read that most of us harbour the assumption that, even though we've changed in the past, who we are today is who we will always be. "When a forty-year-old looks backward, they say, 'I've changed a lot in terms of my personality, in terms of my values, in terms of my preferences,'" says psychologist Dan Gilbert. "But when thirty-year-olds look forward, they say, 'I don't expect to change a lot on any of those dimensions.'" Our identities feel fixed, but science says we are always becoming new versions of ourselves, shedding our values with our skin cells.

I suppose we go into committed relationships the same way, blind to the possibility that we—or our partners—will change in any substantial way, dizzy with hope and presumption and so intoxicated by new love that it is easy to believe tomorrow will look more or less like today, that love will always buoy us.

Anniversaries are the closest thing we have to implying that love can be measured—in years or in gifts and celebrations. They contain all of our ideas about what a relationship should look like at one year or five years or fifty—all the things you should have done, all the feelings you should feel.

I've always thought anniversaries did nothing but sustain the illusion that love could be made permanent. But maybe they are also a way of looking backward and remembering that nothing is permanent, that change is inevitable. Maybe an anniversary is not about marking the passage of time, but instead appreciating that the time has been passed together. Maybe my sister has gotten this right.

I could not have known that the night of the Halloween parade and the PBRs and the Minnie Mouse ears contained the awful car ride from Seattle. Or that the car ride contained the night of the yoga pants and the Thai takeout. There was also the night of my bike accident. The night we decided to live together, and the night, weeks later, when Mark unpacked the last box. There were all the nights we had nothing to cook and no one wanted to go to the grocery store. And one awful evening spent in the animal ER after the dog found a cannabis cookie on the sidewalk. There was, just a few months ago, a warm July evening spent kissing behind the observatory until a security guard walked by with his flashlight and we straightened our clothes and got back on our bikes. I cannot see into the future with Mark, or guarantee there is a future at all, but I can celebrate this accumulation of nights. Nights like nesting dolls, each contained in the first, each inconceivable from the start, stacking up to something unmeasurable, something bigger than the both of us.

# Late Love Song, with an Orange: A Cento

## MAUREEN HYNES

We who are paired[1]
scarcely talking, thoughts pass between us[2]
We had to drink spilled moon from the lake for courage[3]
Nothing was speaking to me, but I offered and all was well.[4]
I married her, my face upright to the sky[5]

My glass I lift at six o'clock, my darling,[6]
my heart of mayonnaise[7]
We are in easy understanding.[8]
This summerbed is soft with ring upon ring
of wedding, the kind
that doesn't clink upon contact[9]
You can tell
I hear it, too, by the look on my face:
That inaudible thumping[10]
Now I'm a bird in the nest of your lap[11]
When you show yourself to the woman
you love, you don't know your fear—[12]
happiness is a kind of fear[13]

here, now here, closer like a mouth
opening and closing, opening and closing[14]
naked
as a heap of clothes, still whispering *undress me*[15]
body hair glistening with a thousand arts[16]
I offer a necklace of tears, orgasms, words[17]
or the soft babble of a kiss.[18]

O for a life of Kisses
*Instead of painting volcanoes!* [19]
joy in my mouth like a peppered bird [20]
This means laughter
or wings [21]

I will be standing at the edge
of that fathomless crowd with an orange for you [22]
the way a woman stands
when you meet her at an unexpected corner [23]

# Maximum Security

## SUSAN MUSGRAVE

How many brides, on leaving the chapel, have to toss the bouquet over a fourteen-foot-high perimeter fence? And how many bouquets, flying clear of the razor wire, fence alarms and leaky radar systems, are eventually caught by a two-hundred-and-fifty-pound uniformed guard with an M-16 rifle in his trigger hand?

*Married in white, you will do all right.* My first marriage had not worked out quite like it was supposed to. *Married in red, you will wish yourself dead.* Neither had my second. This time I chose the colour purple, something criminally expensive. You only get married, I told myself, for the third time once.

*Something old, something new, something ... stolen? ... something blue.* I considered stealing a copy of Stephen's recently published novel, *Jackrabbit Parole*, to carry to the wedding, but didn't want my Big Day to be one where I got arrested. Like Mae West said, marriage is a great institution. I was ready for marriage, but I was not ready for an institution yet.

I went shopping with my daughter, Charlotte, who was to be my flower girl. At the Kiddie's Carousel the saleslady glowed at the mention of a wedding, and asked, "Where will it be held?"

I told her. Kent Institution. She turned a whiter shade of pale than Charlotte's dress. Same with the lady in the shoe store where Charlotte, with her four-year-old eye for fashion, insisted that her shoes be any colour other than her dress. "I don't want to be all white, white, white," she told me.

We settled for black patent pumps—and she was right.

I rattled on to the lady in the cake shop about wedding bars instead of bells.

In the Olde Golde Shoppe, where I bought antique wedding rings, the young clerk asked, "Who's the lucky man?"

I told him. The clerk took my money and ran.

The day before the wedding Charlotte and I went to Mission. On the way, we stopped at a five-and-dime store to buy masks.

Charlotte, who knew the media would be there, had suggested we drive up to the prison wearing masks, and at first I thought it a good idea. Then I remembered I was being married inside a maximum-security penitentiary, where jokes have a tendency to be misconstrued. I explained to Charlotte how

Stephen was in prison because *he* had worn a mask, and how maybe we ought to leave ours in the trunk, along with the squirt gun she had been dying to surprise him with. She agreed, stoically. "The prison might think we're robbing them," she said.

At Andy and Sharon's house, the evening before my nuptials, we drank champagne and feasted. The children played.

Sabrina: "Kiss. Hug. Ring. Zzzz, Zzzz, because they sleep together."

Charlotte: "Well not yet 'cause he's in jail."

Sabrina: "It doesn't matter. They will dance."

At least I didn't have to worry about Stephen having a stag party where his friends would get him tanked and leave him tied naked to a pine tree miles away from the church. The heart, in most cases, has no certainty, but I could be certain of one thing at least: Stephen would be waiting for me at the altar.

Early Sunday morning, Alex arrived to take pictures of the wedding party having breakfast. Still in my dressing gown, I hardly touched my waffle. I had decided I would get dressed in Agassiz—that way there was less chance of getting nervous perspiration on my ensemble.

When you are marrying a good escape artist, you need a good makeup artist, Joyce told me, but I was too anxious to laugh, and besides, it would have cracked my foundation. I steadied my hands long enough to find, at the bottom of my purse, the Exclusive Maybelline Dial-a-Lash Mascara I had bought after seeing the advertisement in *Vogue*. "Lets you control the amount of mascara you put on your lashes," it said. "Dial a lower number for a Nature-Girl look. Dial a higher number for a Glamour-Girl look."

"Here. Joyce, you do it," I said.

Charlotte was applying copious amounts of Le Pout to her lips. I asked if I could borrow some. She looked at me patiently and suggested, in the interest of longevity, that I use a wax-heavy lipstick formulation instead of gloss.

"She's right, you know," said Joyce.

Charlotte is always right.

In the visitors' lot outside the institution, I parked. Charlotte tore across the parking lot, practising her "horrible face." She had written to Stephen a week before saying, "Let's make horrible faces when you marry Susan Musgrave." Even without her mask, Charlotte was a contender.

I reparked. There was no way, today, I would get the car in straight. It was time to start thinking straight, though—there were difficult times ahead. I had to sign my name in the visitors' book at the front gate, for instance. My name completely escaped me.

My usher, Jill, a prison guard, reminded me. After she walked me through the metal detector where I lit up the alert panel to the highest number, ten (it was my French garters. I just knew it), she hand-scanned me for further concealed weapons. Charlotte followed, clutching my freesias with unusual fervour. I prayed she had not decided to slip her squirt gun into the bouquet at the last moment.

The barriers slammed open and we passed through. The "front gate" is a building separate from the prison itself, and we had to walk out into the bold October morning to launch our final assault. They say the road to the house of a friend is never long, but the path to the front door of a prison on your wedding day is endless.

Charlotte said goodbye to me and the seagulls that had been circling us, hoping for handouts. She and my family went one way. I was escorted to the women's washroom where I was to be kept until the appointed time. The cameras followed me in. I borrowed a comb (I had to leave my purse in a locker) and checked out the Glamour-Girl look in the mirror. I liked it. Then I looked for a blemish. What Most Important Day of Your Life would be complete without the world's most uncompromising pimple erupting on your face?

I had to look hard. But I found one. Right on the very end of my nose. Of course my disaster cream was in that locker ...

Meanwhile, Stephen, in the chapel, was welcoming his new in-laws to prison. Apart from my mother and sister, our guests included four of his friends from inside, and newscasters from three TV stations, including Bob McKeown and a crew from CBC's *The Fifth Estate* who were covering "our story." My mother broke the ice by sitting on the outlaws' side.

I had never seen Stephen dressed up before. I had bought him a suit— Giorgio Armani—a shirt, tie, belt, puff, socks and new underwear at British Importers in Victoria. His shoes cost $225—each. I wanted him to be the best-dressed man in prison.

Jill, who was waiting with me outside the chapel, said, "I told him he looked like Clyde. He said, 'Yeah. I'm waiting for Bonnie.'"

I didn't recognize him. When I stepped into the chapel and stood in the glare of flashbulbs, I panicked, like Bonnie Parker up against her first bank. I couldn't find Clyde. Instead of "Okay, everybody. This is a robbery. Reach for the sky!" I cried, "What do I do now?" to the room at large.

I could just make out the Reverend Arnie in his white robes, and Perry, a black muscle builder (most grooms have a best man, but Stephen had a best bodyguard), on the horizon. And then I found Stephen, a few feet in front of me at the altar —where I had expected him to be, after all—looking more nervous than the first time he had robbed a bank with a Czechoslovakian .38 and his sister's nylon over his face. Charlotte took my hand and led me to my intended.

Two guards stood watch over the cake knife that Stephen had obtained with some difficulty, while Stephen and Charlotte exchanged "horrible faces" and Stephen and I exchanged vows. I even got both our names right. Later, in the trailer, we would hear our vows repeated on BCTV, as the camera scaled the guard towers and scanned the coiled miles of razor wire surrounding the prison.

At the short reception, Charlotte helped cut the cake and helped eat most of the icing. Grand Marnier icing. It was the only liquor we had; someone proposed a toast and we ate to a lifetime of happiness.

At two o'clock Stephen was taken to change into prison greens. I was taken out to the front gate to have my honeymoon suitcase inspected. The mentholated cough drops (Xaviera Hollander recommends these as being an interesting accompaniment to certain sexual practices) were impounded, as was my nail file. Under protest I was allowed to keep my dental floss. Floss is forbidden in prison.

What honeymoon would be complete without floss? These and other questions (would there be pen and paper in the trailer?) filled my mind as I waited for Stephen to be photographed for the cover of *Vancouver* magazine. I had told him to take his time over the photograph, even if it did cut into our honeymoon. We had, after all, the rest of our lives together. At least until we reached the age of seventy-five.

Stephen had written to me about a couple like ourselves, very much in love, both writers. They had lived a full, rich life and then, at age seventy-five, had gone to Tahiti to die in a suicide pact. Stephen thought this was very romantic. I said I hoped he grew less romantic with age.

Then, after two years, there we were—alone. Well, not entirely alone. There were still the visitors and communications officer, who had come along to show us how the light switches and the television worked.

I tried to take a new-wifely interest in the groceries. We had enough white bread to feed the prison population. We had Eggo waffles and green apples. Leaving a brown bag full of white bread outside our front door (I hoped it would be returned to the kitchen), I found myself considering the nutritive value of dental floss.

Finally, we were really alone. Nothing, not even our heartbeats, would be monitored over the next seventy-two hours.

We were deeply engrossed in a rousing game of Yahtzee—earlier in the week Stephen had told a *Maclean's* reporter that the honeymoon would be "three days of Yahtzee and *Late Night with David Letterman*"—when the telephone rang. And rang persistently. Stephen had to get dressed (okay, it was strip Yahtzee) and show himself for count. On his way back from being counted he tossed some potatoes into the oven.

We stayed up to watch the 6:00 p.m. news. Seeing ourselves getting married on TV made it, at last, seem real. I had been too nervous, at the time, to have feelings other than nervousness. Now it felt permanent. Forever. As permanent as forever gets—at least until we got to Tahiti. Television allowed emotion to be recollected in tranquility.

The evening turned out to be anything but tranquil. As the camera came to light upon a small bird perched on the wire, something else, slightly larger, lighted upon our roof. This time I put my clothes on. The seagulls had raided the bag full of bread and were having a party of their own above.

We took up where we had left off at Yahtzee. I was on the verge of winning my first game when there came, from the other side of the fence, a series of small explosions. Unmistakably gunfire. I hit the floor.

I am a poor loser. I didn't think it funny when Stephen pulled me up again and said it was nothing personal, only routine target-practice time for the guards.

Life in the Solicitor General's lane. A few minutes later we had a spectacular explosion of our own when two baked potatoes burst in the oven because someone had forgotten to prick them.

It didn't matter.

We danced.

# Wedding Clothes &
# Marriage Blanket

## JOANNE ARNOTT

In December 1999, I was a single mom on welfare, in Richmond, BC. I had joint custody of my four boys, ages three to thirteen, who lived with me half-time and with their father half-time. For me this meant, in practical terms, that some weeks I was a very busy woman, and other weeks, I languished.

Over the preceding three years I had, one by one, dropped all of my old community involvements. Many friendships, relied upon through crises, had since become inactive, in part due to my relocation and in part as a natural process, as all of us moved on to pursue the sort of peacetime activities that people do: work and school, family life, creative and spiritual pathways reabsorbing us. Single now for almost four years, I enjoyed many elements of my independence. At the same time, I was done with spending so much of my time managing loneliness.

I was intrigued by the idea of advertising myself on a singles line, a telephone-based dating service found through ads in the *Georgia Straight* or one of the community papers. How would I describe myself? An award-winning poet? Intelligent, but barely educated? A Manitoba emigrant of mixed ancestry, not much for drinking, not into bingo? "Single mom on welfare" was both true and in my face: I could hear myself making excuses: *I can't get together on Tuesdays, I have to go to the food bank. I can't afford to buy a coffee, sorry, would you like to meet outside the public library?* Ready to move out of hibernation, I found myself baffled at how to communicate my virtues.

From time to time, throughout the fall, there in my basement apartment, I found my thoughts and feelings returning to a fellow I'd travelled with—and promised to marry—almost twenty years before. Maudlin songs of remembered love, on television ads and the radio, brought unexpected tears.

Nick and I had first met at university in Windsor, Ontario, when I was nineteen. He was a foreign student from Indiana, completing a master's degree in fine arts, and I was a hungry undergraduate, honing my poetry. The contrast between his oversized, vibrant paintings and his shy, unobtrusive self caught my attention. Through the round of New Year's festivities in 1980, we became a couple.

Over the course of our few years together, I had twice travelled to visit him at his parents' home in Evansville, Indiana, and together we'd visited my parents' homes in the West. Dad was living with my stepmom and youngest brother in the town nearest to the land he'd grown up on, and where I'd lived for a half-dozen years of my girlhood. The Assiniboine River, passing just outside of town, always looked, smelled and felt like home to me. Ma had a tiny room in Vancouver. While visiting, we stayed in my sisters' apartments and spent time with my grandparents in East Van. We travelled the width of the continent together during that first summer, hitchhiking all the way across southern Canada, coast to coast.

Poverty and the combined forces of hunger, homelessness and Nick's diabetes would often undermine our various plans, particularly after our travels concluded and I returned to school. Nick's student visa was no longer in force, and he moved to an aging hotel in Detroit. We traded disappointments in our fleeting succession of breakups and reunions. But we'd also sing together late in the night, songs I'd taught him at the side of a hot summer highway. I'd feel his hand on my belly in sleep.

We hadn't seen one another since the early 1980s, and hadn't had contact since the early 1990s. Nick was living in Seattle, Washington, just a few hours' drive from where I now lived. I wasn't sure what kind of reception I might get if I contacted him again, but it would cost me nothing to check with directory assistance in Seattle. So I did.

There he was.

And so was the lure of all that had been sweet between us, tempered by our history of nearmisses, joined with the goad of loneliness. I waited a week, maybe two, but I did call. We promised to exchange Christmas cards, but he forgot to ask for my address or my phone number. So a week or so later, I called again.

Nick wrote me a letter, acknowledging the power of our past relationship, and expressing his anticipation of much more happiness to come. Even before it arrived, however, I was aquiver at what might already be underway.

My friend, poet Greg Scofield, recently returned to the prairie, listened to me on the telephone as my emotional world began to tumble and cascade. While our growing up years had been quite different, and Greg's ties to the larger Métis cultural life were more firm, we clearly recognized one another and the worlds evoked by one another's words. Our families' roots grew from the same prairie soil. He encouraged me to enjoy myself, however it might turn out. He added an essential piece of advice that December: "Put those feelings into a poem."

Nick and I soon began spending time together on a regular basis. Sometimes he visited me and my boys in Canada, and sometimes I stayed in his art-filled apartment in Washington. Nick bought a blue Caravan to ease the cross-border visiting. Almost immediately, again at Nick's initiative, we started to plan a journey.

In the late spring, we drove down the coast together, some nights camping, some nights staying in a bed and breakfast, some nights sleeping in a motel. We traded stories of the time between, comparing versions of shared memories, discovering each other more deeply. Driving from the seaside highway in early June, turning east from the beach and rising up the side of a mountain, we arrived at the snowbound Crater Lake. We stood enchanted in the snowfall, wearing our summer clothes, feeling the wild presence of that ancient place. Later in the interpretive centre, we heard for the first time the story of the crater's formation, and of how Coyote's desperate love for the Moon filled the lake to the brim with his tears. As the story goes, Coyote fell in love with the Moon. Coyote's love was complete, all-involving. But Coyote's love was also exclusive, like greed: Coyote wanted not just to love the Moon, but to own the Moon, and to keep the Moon as a solitary pleasure for himself. He failed. The Moon is, of course, for everyone.

In years past, Nick and I had both played Coyote, and we'd taken turns embodying the elusive Moon. By being reminded of the acknowledged foolish reaches of love, the possibility of enacting a different version of the old story opened up for us.

As Nick drove us north through Oregon on our return journey, I sat with my thirty-nine-year-old bare feet propped on the dash, feeling replete. A spark had been lit inside me, an inexorable process of life, newly begun: it would be weeks before science could confirm it, but I felt a new child's presence, which I welcomed with primordial enthusiasm.

How to think about our past was a topic of many of our conversations. The litany of misconstrued intentions made it clear that we both needed to ask a lot more questions of one another before making life-altering choices. But to say it was all a mistake seemed disrespectful. I wasn't about to sweep the intervening decades away, along with my four young children. What felt right for me was a longer view of a passage through difficult terrain: Nick and I had matured toward a possibility glimpsed, grasped and lost in the earliest moments, and now could try again.

Some of what had proved difficult in the past we now prepared to conquer. The presence of the international boundary between us made a necessity of marriage in order just to be together. Although neither of us had married or immigrated before, we were prepared to take on the bureaucracies with all of the patience and persistence that we could muster.

Shopping for our wedding clothes in the following months was not a departure from our now usual ways of passing time together. Nick, a visual artist, enjoyed visiting second-hand shops in search of lace and other fabrics to use in his paintings. I had yet to develop an enjoyment of clothes shopping, but in Nick's company it became for me a lighthearted venture too.

I found a creamy white dress with cascades of gauzy fabric, seed pearls across the bodice and beautiful sleeves, clean and undamaged, in a trendy shop in the University District of Seattle. Nick picked up a blue suit and a dress shirt in the same shop. As this was my first and probably only wedding, I decided to go for the whole dress-up party.

At a Richmond consignment store, I found three colourful vests, three white shirts and three pairs of pants in good condition for my younger sons. At the Salvation Army store, I found a blue suit, white dress shirt and black shoes for my firstborn son, Stuart. The only purchase that I made new were three pairs of soft leather walking boots, each with an embroidered motif at the ankle from a discount shoe store at a Richmond mall for my younger boys. The only purchase that Nick made new was a lovely little diamond ("brilliant, like you") set in a white gold band. I called it my "rainbow blaster." I used it to amuse my children and, as time went on, to fend off the sometimes bemused stares of strangers reacting to the combination of my greying hair and fertile belly.

I called my friend Flo Robertson after a decade of lapsed contact. We'd both lived in a housing co-operative in the Downtown Eastside of Vancouver and become friends while making policy together, sharing life stories as mothers and daughters over cups of hot tea. Although Flo was of the Nlaka'pamux people of British Columbia, and I was a Winnipeg-born mixed blood, we were both urban persons of mixed race, with palpably weak connections to more traditional communities. We shared a family feeling from the start and plenty of humour. When I wondered at the ease of our return to active friendship after so long a silence, she said, "Ten years? Ten years is nothing when it's love."

Besides her decades of work in child care and social work, Flo was an expert at beadwork and making cakes. She happily agreed to make our wedding cake.

Flo suggested that we consider a marriage blanket ceremony. Gifts of blankets and their ceremonial use in weddings, funerals and at other important times is a practice continued by Sto:lo, Cree and many other modern First Nations people. Once upon a time, these blankets were always handmade, woven from indigenous plant life, or woven from animal hair or—in other regions—made from skins. Today the role is largely symbolic, usually filled by colourful store-bought blankets. As I had been wrapped in a blanket in healing ceremonies in the past, I was deeply aware of the power of the gift she was offering, and I felt honoured. In making such an offering, Flo was taking on the role of a family elder.

Greg continued his role as long-distance confidant/adviser. With better knowledge of Métis traditions than I had, Greg was a good person to consult about specifically Métis matters—for example, to ensure our respectful handling of our Métis sashes. The traditional sash weaves five colours—red, green, blue, yellow and white—symbolic of the four directions plus the self. There is no end to what these five colours are associated with. The five petals on the Métis beadwork flowers symbolize the source cultures that fed into the birth of the Métis Nation. For me, the sashes represent the different ways that my immediate family has found to get close to our roots. Being a brown-skinned girl regularly recognized for my "aboriginal" cheekbones, I have identified most with the Indigenous and Métis elements of our ancestral inheritance. My years in my father's home country, with the green pump in the kitchen and mixed-blood relations around me—albeit with no one acknowledging race—helped. One of my sisters, more urban, white-skinned and green-eyed, studied Old Irish, both as a language to speak and as a wealth of traditional songs to sing.

Like many mixed-race families—though by no means all—earlier generations of my family bowed to the pressures to assimilate, and I know of no material representations of culture that have been preserved or passed on. Thus, my Métis sashes, like so much else in life, were acquired second-hand. When I brought them home, I cleansed them with smudge and prayed to restore their sense of purpose, to rehabilitate the cast-off regalia in the same fashion that I was attempting to rehabilitate both my family members and myself.

After further discussions with Flo, I approached a respected Métis woman, Amy Wuttunee Eustergerling, to lead the ceremony. Amy agreed, helping to fill out our ideas of incorporating the sash and the marriage blanket into the ceremony, and generously adding from her own traditions and knowledge. Nick and I also approached Clare Ash, a local marriage notary, to perform those formal elements of the ceremony that would satisfy the Government of Canada, a necessary step for Nick to obtain status as a landed immigrant and a permanent resident. With these two representatives of different communities agreeing to perform the wedding for us, the planning moved into a new phase. For the venue, we settled on the Eco-Pavilion, in Strathcona Community Gardens, a spacious and comfortable garden shed harbouring drying plants and implements, along with the tables, chairs and gathering space required.

Friends joined in the spirit of the wedding, gathering many small items from second-hand shops on Vancouver Island, from costume jewellery to high-heeled shoes to lacy lingerie and a small purse, and provided me with a shimmering honeymoon dress, along with tablecloths, thank-you cards and a guest book. The invitations were made and tendered, featuring a playful little painting by Nick: a version of us standing in a distinctive West Coast landscape under an arch made of lace, with the words "Welcome to Forever / Joanne and Nick" painted across the sky.

As the months passed and our plans finalized, it became clear that the wedding dress would not be able to accommodate the gestating child that I carried. I brought the dress to a Filipina tailor who owned a little shop in central Richmond. She listened to my pleas, frowned over the calendar, the dress and my belly, and agreed to take on the job. She also agreed to put together a simple veil compatible with the materials and design of the dress. When I returned for a fitting, I was delighted. Her careful, painstaking hours of work had rendered the dress a comfortable fit, useful once more. She told me, "I want you to know this is a MIRACLE I performed here! I made a miracle for you!"

Nick's parents travelled up to be with us from southern Indiana. The Zenthoefers are an old German-American family, one-time owners of the local tavern, the kind of family that gathers in gladly at every opportunity. Good-hearted and highly social people, Carl and Doris are easy to be with, and it was good to see them again after so many years. We shared burgers and laughter in Seattle and sat on beds in a motel room, sipping beer. They reminisced about my husband—their firstborn child—as a greedy breastfeeding infant, much to my delight. Nick caught a glimpse not only of his past, but of what the near future held for him with the birth of his first child.

In the November evenings before the wedding took place, my son Stuart and I prepared for the ceremony by making tobacco ties together. Tobacco opens communication with the Creator, and with the Grandmothers and Grandfathers. Making the small cotton twists of tobacco-filled cloth are a necessary preparation for, and part of, many ceremonies. We discussed the changes underway in our family, the upcoming ceremony and the gifts for the family and friends who would soon gather. At our final sitting, Nick joined us, and we taught him as we had been taught, the how and the why of making tobacco ties.

The night before the wedding, Nick's mom, Doris, spoke of her family, and told us that her family was of mixed blood like mine. I remembered many years before when I was a nervous girl visiting her home, how she had tried to open a conversation with me about race. I was so afraid of what she might say about my worth or lack thereof that I'd ended the conversation prematurely. Nick said later that he'd always thought she was Irish, and couldn't say if he'd been told the truth and forgotten, or had never been told at all.

At the pavilion in the damp community garden, I waited nervously, instructing my children in hushed tones, and greeting our guests as they began to trickle in. Out-of-town guests and local, but rarely seen, loved ones arrived. Flo arrived early with the cake: below an arch decorated with rings and birds, a tiny couple stood carefully wrapped by Flo in a marriage blanket of their own.

Amy initiated the ceremony with an opening prayer, with voice and with drum. She was followed by Clare, who oversaw the ceremonial exchange of rings and vows. My elder sister sang a traditional love song for us in Irish.

Amy performed a smudge ceremony, cleansing Nick and me, wafting the smoke of burning medicine plants over each of us with the strokes of an eagle feather. At Amy's sign, I symbolically extended the Métis family to include my new husband by encircling his waist with a sash.

With Flo's assistance, Amy smudged the blanket. Geometric patterns in red, turquoise, beige, blue and black created a vibrant, earthy feel, and as the blanket was turned, a different combination of diamonds, triangles and arrows was revealed. To my eye, the blanket looked warm, durable and beautiful. Nick and I were called forward again, and the two women enfolded us in our new marriage blanket.

"Treat this blanket with reverence," Amy told us. "Treat it with respect, because it is your marriage. You were two, with two different lives, and now you are joining your lives together. Now you are one. The blanket represents that. You have to respect yourselves and your marriage, and consider yourselves one now, in everything you do. This blanket covers you, in the same way that your marriage will cover you. Treat it with respect." Amy lifted her drum again, and sang two songs, one in Cree and one in English.

Then, with a few closing words, the ceremony was done.

Today the marriage blanket is kept, clean and safe, at the top of our bedroom closet; it goes where we go. While most of the tobacco ties went home with our guests, a few still grace the family altar, a blending of Indigenous with non-Indigenous spiritual traditions. One tie, encompassing a small prairie river stone, I wear around my neck on a long strip of leather. It gently beats against my belly as I move through my days.

Our youngest children, blue-eyed Flora, dark-eyed Jules, sometimes romp around in the wedding veil, decorate themselves with the costume jewellery and toddle around in the high heels. Each weekday morning, I tie the last of the new boots that I had bought for my sons to my smallest child's feet. The gold-embroidered purse that carried my cigarettes on that one day now dangles from a small boy's arm, stuffed with toy cars.

From time to time, when I have a poetry reading, Nick and I leave the youngest children in the care of their brothers. I put on my honeymoon dress, and we drive to the venue together. He sits in the crowd sipping a drink, and I move to the stage, stand before the mike, feel the heat of the spotlight upon me.

To warm up the crowd and myself, I might ask, "Do you like my dress?"

I search for Nick's face through the crowd. When I spot him, I retell the story of my love for him, and read a poem I wrote during the first twelve months of our reunion.

Returning

the creekbed shifts her hips
in anticipation and longing
for the salmon who will hurl
and spend themselves
on her rocks
in her cool waters

# The Joy of the Ancient Marriers

**ANDREAS SCHROEDER**

On August 8, 2007, Sharon Elizabeth Brown and I, Andreas Schroeder, were legally married in a modest ceremony in our home in Roberts Creek, BC. We were attended only by two elegant young women and a provincial marriage commissioner.

This simple fact—seen from a high perch overlooking the history of marriage in Canada over the past half-century—is not particularly momentous. Not even if you consider that Sharon and I were both sixty-one years of age, had already lived together for thirty-three years, and those two elegant young women were our fully grown daughters. But the event was emblematic of a slow but relentless seachange in Canada's marriage statistics: it may not be long before it'll be as radical to *get* married as it was radical in the sixties not to.

When Sharon and I decided to merge our lives and move into a Toronto apartment in 1976, just before we both turned thirty—an act that in earlier times would have been immediately preceded by a wedding—the gulf between us and the tradition of marriage seemed unbridgeable. Having already rejected the God of our intensely religious fathers, we were easily suspicious of the proprietorial interest both the Church and the State insisted on taking in what seemed to us a very personal matter. Indeed, the rites of an officially sanctioned marriage seemed to us more like a governmental roundup in which we would be cornered, hog-tied, branded and shackled together, while some bureaucrat preacher stood above us in the dust, intoning the conditions under which this bondage was to be endured. Submitting to this ceremony would have sent a billboard-sized message of apostasy and surrender to our families, relatives and friends. It was a message that I, for one, was determined not to send.

Not that shacking up in the sixties was a new phenomenon. In fact it was already a growing trend, at least outside our own immediate communities. But within them—within our wider families and the Church—it was still as rare as syphilis, and about as acceptable. Our fathers considered our children, once they were born, to be bastards, and mine, in particular, had little time for them. Sharon's father proved less doctrinaire about the children, but refused to let us sleep together under his roof during Christmas visits, even after we'd been living together for more than a decade.

Aside from avoiding the wrong meta-message, I wanted my relationship with Sharon to remain "voluntary"—not coerced. I wanted to feel, returning home every night, that I was doing so of my own free will. I also wanted our relationship to reflect at least something of what we were learning from the ethos of the time. It's fashionable now to dump on the sixties, but many of us experienced that era, for all its foolishness, as enormously liberating. People forget how anthropoidal the fifties actually were. Young females mostly stood around in groups preening and giggling, while young males stood around in gangs, fighting or smashing beer cans against their foreheads. You couldn't get a decent conversation going between the sexes to save your soul. Once the sixties got into its groove (and don't forget that in Canada, the sixties mostly happened in the seventies), you actually could. Fraternities and sororities virtually atrophied. I'm not saying that was the whole story, but it gives you an idea.

Here's an excerpt from "The Good Wife's Guide," published in *Housekeeping Monthly* in 1955. It advises wives on how to greet their husbands returning home from the office. "Let him talk first—remember, his topics of conversation are more important than yours. Don't complain if he's late for dinner or even if he stays out all night. Arrange his pillow, or offer to take off his shoes. Speak in a low, soothing and pleasant voice.

"Don't ask him questions about his actions or question his judgment or integrity. Remember, he is the master of the house and as such will always exercise his will with fairness and truthfulness. You have no right to question him. A good wife always knows her place."

I rest my case.

The Church's marriage vows didn't spell this out quite so explicitly, but they were clearly singing from the same hymnal. The bride was required to "love, honour and obey" her new husband, while the groom was only required to "honour and protect" his new wife. Both Catholic and Protestant marriage vows in those days still took their marching orders from Ephesians 5:22–24, in which the Apostle Paul laid down the law with his usual categorical paternalism: "Wives, submit to your husbands as to the Lord. For the husband is the head of the wife as Christ is the head of the church, his body, of which he is the Saviour. Now, as the church submits to Christ, so also wives should submit to their husbands in everything."

It's tempting to assume that our fathers' take on this issue was identical, but we'll never know because neither Sharon nor I ever managed the nerve to introduce them to each other. And since we'd never formalized our relationship, they never saw reason to ask. Sharon's father was a tall, bulky, hard-drinking, glad-handing Anglican priest, while mine was a diminutive, tightly laced Mennonite deacon. If my father had ever set foot in an Anglican church, one look would have confirmed the obvious—that Anglicans were rampant idol worshippers—and if that hadn't done the job, the first welcoming clout on his back from Sharon's gregarious father would have poleaxed him. The two men's take on their religious calling differed so fundamentally that it was hard to imagine a compromise. My father believed profoundly in the Direct Call from God, as experienced by Solomon or Zacchaeus. Sharon's father believed that becoming a priest was simply a career choice, one he had chosen in preference—after his retirement from the air force—over his second option, becoming a Seagram's salesman. (There were some who insisted he'd never chosen one to the exclusion of the other.)

Sharon's own take didn't entirely coincide with mine, but the similarities were greater. She would have agreed to marry, provided she didn't have to change her name or promise to obey anyone. Also, Sharon would certainly have refused a church wedding. This had more to do with her aversion to hypocrisy than her quarrels with theology. While she had developed profound doubts about the existence of a conventional God and the Holy Trinity—not to mention Virgin births and resurrected Saviours—she still respected the institution enough to refuse to treat it like wallpaper. She suggested we—at some point—come up with some sort of secular ceremony that would simply affirm and celebrate that we were committed to each other in a lifelong relationship. We travelled some distance down that road, sitting in our hot tub or on our deck, free-associating about what such a ceremony would look like, but we could never quite agree on its contents. I kept making suggestions that gave the distinct impression I was still trying in various ways to subvert the tradition, while Sharon wanted at least some of its formality and reverence kept intact. In effect, she wanted an actual wedding, while I was promoting something like an anti-wedding. Probably still shadow boxing with the Mennonite Church, regardless of how completely I thought I'd escaped its clutches.

None of this, fortunately, interfered with our own relationship. We might have worried, briefly, about the reception our children would eventually get at school, but by the time they got there, all but one of the four couples on our short rural street turned out to be unmarried, and the students' preoccupation at school was with divorce and separation, not marital status. Out in the secular world we were now becoming less and less uncommon—the number of common-law marriages was more than doubling every two decades in Canada (more than tripling in Quebec), and the rate of legal marriages was plateauing. (Shortly after the millennium, it actually began to drop.)

So we kept on trucking, rising relentlessly through the demographic. Even the YWCA, which had once denied Sharon a promised job when it was discovered she was living in sin, looked in the mirror and re-proffered its offer. In due course, Revenue Canada added a little box to its marital status section labelled "common-law," and Statistics Canada followed suit a year or so later. By 1981 Sharon no longer qualified as a "spinster," and I'd apparently lost my "bachelor" status. It was almost a little disappointing, this growing inability to offend. Even the normally reliable guards at the US–Canada border didn't seem to care about our marital status anymore.

We began to suspect we'd been co-opted. We seemed to have lost our position just ahead of the curve.

I began to think it might be time again to start wearing a tie.

---

Sometimes I wonder whether there's something like a mid point in our lives when we start dragging back the things we spent the first half of our lives throwing out. Is there a component in our beliefs and principles that stretches readily during our first three or four decades, then starts contracting again? Can it be true (as Michael Ulmer warned in a *Globe and Mail* column) that, metaphorically speaking, we all eventually lawn bowl?

Our stand on marriage in the sixties was based, first and foremost, on the notion of gender equality. But gender equality can be a many-splendoured thing. In keeping with our generation's suspicion that most gender inequality is learned (and that our governments and leaders were actually promoting it), Sharon had enrolled in a night school auto-mechanics course, and I had learned how to sew. When we eventually merged our lives, we not only merged our considerable libraries, but also Sharon's long-handled Husky socket wrench, her 16-ounce Craftsman claw hammer, and my Bernina 830 sewing machine. We knew plenty of parents who were giving their newborn boys dolls, and their newborn girls toy trucks. Almost everyone subscribed to the notion that both genders should cook, clean and child-raise—though I'd have to admit I heard a lot more about this in theory than I saw in practice.

We assumed, of course, that parents' initial reports of the boys using their dolls as machine guns and the girls diapering their toy trucks was to be expected in a transitional phase. So was the fact that, once we'd started living together, Sharon's vastly superior cooking skills and my significantly more intuitive grasp of auto repair and carpentry tended to mean—in the interests of saving time and effort when both were in short supply—that I fixed the house and car, and she cooked the meals. We might have questioned this arrangement more vigorously if either of us had felt the other to be taking advantage, but we were both eldest siblings with built-in take-charge instincts, which made these compromises easier to ignore.

Besides, most of our friends were reporting the same experiences.

Then there was the drug issue. During the sixties and seventies, almost everyone we knew was smoking, snorting, inhaling or ingesting illegal drugs of some sort—ourselves included. So we knew from direct experience that the anti-drug nonsense being peddled by the authorities was just so much propaganda. The few drug fatalities we actually saw were vastly outnumbered by deaths due to alcohol or tobacco. We found ourselves intuitively dividing the world into stoners and straights. And yet, when we began to have kids, we found it not quite so easy to condone unbridled dope smoking when it interfered with our own child-raising agendas. A certain amount of hair splitting became necessary. Perspectives became more nuanced. Once again it wasn't the whole story, but you get the idea.

One tends to question the herd instincts of other generations or societies long before recognizing one's own, so I'm not sure that we started seriously questioning ours at this stage—or if we did, it certainly wasn't as cynically as it's more recently become. We didn't yet know that, once history has finished with it, even a "progressive" generation rarely turns out to have pioneered more than one or two truly progressive ideas.

But at the very least, practical experience was beginning to wear the sharp edges off some of our sixties ideologies. Perhaps we'd been a touch too categorical in our view of the world. Perhaps—an appalling thought—lawn bowling wasn't entirely as absurd as it looked.

---

I don't normally worry too much about the mind-brain dichotomy—it can be a dangerous concept, especially if you try thinking about it while riding a motorcycle at high speeds, which I often do. But every now and then my mind relents and lets me in on what it's been doing with my life while I've been too busy to pay attention, and something like that happened during the final preparations for our sixtieth birthday party in November 2006. What had started off as plans for a relatively modest party quickly ballooned in exactly the same way that weddings tend to do, and once the guest list exceeded three hundred, it did begin to dawn on me that, perhaps, something was happening here, but we didn't know what it was, did we, Mr. Jones?

Two days before the party I finally consulted my elder daughter, Sabrina.

She was, of course, immediately fascinated. Getting to consult with your biological father on the topic of proposing to your biological mother is something that normally happens only in science fiction stories involving time warps. This was messing with metaphysics; this was overcoming entropy.

"A wicked idea, Father," she enthused. "It would be so unexpected—especially from you. People would absolutely freak." She patted me encouragingly on the back. "So why are you doing this, exactly?"

I retired to my desk to jot down some preliminary notes.

Then there was the matter of a ring. Like all men who hate shopping, I've always relied on Sharon for advice on all my haberdashery purchases, so buying a ring without consulting her was unthinkable. My solution, since I've always liked working with wood, was to cut and grind away at a piece of six-by-six-inch cedar until it eventually resembled a miniature napkin ring, hopefully ennobled by being placed on the satin lining of a former Eddie Bauer watch gift box. A temporary engagement device.

On the evening of the party I was about as ready as I was ever likely to be, though still not entirely convinced this was going to happen. I waited for an opportunity between the announcements, the speeches, the roasts and the potluck dinner, but kept missing my cue. There was a pause while Sharon and her musically inclined brothers teamed up to sing a bowdlerized version of "California Dreamin'" ("All of us are Browns … hm hm hm hm … and we're turning grey"), but I slipped up on that one too. Finally, when the intermission arrived and the band began to set up for the dance to follow, I decided I'd flubbed it. Sabrina's face was a big question mark.

"I think the mood's changed," I shrugged.

She gave me her best spine-stiffening look. "You can change it back," she said. "If you really want to."

I watched the band members hauling speakers onto the stage for a while. People drifted idly among the tables in the hall, chatting and laughing. A few—the non-dancers, the ones who had a long drive home—were leaving. Finally I picked up a cordless mike and climbed onto the stage. I asked for everyone's attention and I got a bit of that, but most people obviously thought I was just going to make a few announcements. The hubbub didn't subside much.

I started in blindly. I began talking about my thirty-two years of living with Sharon, about all the projects we'd undertaken together, about our children and what they meant to us. About how Sharon designs things and I build them; how she cooks and I clean up; how she obeys the law and I try not to.

It was the women in the audience who first sensed what was happening. They began swinging around in their seats like compass needles. The hubbub diminished. People shushed other people.

I said that Sharon sometimes claimed I'd rescued her from certain demons, and I didn't know about that, but that she'd certainly rescued me from a bunch of mine. And that, even after three decades together, every time I woke up in the morning and looked at her lying there beside me, I still felt like the luckiest guy on the planet.

There were assorted shrieks, and some loud shouts of encouragement. People were beginning to suspect where this was headed. I could see anticipation on every face. I said a bunch of other things I don't recall with any certainty, something about being children of the sixties, when it hadn't seemed all that important, but now that the Church, if not the State, was off our backs, and the trend was in the opposite direction, and wearing ties might become necessary just so they don't disappear—drivel of that sort— and then I finally said, "So Sharon, the concept of waiting for the right time hardly begins to explain the glacial pace at which I've approached this issue, but anyway, I'm finally getting around to saying, formally, in public, before assembled friends, that if you're so inclined, you know, and if you figure you could put up with me for another three decades, would you, like, you know … would you … marry me?"

The place went bananas.

I couldn't see Sharon very clearly through the uproar, but she was laughing and hugging our younger daughter Vanessa, who was practically fibrillating. When we finally managed to reach each other, Sharon gave me a big kiss and a friendly punch.

"You dog!" she said fondly.

Being a literalist, Vanessa looked a bit anxious. "So what's your answer, Mom? Are you gonna do it?"

Sharon took her good sweet time. "Oh, all right," she finally grinned.

The hall exploded into cheers and applause.

---

Wedding vows have always struck me as particularly potent indicators of where a society stands on a lot more issues than just marriage. On the assumption that Sharon and I would have to take an axe and a machete to the vows currently on offer by our provincial government, I consulted a selection of my married friends from other ethnic or religious backgrounds to discover the current status of their marriage traditions.

The most common feature—common to eleven of my twelve queries— was the question-and-answer format. "Do you, (groom), promise to take this woman, (bride) …" etc., etc. Even the Moonies and the Scientologists use it.

Only the Sikhs don't. Trouble in paradise can usually be traced back to differences between what the bride and the groom are obliged to promise.

I discovered that most progressive forms of Christianity began dropping the promise to obey from the bride's vows around the 1960s. Today, only a few ultra-traditional or evangelical Christian churches still insist on it. Mike Huckabee, 2008 US presidential candidate, garnered the greatest applause during a South Carolina Republican leadership debate when he defended his view that a wife should submit herself to the will of her husband. Another vigorous defender of men's rights was the Unification Church's Reverend Sun Myung Moon, who called husbands "subjects" and wives "objects." In order to qualify as an "absolute object," the UC requires the wife to demonstrate absolute faith in, love for and obedience to her subject.

Orthodox Jews don't come right out and say it, but in their ceremony the groom gives a ring to his bride and says, "You are consecrated to me, through this ring, according to the religion of Moses and Israel." There's no provision for a similar claim by the bride. Also, a man can divorce his wife unilaterally, but a wife can't divorce her husband without his consent. More progressive Jewish traditions have addressed the former issue by having the bride reply with an identical or similar statement, and the latter by decreeing that her husband can no longer arbitrarily refuse her a divorce if she wants one.

In the Sikh marriage ceremony, no vows are spoken; bride and groom merely circle the Sikh holy book (Adi Granth) four times while the priest recites a sacred hymn to musical accompaniment. In its traditional form, the bride walks behind the groom, indicating her unequal status—still the most common form today—but more progressive temples have begun to permit the couple to circle the Adi Granth side by side.

Mormons don't get married, they get "sealed." They're instructed to join hands in a "Patriarchal Grip" (there are detailed instructions), after which the following exchange takes place. "Brother (name), do you take Sister (name) by the right hand and receive her unto yourself to be your lawful and wedded wife?" (I do.) "Sister (name), do you take Brother (name) by the right hand and give yourself unto him as his lawful and wedded wife?" (Hmmm. Should she?) On the positive side, Mormon marriages come with a bonus—the automatic power to "come forth in the morning of the first resurrection clothed in glory, immortality and eternal lives." It's apparently activated as soon as you do the Patriarchal Grip.

Quakers and Icelanders have always promoted equality between the sexes, so they put identical questions to both bride and groom. The Buddhists, in a stroke of genius, solve the problem by simply having the couple reply to each question in unison. And the Scientologists, while apparently promoting equality, do so with a twist. Question to the bride: "Do you take his fortune at its prime and ebb and seek with him best fortune for us all?" (I do.) Question to the groom: "Girls need clothes and good and tender happiness and frills. A pan, a comb, perhaps a cat. All caprice, if you will, but still they need them. Will you provide?" (I will.)

———

Once we'd paid our hundred dollars plus GST at the Government Agent's Office and received our marriage licence ("Don't lose it or you'll have to pay again"), we braced ourselves for the inevitable. But the pamphlet containing the civil marriage ceremony surprised us. *The state of matrimony as understood by us*, it read, *is a state ennobled and enriched by a long and honourable tradition of devotion, set in the basis of the law of the land, assuring each participant an equality before the law, and supporting the common rights of each party to the marriage.*

"That doesn't sound so bad," Sharon mused.

*There is assumed to be a desire for a lifelong companionship, and a generous sharing of the help and comfort that husband and wife ought to have from each other, through whatever circumstances of sickness or health, joy or sorrow, prosperity or adversity, the lives of these parties may experience.*

"Looks like a real writer's infiltrated the bureaucracy," I marvelled. "Direct and to the point. Almost elegant. How did this happen?"

After correcting one typo and erasing one syntactical blemish, we were able to use the entire ceremony as written.

Miracles still occur.

We could have used a miracle in our actual wedding preparations, but one has to be realistic. I wanted us to come roaring into the hall on a motorcycle, and Sharon wanted to lay loaves and fishes on sufficient multitudes that the logistics couldn't be made to synchronize. We finally decided to scrap the whole huge-wedding approach and just do it for us. As soon as that decision was made, we both felt relieved. We were becoming too old for the six-month hysteria that characterizes most wedding preparations.

At this point, our daughters took over. I'd like to say, parenthetically, that it's not a half-bad idea to wait to get married until one has two grown-up daughters to take on the preparations. Sharon and I were banished to the cottage while the girls cleaned and decorated the house, and then they spent the rest of the day cooking and baking like dervishes. They organized a shower for Sharon, and a stag for me (at which they were granted honorary stag status), and we had some wonderful conversations and reminiscences. They pumped me for hours about the early years when Sharon and I were courting, and what had gone on when they were babies. At one point Sabrina asked me what I'd have done with my life if I hadn't decided to become a writer. I said I'd probably have become a blues musician, playing tenor sax.

It was raining on the day of the wedding, but it miraculously cleared up just before the marriage commissioner arrived. She turned out to be a delightful person, not at all bureaucratic, and quite game to go along with whatever ceremonial idiosyncrasies we had in mind. Not counting the fact that I accidentally filled out one of the documents in such a way that I temporarily married Vanessa, it all went off without a hitch. We finished the day with a sumptuous meal of marinated lamb popsicles in a fenugreek cream curry, several bottles of Church & State '05 Merlot and a set of real wedding rings.

And the following Christmas, Sharon and the girls gave me—hold still for it—a Buescher Aristocrat tenor sax.

# Notes on Essays and Poems

**In "Cover to Cover," by Fiona Tinwei Lam:**
The Free Dictionary, s.v. "cover," http://idioms.thefreedictionary.com/cover.
Mary Bess Kelly, "Divorce cases in civil court, 2010/2011," Statistics Canada, 2012,
http://statcan.gc.ca/pub/85-002-x/2012001/article/11634-eng.htm.
William Blackstone, *Commentaries on the Laws of England*, vol. 1 (1765), 442–5, quoted in
Jone Johnson Lewis, "Blackstone Commentaries," ThoughtCo., updated March 18, 2017,
https://www.thoughtco.com/blackstone-commentaries-profile-3525208.
Myth of Aristophanes from the *Symposium* by Plato, as set out in *Lapham's Quarterly*,
https://www.laphamsquarterly.org/eros/platos-other-half.

**In "Dear Son," by Betsy Warland:**
Betsy Warland, "Small Stranger," in *A Gathering Instinct* (Williams-Wallace, 1981).
Warland, excerpt from "I am unwrapping myself from you," in *A Gathering Instinct*.
Warland, from "aflame," in *open is broken* (Longspoon Press, 1984).
Warland, from "zero gravity," in *What Holds Us Here* (Buschek Books, 1998).
Warland, "Clack/clack," in *Force Field: 77 Women Poets of British Columbia*, ed. Susan
Musgrave (Mother Tongue Press, 2013).
Warland, *Oscar of Between* (Halfmoon Bay: Dagger Editions, 2016).

**In "Bees of the Invisible," by Kara Stanley:**
Yuval Noah Harari, *Sapiens: A Brief History of Humankind* (Toronto: McClelland &
Stewart, 2016), 147.
Lou Reed, "Some Kinda Love," performed by The Velvet Underground, TTG
Studios, 1969.
Rainer Maria Rilke, *Where Silence Reigns: Selected Prose* (New York: New Directions, 1978).

**In "In *Anna Karenina* Furs," by Susan Olding:**
Leo Tolstoy, *Anna Karenina*, trans. Richard Pevear and Larissa Volokhonsky (New
York: Penguin, 2002).
Tammy Worth, "Why Women Cheat," WebMD, https://www.webmd.com/sex
-relationships/guide/why-do-women-cheat#1.
Gary Saul Morson, *"Anna Karenina" in Our Time: Seeing More Wisely* (New Haven: Yale
University Press, 2007), 65.
"Which Anna Karenina Character Are You?," SelectSmart, October 2007, http://www
.selectsmart.com/FREE/select.php?client=Karenina.
James Hynes, "Reading *Anna Karenina*," *Salon*, July 11, 2005, https://www.salon.com
/2005/07/11/tolstoy_2/.
Leo Tolstoy, *Recollections and Essays*, trans. Aylmer Maude (London: Oxford University
Press, 1961), 81–82.

### In "This Is a Love Story," by Michelle Kaeser:
Graham Greene, *The End of the Affair* (1951; repr., London: Vintage Books, 2004).
Douglas Adams, *The Restaurant at the End of the Universe* (1980; repr., London: Pan Macmillan, 2016), 57.
Andrew Reagan et al., "The Emotional Arcs of Stories Are Dominated by Six Basic Shapes," *EPJ Data Science* 5, no. 31 (2016), https://epjdatascience.springeropen.com/articles/10.1140/epjds/s13688-016-0093-1.

### In "On Being a Couples Therapist," by Toni Pieroni:
Ellyn Bader and Peter Pearson, "Facing Our Fears: Why We Avoid Doing Couples Therapy," *Psychotherapy Networker*, November/December 2011, https://www.psychotherapynetworker.org/magazine/article/312/facing-our-fears.

### In "Are You Still Married?," by Lesley Buxton:
Tim O'Brien, *The Things They Carried* (Boston: Houghton Mifflin Harcourt, 1990).
The Compassionate Friends, *When a Child Dies—2006 Survey Summary*, April–May 2006.

### In "As Women Scorned," by Lauren McKeon:
Margarita Tartakovsky, "A Glimpse into Marriage Advice from the 1950s," *Psych Central*, February 27, 2012, https://psychcentral.com/blog/archives/2012/02/27/a-glimpse-into-marriage-advice-from-the-1950s/.
"How to Move On after Divorce, and How Long It Really Takes," *Huffington Post*, July 30, 2013, https://www.huffingtonpost.com/2013/07/30/how-to-move-on_n_3679198.html.
Elizabeth Bernstein, "After Divorce or Job Loss Comes the Good Identity Crisis," *Wall Street Journal*, July 30, 2013, https://www.wsj.com/articles/SB10001424127887324354704578635900864791348.

### In "On Anniversaries," by Mandy Len Catron:
Daniel Gilbert interview quote, from Stephanie Pappas, "You May Not Recognize Yourself in 10 Years," Live Science, January 3, 2013, https://www.livescience.com/25951-future-change-more-than-expected.html.

### In "Late Love Song, with an Orange: A Cento," by Maureen Hynes:
(1) Jane Munro (2) Joanne Kyger (3) Sue Goyette (4) Muriel Rukeyser (5) Erín Mouré (6) John Berryman (7) Mary Ruefle (8) Joanne Kyger (9) Brenda Shaughnessy (10) Laura Kasischke (11) Catherine Graham (12) Brenda Shaughnessy (13) Maleea Acker (14) Catherine Graham (15) Barry Dempster (16) Nicole Brossard (17) Alicia Suskin Ostriker (18) Barry Dempster (19) Mary Ruefle (20) Maleea Acker (21) Erín Mouré (22) Mary Ruefle (23) Dionne Brand.

### In "The Joy of the Ancient Marriers," by Andreas Schroeder:
"The Good Wife's Guide," *Housekeeping Monthly*, May 1955, quoted in Angel Chang, "This 1955 'Good House Wife's Guide' Explains How Wives Should Treat Their Husbands," LittleThings, https://www.littlethings.com/1950s-good-housewife-guide/.

# Acknowledgements

Thank you to the publishers and editors of the following magazines and books where these poems and nonfiction pieces have previously appeared:

A version of Joanne Arnott's "Wedding Clothes & Marriage Blanket" appeared in *My Wedding Dress: True-Life Tales of Love, Laughter, Tears and Tulle*, edited by Susie Whelehan and Anne Laurel Carter, Vintage Canada, Random House, 2007.

Jagtar Kaur Atwal's "Finding a Way Out" appeared in *Room*, issue 39:1, 2016.

Ronna Bloom's "Let's Get Married" was published in *The More*, Pedlar Press, 2017.

Lesley Buxton's "Are You Still Married?" appeared in *Hazlitt*, September 17, 2015.

Kevin Chong's "Every Stepfather Has His Day" appeared in *The Walrus*, June 16, 2017.

Lorna Crozier's "My Last Erotic Poem" was published in *Small Mechanics*, McClelland & Stewart, 2011.

Michael Crummey's "Getting the Marriage into Bed" was published in *Under the Keel*, House of Anansi Press, 2013.

Barry Dempster's "Valentine's Day" appeared in *Love Outlandish*, Brick Books, 2009.

Jane Eaton Hamilton's "On the Piano" was published in *Out Proud: Stories of Pride, Courage, and Social Justice*, ed. Douglas Gosse, Breakwater Books, 2014.

Maureen Hynes' "Late Love Song, with an Orange" was published in *In Fine Form, 2nd Edition: A Contemporary Look at Canadian Form Poetry*, eds. Kate Braid and Sandy Shreve, Caitlin Press, 2016.

Michelle Kaeser's "This Is a Love Story" appeared in *The New Quarterly*, issue 144, fall 2017.

Fiona Tinwei Lam's "Cover to Cover" appeared in *The New Quarterly*, issue 144, fall 2017.

Evelyn Lau's "Fireworks" was published in *Treble*, Polestar, 2005.

Lauren McKeon's "As Women Scorned" appeared in *Hazlitt*, January 4, 2016.

Susan Musgrave's "Maximum Security" was published in *Great Musgrave*, Prentice-Hall, 1989.

Susan Olding's "In *Anna Karenina* Furs" appeared in *Maisonneuve*, March 22, 2013.

Elise Partridge's "Gifts" was published in *The Exiles' Gallery*, House of Anansi Press, 2015.

Miranda Pearson's "Lice" was published in *Prime*, Beach Holme Publishing, 2001.

Rachel Rose's "Cleave" was published in *Marry & Burn*, Harbour Publishing, 2016.

Andreas Schroeder's "The Joy of the Ancient Marriers" was published in *Slice me some truth: an anthology of Canadian creative nonfiction*, eds. Luanne Armstrong and Zoe Landale, Wolsak & Wynn, 2011.

Karen Shklanka's "La Cumparsita" was published in *Sumac's Red Arms*, Coteau Books, 2009.

Jane Silcott's "Cooking Class & Marriage Lessons" was published in *Sustenance: Writers from BC and Beyond on the Subject of Food*, Anvil Press, 2017.

Anne Simpson's "Third Sutra" appeared in *The Malahat Review*, vol. 180, fall 2012.

Chris Tarry's "The Good Man" appeared in *Grain*, winter 2014.

Rob Taylor's "The Time of Useful Truths" was published in *The Other Side of Ourselves*, Cormorant Books, 2011.

Russell Thornton's "Arrivals, Departures" was published in *Birds, Metals, Stones & Rain*, Harbour Publishing, 2013.

Ayelet Tsabari's "The Marrying Kind" appeared in *Room*, issue 33:2, 2010.

Bronwen Wallace's "The Woman in This Poem" was published in *Signs of the Former Tenant*, Oberon Press, 1983.

Samra Zafar's "The Good Wife" appeared in *Toronto Life*, February 17, 2017.

Thank you to our wonderful publisher, Vici Johnstone, and to the hard-working and dedicated staff at Caitlin Press: Emily Stringer, Michael Despotovic and Cara Cochrane. Independent publishers like Caitlin Press are vital to keeping literary wheels turning across the country. Thank you to everyone who submitted work to *Love Me True*. We wish we could have made a book twice as big. We are grateful to all our amazing contributors for courageously delving into intimate territory with such honesty. And finally, thank you to our partners and our families. Loving true makes our worlds go round.

# Contributors

**Luanne Armstrong**, MFA, PhD, is a writer and editor. She is the author of twenty-one books, including poetry, novels and children's books. She has been nominated for numerous prizes and awards. She has published many stories and essays in magazines and journals. She has also contributed essays to many anthologies. Together with Zoe Landale, Luanne has edited the collection of Canadian nonfiction, *Slice me some truth*.

**Joanne Arnott**, a Métis/mixed-blood writer, is mother to six young people and author of six books of poetry. *Wiles of Girlhood* (Press Gang) won the League of Canadian Poets' Gerald Lampert Award (1992). Her books in print: *Steepy Mountain Love Poetry* (Kegedonce, 2004), *Mother Time* (Ronsdale, 2007), *A Night for the Lady* (Ronsdale, 2013) and *Halfling Spring: An Internet Romance* (Kegedonce, 2014). She also published an illustrated children's book (*Ma MacDonald*) and a collection of short nonfiction (*Breasting the Waves*), and edited *Salish Seas: An Anthology of Text + Image* (Aboriginal Writers Collective West Coast, 2011). Joanne is currently poetry editor for *Event* magazine. She received the Vancouver Mayor's Arts Award for Literary Arts, 2017, alongside Tsleil-Waututh poet Wil George (Wil to Write). Nick Zenthoefer died on March 31, 2016.

**Jagtar Kaur Atwal** lives and writes in Cambridge, Ontario, and has recently started painting images that reflect her life experiences. She has been published in *Room* magazine and *The New Quarterly*.

**Donna Besel** loves writing of all kinds. Her collection of short stories, *Lessons from a Nude Man*, captured a fourth-place spot on McNally Robinson Bookstore's 2015 bestsellers list, and nominations for the Margaret Laurence Award for Fiction and Most Promising Manitoba Writer. Her work has also earned national recognition from the CBC Literary Prizes, the Great Canadian Literary Hunt and *Prairie Fire*. Recently, Canada ReLit Awards long-listed her book for their annual prize and the University of Manitoba featured her in its alumni magazine in an article about overcoming adversity.

**Ronna Bloom** has published six books of poetry, most recently *The More* (Pedlar Press, 2017). Her poems have been translated into Spanish and Bengali, recorded by the Canadian National Institute for the Blind and used in films, by architects, in education and health care. Her work appears in "Poetry is Public" and in the Toronto Public Library Poetry Map. She is currently poet-in-community at the University of Toronto and poet-in-residence at Mount Sinai Hospital and in the Sinai Health System in Toronto. www.ronnabloom.com

Lesley Buxton studied theatre in London, England, and travelled extensively before settling down in Penticton, BC. She has worked as a writer in a number of capacities: as a playwright, a short-fiction author, a newspaper columnist and theatre critic. Her short stories and essays have appeared in a variety of literary journals including *The Antigonish Review*, *The Fiddlehead*, *The New Quarterly* and *Hazlitt*. She has an MFA in creative nonfiction from the University of King's College in Halifax, Nova Scotia. Recently she completed a memoir, *One Strong Girl*, based on her blog, *Fall On Me, Dear*.

Originally from Appalachian Virginia, Mandy Len Catron now lives in Vancouver, BC. Her writing has appeared in the *New York Times*, the *Washington Post*, *The Rumpus* and *The Walrus*, as well as literary journals and anthologies. Her article "To Fall in Love with Anyone, Do This" was one of the most popular articles published by the *New York Times* in 2015. *How to Fall in Love with Anyone: A Memoir in Essays* is her first book.

Kevin Chong is the author of six books, including the memoir *My Year of the Racehorse* and the novel *The Plague*. His work has been shortlisted for the Hubert Evans Prize and a National Magazine Award. His writing has recently appeared in the *The Walrus*, *The Rusty Toque* and *Cosmonauts Avenue*.

An officer of the Order of Canada, Lorna Crozier's latest book of poetry, *What the Soul Doesn't Want*, came out in 2017. Her poetry has received many awards, including the Governor General's Award for Poetry, and she has been invited to read her work on every continent except Antarctica. She lives on Vancouver Island with writer Patrick Lane and two fine cats.

Michael Crummey has published ten books of poetry and fiction. His first novel, *River Thieves*, was a finalist for the Giller Prize and won the Winterset Award. *Galore* won the Canadian Authors Association fiction prize and the Commonwealth Prize (Canada and Caribbean region). *Sweetland* was a national bestseller and a finalist for the Governor General's and Winterset Awards. *Little Dogs: New and Selected Poems* was published by House of Anansi in the spring of 2016. He lives in St. John's.

Barry Dempster, twice nominated for the Governor General's Award, is the author of sixteen collections of poetry, two volumes of short stories, two novels and a children's book. In 2010 and 2015, he was a finalist for the Ontario Premier's Award for Excellence in the Arts. He was also nominated for the 2014 Trillium Award for his second novel, *The Outside World*. His most recent book is the poetry collection *Late Style*, published by Pedlar Press.

Eufemia Fantetti is in love with essay collections and anthologies. She holds an MFA in creative writing from the University of Guelph and also attended the Writer's Studio at

Simon Fraser University. Her book *A Recipe for Disaster & Other Unlikely Tales of Love* was runner-up for the Danuta Gleed Literary Award and winner of the Bressani Prize.

**Jane Eaton Hamilton** is the author of nine books of creative nonfiction, fiction and poetry, including the 2016 novel *Weekend* and two prior collections of short fiction. Their memoir was one of the UK *Guardian*'s Best Books of the Year and a *Sunday Times* bestseller. They are the two-time winner of Canada's CBC Literary Prize for fiction (2003 and 2014). They have had a notable in BASS and BAE (2016) and have appeared in *The Journey Prize, Best Canadian Short Stories* and *Best Canadian Poetry*. Their work has also appeared in publications such as *Salon, The Rumpus, The Missouri Review*, the *New York Times* and *The Sun*.

Toronto poet and essayist **Maureen Scott Harris** has published three collections of poetry: *A Possible Landscape* (Brick Books, 1993), *Drowning Lessons* (Pedlar Press, 2004), awarded the 2005 Trillium Book Award for Poetry, and *Slow Curve Out* (Pedlar Press, 2012), shortlisted for the League of Canadian Poets Pat Lowther Award. Her chapbook *Waters Remembered* (Espresso) was published in 2015. In 2016 *Sussurri dall'acqua*, a bilingual Italian-English selection from *Drowning Lessons*, was released, and her poem "Will's Diaries: Enkroetschment 1, How To Begin" was long-listed for the CBC Poetry Prize.

**Maureen Hynes**' poetry collection *Rough Skin* won the League of Canadian Poets' Gerald Lampert Award for best first book of poetry by a Canadian. Subsequent collections are *Harm's Way* and *Marrow, Willow*. Her most recent book, *The Poison Colour*, was nominated in 2016 for both the Pat Lowther and Raymond Souster Awards. Her poetry has been included in over twenty anthologies, including *Best Canadian Poetry in English* 2010 and 2016, and twice long-listed for the CBC Canada Reads poetry contest. Maureen teaches creative writing at the University of Toronto, and is poetry editor for *Our Times* magazine. www.maureenhynes.com

**Michelle Kaeser**'s fiction and essays have appeared in publications across the country, including *The Feathertale Review, The New Quarterly, Prairie Fire, Grain, Maisonneuve* and others. Her debut novel, *The Towers of Babylon*, is forthcoming in 2019.

**Chelene Knight** was born in Vancouver and is a graduate of the Writer's Studio at Simon Fraser University in multiple genres. In addition to being a workshop facilitator for teens, she is also a regular literary event organizer and host. She has been published in various Canadian and American literary magazines. Chelene is currently the managing editor at *Room* magazine. *Braided Skin*, her first book (Mother Tongue Publishing, 2015), has given birth to numerous writing projects including her second book, *Dear Current Occupant* (forthcoming with BookThug, 2018). She was one of the judges for the 2017 Vancouver

Writers Festival Contest, and is working on a novel set in the Strathcona neighbourhood of Vancouver known as Hogan's Alley.

**Evelyn Lau** is the Vancouver author of twelve books, including seven volumes of poetry. Her memoir, *Runaway: Diary of a Street Kid*, published when she was eighteen, was made into a CBC movie. Evelyn's prose books have been translated into many languages; her poetry has received the Milton Acorn Award, the Pat Lowther Award, a National Magazine Award and a Governor General's nomination. She served as 2011–14 poet laureate for the City of Vancouver. Her most recent collection is *Tumour* (Oolichan, 2016).

**Ellen McGinn** divides her time between Saturna Island and Vancouver. A graduate of the University of British Columbia's MFA program, she has published a book of poetry, *From Dark Horse Road*, and her plays, *Comfort Me with Apples* and *Love Letters for Georgia*, were produced in the Vancouver and Victoria fringe festivals. Her new play, *Antarctica Welcomes International Women's Year 1975*, is in development.

**Lauren McKeon** is an award-winning writer and editor. Her first book is *F-Bomb: Dispatches from the War on Feminism*. She is a digital editor at *The Walrus*.

**Monica Meneghetti**'s memoir, *What the Mouth Wants: A Memoir of Food, Love and Belonging* (Dagger Editions, 2017) is excerpted in *Absent Mothers* (Demeter Press, 2017) and *Sustenance* (Anvil Press, 2017). Monica's fiction, poetry and creative nonfiction can be found in *CBC Canada Writes*, *CBC Hyperlocal*, *Trivia: Voices of Feminism*, *Plenitude Magazine*, *The Winnipeg Review*, *Prairie Journal*, *Prairie Fire*, *Filling Station* and *Canadian Alpine Journal*. Her translation, *The Call of the Ice* (Mountaineers Books, 2014) was a 2015 Banff Mountain Book finalist. Several composers use her poetry in their scores. She teaches writing at Langara College, on unceded Coast Salish territory.

**Jane Munro**'s sixth poetry collection, *Blue Sonoma* (Brick Books, 2014), won the 2015 Griffin Poetry Prize. Her previous books include *Active Pass* (Pedlar Press, 2010) and *Point No Point* (McClelland & Stewart, 2006). Her work has received the Bliss Carman Poetry Award and the Macmillan Prize for Poetry, was nominated for the Pat Lowther Award and is included in *The Best Canadian Poetry 2013*. She is a member of the collaborative poetry group Yoko's Dogs, who have published *Whisk* and *Rhinoceros*. She lives in Vancouver.

**Susan Musgrave** has published more than thirty books and received awards in six categories—poetry, novels, nonfiction, food writing, editing and children's books. She lives on Haida Gwaii and teaches poetry in the University of British Columbia's Optional-Residency MFA in Creative Writing Program. Her most recent book, *A Taste of Haida Gwaii: Food Gathering and Feasting at the Edge of the World*, won the Bill Duthie Booksellers'

Choice Award at the 2016 BC Book Awards, and was the gold winner in the Regional Cookbook category at the Taste Canada Awards, November 2016. She married in 1987, and is still married to Stephen Reid.

**Lorri Neilsen Glenn**'s books include nine collections of poetry, creative nonfiction and scholarly work, along with four anthologies. Lorri's acclaimed workshops in memoir, creative nonfiction and poetry have been held in Chile, Greece and Ireland, and across Canada. *Following the River* (Wolsak and Wynn, 2017) tracks her search for stories of her Indigenous grandmothers and their contemporaries in nineteenth-century Red River. Former Halifax poet laureate, she lives in Nova Scotia. Find her on Twitter @neilsenglenn

**Juliane Okot Bitek** is a poet. Her *100 Days* (University of Alberta Press, 2016) was nominated for the Dorothy Livesay BC Book Prize, the Pat Lowther Award, the Robert Kroetsch Award for Innovative Poetry, Canadian Authors Award for Poetry and the Indie Fab Book of the Year Award, for which it won the gold prize. She lives and loves in Vancouver.

**Susan Olding** is the author of *Pathologies: A Life in Essays*, selected by 49th Shelf and Amazon.ca as one of one hundred Canadian books to read in a lifetime. Her writing has won a National Magazine Award (Canada), and has appeared in *The Bellingham Review*, *The Los Angeles Review of Books*, *Maisonneuve*, *The Malahat Review*, *The New Quarterly* and the *Utne Reader*, and in anthologies including *Best Canadian Essays 2016* and *In Fine Form 2nd Edition*.

**Elise Partridge** was born in Philadelphia in 1958, and moved to Vancouver in 1992 when her husband-to-be began teaching at the University of British Columbia. She was the author of three books of poetry: *Fielder's Choice* (Véhicule, 2002), *Chameleon Hours* (Anansi and Chicago, 2008) and *The Exiles' Gallery*, published by Anansi shortly after her death in 2015. In 2017 New York Review Books published her collected poems, *The If Borderlands*. Her poems appeared in *The New Yorker*, *Poetry*, *The Walrus*, *The Fiddlehead* and many other periodicals, and have been selected for *Best Canadian Poetry* and other anthologies.

**Miranda Pearson** is the author of four books of poetry, most recently *The Fire Extinguisher*, which was a finalist for the 2016 Dorothy Livesay BC Book Prize. The poem "Lice" is from her first collection, *Prime* (Beach Holme, 2001). Miranda lives in Vancouver. www.mirandapearsonpoetry.com

**Toni Pieroni** has been a psychotherapist in private practice in Vancouver, BC, for the past twenty-four years, working with individual adults and couples. She became a therapist in her early forties following a twenty-four-year career as a dental hygienist. She knew it was time to make a change when she became much more interested in her patients' lives than in their teeth. She has also been interested in environmental and social justice work and has led workshops and retreats based on the work of eco-philosopher, Joanna Macy. She and her husband, Larry, love hiking, biking, backpacking and getting away in their camper van whenever they can.

**Rachel Rose** is the author of four poetry books. Her most recent collection, *Marry & Burn* (Harbour), received a 2016 Pushcart Prize and was nominated for a Governor General's Award. Her nonfiction book, *The Dog Lover Unit: Lessons in Courage from the World's K9 Cops*, was published in fall 2017 by St. Martin's Press/Thomas Dunne Books, as was the anthology she edited, *Sustenance: Writers from BC and Beyond on the Subject of Food* (Anvil Press). http://rachelsprose.weebly.com/

**Tana Runyan** lives and writes in Vancouver. Her book of poetry, *Arithmetic of Surrender*, was published by Exile Editions. She is retired from a working life in libraries and tutoring. Both she and her husband are grateful cancer survivors.

**Andreas Schroeder** has made his living as a freelance writer in BC for the past fifty years. His twenty-five books include works of fiction, creative nonfiction, poetry, history, translation and literary criticism. For a dozen years (1990–2002) he was the "resident crookologist" on CBC Radio's *Basic Black* show, and he has won or been shortlisted for over a dozen literary awards, including the Governor General's Award for Nonfiction (1977), the Seal Books First Novel Award (1984) and a Canadian Association of Journalists Best Investigative Journalism Award (1991). In 2013 the Writers' Union of Canada honoured him with the Graeme Gibson Award (given only three times in its history) for the thirty-three years he spent leading the union's successful crusade for the Public Lending Right. He held the Rogers Communications Chair in Creative Nonfiction in the University of British Columbia's Creative Writing Program from 1993 until his retirement in 2017.

**Karen Shklanka** is a writer and Argentine tango dancer, who works as an addiction medicine consultant. She is a clinical assistant professor at the University of British Columbia, and teaches behavioural medicine and physician resilience. Previously, she was a family physician in Salt Spring Island, BC, and Moose Factory, Ontario. She has an MFA in creative writing; her first book of poetry, *Sumac's Red Arms* (Coteau, 2009), was a finalist for the ForeWord Review Book of the Year prize; and two long poems from her second book, *Ceremony for Touching* (Coteau, 2016), were long-listed for the 2012 CBC Poetry Prize.

**Anne Simpson** writes poetry, fiction and essays. Her second book of poetry, *Loop*, won the Griffin Poetry Prize; her fifth book of poetry, *Strange Attractor*, is forthcoming. She has also written novels, most recently *Falling*, which won the Dartmouth Fiction Award. Her book of essays, *The Marram Grass: Poetry and Otherness*, is about poetry, art and philosophy. She has been a writer-in-residence at universities and libraries across the country.

**Kara Stanley** lives, works and plays on the Sunshine Coast with her musician husband, Simon Paradis. She is a contributing songwriter to the 2013 Stanton Paradis CD *Good Road Home* and the 2015 Simon Paradis CD *Mouthful of Stars*. *Fallen: A Trauma, a Marriage, and the Transformative Power of Music*, which was included on CBC's list of Best Books of 2015, is her nonfiction account of her husband's life-altering accident that resulted in a severe brain and spinal cord injury and the role music plays in his ongoing recovery. Her first novel, *Ghost Warning*, was released in September 2017.

**Chris Tarry** is a Peabody Award-winning writer, a five-time Juno Award-winning jazz musician and author of the short story collection *How to Carry Bigfoot Home* (Red Hen Press, 2015). His fiction and nonfiction has been published widely. Along with writing and music, Chris also produces podcasts. He is the cocreator and sound guru behind the serialized kids' audio show *The Unexplainable Disappearance of Mars Patel*, one of the top audio fiction podcasts publishing today. www.christarry.com

**Rob Taylor** is the author of the poetry collections *"Oh Not So Great": Poems from the Depression Project* (Leaf Press, 2017), *The News* (Gaspereau Press, 2016) and *The Other Side of Ourselves* (Cormorant Books, 2011). *The News* was a finalist for the 2017 Dorothy Livesay Poetry Prize, and *The Other Side of Ourselves* won the 2010 Alfred G. Bailey Prize. In 2015 Rob received the City of Vancouver's Mayor's Arts Award for Literary Arts, as an emerging artist. He lives with his wife and son in Vancouver, where he coordinates the Dead Poets Reading Series.

The title story of **Yasuko Thanh**'s collection *Floating Like the Dead* (McClelland & Stewart, 2012) won the 2009 Journey Prize and was chosen as a *Quill & Quire* Best Books of 2012. Her second book, the novel *Mysterious Fragrance of the Yellow Mountains*, won the 2016 Rogers Writers' Trust Prize and the Victoria Butler Book Prize, and was shortlisted for the Amazon First Novel Award. She holds an MFA from the University of Victoria and lives with her two children in Victoria, BC. She's currently working on a memoir called *Mistakes to Run With*, forthcoming with Penguin Random House in 2018.

**Russell Thornton**'s *The Hundred Lives* was shortlisted for the 2015 Griffin Poetry Prize. His *Birds, Metals, Stones & Rain* was shortlisted for the 2013 Governor General's Award for Poetry, the 2014 Raymond Souster Award and the 2014 Dorothy Livesay BC Book Prize. His other titles include *The Human Shore, House Built of Rain, A Tunisian Notebook* and *The Fifth Window*. He is the cotranslator of *Poems from the Scythian Wild Field: A Selection of the Poetry of Dmytro Kremin* (2016). His latest collection is *The Broken Face*, due out in 2018. He lives in North Vancouver.

**Ayelet Tsabari** was born in Israel to a large family of Yemeni descent. Her first book, *The Best Place on Earth* (HarperCollins) won the Sami Rohr Prize for Jewish Literature and the Edward Lewis Wallant Award, and was long-listed for the Frank O'Connor International Short Story Award. The book was a *New York Times Book Review* Editors' Choice and a *Kirkus Reviews* Best Book of 2016, and has been published internationally. Excerpts from her forthcoming book have won a National Magazine Award and a Western Magazine Award. She lives in Toronto.

**Bronwen Wallace** was a poet, short story writer and essayist from Kingston, Ontario. She wrote five books of poetry, including *Common Magic* (1985), *The Stubborn Particulars of Grace* (1987), which contains a sequence that describes her work in a battered women's shelter, and *Keep That Candle Burning Bright and Other Poems* (1991). Her book of short stories *People You'd Trust Your Life To* (1990) depicts with toughness and compassion the Kingston of cheap apartments, laundromats, fast food and domestic violence. Her columns on feminist thought for the *Kingston Whig-Standard* are collected in *Arguments with the World* (1992). She passed away in 1989.

**Betsy Warland** has published twelve books of creative nonfiction, poetry and lyric prose. Her bestseller book of essays *Breathing the Page: Reading the Act of Writing* was published in 2010. *Oscar of Between: A Memoir of Identity and Ideas* launched Caitlin Press' Dagger Editions in 2016. A creative writing teacher, mentor and editor, Warland received the City of Vancouver Mayor's Arts Award for Literary Arts in 2016. She is currently mentoring in the Writer's Studio at Simon Fraser University and Vancouver Manuscript Intensive.

**Gina Leola Woolsey** is an award-winning author inspired by the natural world and the complexity of human emotion. She recently completed the biography of Dr. John C. Butt, Nova Scotia's chief medical examiner during the Swissair disaster of 1998. In 2010, Gina launched her writing career with a first-place CBC Literary Prize in Nonfiction. Since then, she's completed an MFA at the University of King's College in Halifax and written her first book while supporting her husband through his health challenges.

**Samra Zafar** is an international speaker, TEDx presenter, human rights activist, scholar, author and founder of Brave Beginnings. After arriving in Canada as a child bride in a forced marriage and escaping a decade of abuse, she pursued her education as a single mother, graduating with a master's degree and winning over a dozen awards and scholarships. Today, she serves as the youngest alumni governor for the University of Toronto. Her story and work have been featured in prominent media platforms, including *Toronto Life*, CTV, CBC, Global News, Yahoo and many others, impacting tens of millions of people worldwide.

# Editors

**Jane Silcott**'s collection of essays, *Everything Rustles*, about love, loss and camping, was a finalist in the BC Book Prizes. Her work has been published in several Canadian literary magazines and anthologies. Her writing has earned her recognition from the BC Book Prizes, the CBC Literary Prizes, the National and Western Magazine Awards, the Creative Nonfiction Collective of Canada and *Room*. She has an MFA in creative writing from the University of British Columbia and a BA in English and creative writing from the University of Victoria. Originally from Toronto, she moved west when she was 19 and now lives in Vancouver with her husband and two children. Jane is a mentor with the Creative Nonfiction MFA Program at the University of King's College, Halifax, and Vancouver Manuscript Intensive. www.janesilcott.ca

**Fiona Tinwei Lam** has authored two poetry books, *Intimate Distances* and *Enter the Chrysanthemum*, and a children's book, *The Rainbow Rocket*, about a child witnessing his grandparent's struggle with Alzheimer's disease. Her prose and poetry appear in over thirty anthologies. Her past work has been shortlisted for the *Event* creative nonfiction prize and City of Vancouver Book Award, and she recently won *The New Quarterly*'s Nick Blatchford poetry prize. She edited *The Bright Well: Contemporary Canadian Poems about Facing Cancer* and co-edited the creative nonfiction anthology *Double Lives: Writing and Motherhood* with Cathy Stonehouse and Shannon Cowan. Her video poems have screened at festivals locally and internationally. She teaches at Simon Fraser University Continuing Studies in Vancouver, BC. www.fionalam.net